CW01083583

ALMOST UNKNOWN

Squadron Leader Tony Gaze OAM DFC★★
Fighter Pilot and Racing Driver

Stewart Wilson

chevron
PUBLISHING GROUP

Tony Gaze
Almost Famous
By Stewart Wilson

Published by
Chevron Publishing Group
ABN 64 003 508 567

Unit 13 Building F
16 Mars Road
Lane Cove NSW 2066 Australia
Published 2009

Copyright © Stewart Wilson 2009

Cover design: Mat Clancy APM Graphics Management
Artwork: Into Images
Printed by WKT Company Limited

ISBN 978 0 9805912 1 7

All rights reserved. Subject to the Copyright Act 1968. No part of this
publication may be produced, stored in a retrieval system, or transmitted in
any form, or by any means, digital, electronic, mechanical, photocopying,
recording, or otherwise, without the prior written permission of the publishers.

CONTENTS

INTRODUCTION

WHEN I STARTED work on this book two-and-a-half years ago, Tony Gaze - who was 86 at the time - reminded me that I'd better not take too long to finish it because he "might not be around for too long." This became a bit of a running gag which I didn't really take seriously because he was in good health, alert and obviously mentally strong.

The gag nearly came unstuck towards the end of 2007 when both Tony and his wife Diana became ill, life-threateningly ill. For a while it didn't look too good for either of them but happily, at the time of writing this, things were looking better.

I hope it stays that way for a long time yet, because in Tony Gaze we have a most remarkable man, an Australian of whom we in this part of the world should be proud. A top-notch and highly decorated Spitfire pilot in World War II and a successful racing driver after it, the list of his achievements is staggering. They are revealed in the pages of this book so there's no need to reiterate them here, but it's true to say that I was continually amazed as I unearthed more and more information about him.

And best of all, he's a lovely bloke. Modest, understated and a gentleman of the old school, the type of man who's becoming a rarity in modern times.

You can't mention Tony without including Diana. The widow of that great Australian racing driver, Lex Davison, she, Tony, Lex and Tony's first wife Kay were all good friends for many years. Tony and Diana got together after tragedy took both of their spouses away and you can tell just by being in their company that they made an excellent match. A classy lady, Diana.

This is my 59th book and the first biography I've tackled. At the start I got advice from several people that I should read a number of biographies by other authors to see how it's done. Obviously I've read biographies before but I chose to ignore that advice and just get on with it, trusting the instincts that had worked well for my previous 58 books and doing my own thing. Hopefully, they've worked this time too!

The title *Almost Unknown* was originally suggested by Tony. It comes from a description of him in another book and is particularly apt. Despite his achievements, Tony never gained the 'household name' fame of many of his contemporaries, despite being at least as worthy as most of them.

Never one for self-promotion, Tony remained what these days might be called a 'quiet achiever', rarely in the public eye but held in the highest esteem by his colleagues in both aviation and motor racing. Perhaps now – with this book – we can finally give Tony Gaze some of the more public recognition he deserves.

I wish to thank Tony and Diana for their patience while this project developed, for their hospitality, help and good cheer. Tony endured the ordeal of sitting with me for many hours being interviewed, providing a great deal of information as well as ideas which led to further research and branches of his story.

I also thank Tony for trusting me with his log books during the whole time I was writing the book. They are arguably any pilot's most treasured possession and the decision to lend them out is not taken lightly, especially when they are so old and fragile .

I'd also like to thank my wife Wendy for her help with this project and ongoing support of my writing life, and the folks at Chevron for agreeing to publish this book. I hope you find something of interest within its pages.

STEWART WILSON
December 2008

FOREWORD

LIKE SO MANY of the exciting and successful things in our lives, the Goodwood Motor Circuit came into being by accident. The lion's share of the credit for the creation of the circuit goes to the 9th Duke of Richmond and Gordon, and rightly so, for it was he who had the energy and the audacity to make it happen.

History relates, however, that it was a chance meeting between the Duke and a young Australian RAF officer that was the inspiration for the project. Not long after the Second World War had ended Squadron Leader F A O (Tony) Gaze suggested to the Duke that the RAF aerodrome at Westhampnett, built on Goodwood farmland, would make a terrific motor racing circuit.

Tony Gaze could hardly have sewn the seeds in a more fertile mind. The Duke, or Freddie March as he was more widely known, had been a successful racer with the MG works team before the war and was by now the President of the Junior Car Club, or the BARC as it is known today.

Tony Gaze, whose brother had gone missing on a wartime sortie from RAF Westhampnett, reckoned that the perimeter roads of the aerodrome would make a great racing circuit and Freddie March needed no further encouragement. Some practice laps of the narrow concrete roads in his own Lancia Aprilia convinced Freddie that Goodwood could indeed have a great motor racing event alongside his already successful horse racing.

Calling on his friend Earl Howe, then President of the British Racing Drivers Club, and other influential contacts within the RAC and the BARC, as well as amateur racer and journalist Tommy Wisdom, he soon had the right people on board.

The project, not without its challenges, consumed a huge amount of Freddie March's time but after eighteen months' hard slog the circuit was ready for its first ever meeting. There were spectator enclosures and a paddock for the cars, but no pit buildings or grandstands. No matter, Goodwood was open for business, and 15,000 people came to watch the races on September 18th, 1948.

It was a good idea, Squadron Leader Gaze. A damn good idea.

LORD MARCH
September 2008

ONE

ALMOST UNKNOWN?

THERE IS A BOOK entitled *Planes of the Luftwaffe: Fighter Aces Volume 1* which on page 159 makes the following statement: "By the end of the war a number of RAF units such as 610 Squadron had been equipped with the high performance Spitfire Mk.XIV. This machine, [the one illustrated] DW-D, was flown by an *almost unknown* Australian ace, Squadron Leader Tony Gaze DFC...."

'Almost unknown' indeed, and despite a litany of remarkable achievements as a fighter pilot with the Royal Air Force during World War II and as a racing driver afterwards.

Consider this: Tony Gaze flew Spitfires almost exclusively during the war and ended it with 12.5 confirmed combat victories to his credit and another four 'probables'; he flew with and was highly respected by luminaries such as Douglas Bader and Johnnie Johnson and was rated by them and others as an exceptional fighter pilot; he has the rare distinction of being awarded the Distinguished Flying Cross "to recognise gallantry whilst flying in active operations against the enemy" three times; he was the first Australian to fly jet aircraft operationally and possibly the first from 'Down Under' to fly a jet at all; the first Australian to shoot down a jet in aerial combat; he escaped from occupied France with the help of the French Resistance; and he was the first Allied pilot to land in France after D-Day, albeit very unofficially!

Tony Gaze may have been 'almost unknown' as far as the public and even many aviation and motor racing enthusiasts are concerned but among his contemporaries he was recognised as being among the best. No finer confirmation of this comes directly from Group Captain Johnnie Johnson, the RAF's top-scoring fighter pilot of the war, who wrote: "I have known this officer throughout his wartime career as a fighter pilot, and during the closing stages of the war he served under me in 12 Group Wing. I consider him to be a pilot of exceptional capability and one who possesses a high standard of technical knowledge."

Then there's Tony Gaze's motor racing career after the war: he became the first Australian to compete in World Championship Grand Prix motor racing, debuting at the Belgian GP in June 1952 driving an ex-Stirling Moss HWM-Alta and sharing the starting grid with luminaries such as Juan Manuel

Fangio, Alberto Ascari, Guiseppe Farina, Mike Hawthorn, Jean Behra and Peter Collins.

He was the driving force behind the establishment of the Goodwood motor racing circuit in England and his racing career saw him competing in Europe, Australia, New Zealand and South Africa in open-wheelers and sports cars including Maseratis, Ferraris and Aston Martins in numerous prestigious events. These included the Australian Grand Prix, Le Mans 24 Hour and even the 1953 Monte Carlo Rally, teamed up with fellow Aussies Lex Davison and Stan Jones in a Holden 48/215.

Tony Gaze also represented Australia in the 1960 World Gliding Championship in Germany and continued gliding well into the 1970s – the list goes on and on, including the awarding of an Order of Australian Medal in the 2006 New Year's Honours List. Not bad for an 'almost unknown' and someone who likes to think of himself as an 'ordinary bloke'! By any measure, this is a very impressive list of achievements by someone who is certainly not 'ordinary'.

Some who have written or spoken about Tony Gaze in the past have described his life as being like something out of a 'Boys' Own Ripping Yarns' adventure story. On the surface, this might appear to be true, but that description trivialises his achievements and those of his contemporaries.

Tony Gaze's life and its achievements are not fiction, they are real. The dangers were real, the blood was real, the bullets were real and the deaths were real. His motor sport career was conducted during an era in which the term 'driver safety' was rarely used and was at best an afterthought. Death and injury were a weekly occurrence at circuits all over the world.

Those who really know Tony Gaze speak of a man of modest and polite disposition but at the same time with steely determination. He was one of the very best fighter pilots of his time and a talented racing driver. They also know him as the true gentleman he has always been.

. . . .

It was probably inevitable that when Frederick Anthony Owen (Tony) Gaze arrived on this earth on 3 February 1920 he would eventually find his way into aeroplanes and racing cars, given his family background. His father Irvine indulged in both activities and his mother Freda had done some competitive driving in England in the very early days.

Tony's paternal grandmother was born in Sydney and his grandfather Frederick Owen Gaze came to Australia from Norfolk in England and settled on a property in Western Australia where he farmed and became involved with gold. Frederick was something of a risk-taker in business and as a result Tony's father and brothers had a sometimes strange life as the family's fortunes rose and fell, apparently with some regularity. The boys' education was at a private school when things were good, but when they went awry they would quickly find themselves at a state school.

Grandfather Gaze eventually made a success of himself, largely through what became his greatest legacy in business as co-founder of the Ezywalkin' chain of retail shoe shops. It became a long-lasting and highly respected business institution with branches around Australia. The Ezywalkin' brand still exists today and provided Frederick Gaze with a source of good and constant income.

Two of Frederick's sons remained in Western Australia on the land but Irvine Gaze went to Melbourne to help manage the rapidly expanding shoe business. But this provided no satisfaction. He quickly discovered that a life of business suits, accountants and double entry bookkeeping was not for him - he yearned for the land and some adventure

Irvine got his wish for adventure in 1914 - shortly before the start of the First World War - when he signed on for the third of Sir Ernest Shackleton's Antarctic expeditions. Shackleton's first had been as a member of Robert Scott's unsuccessful attempt in 1901-04 to be the first to reach the South Pole. Scott made it to the Pole at his second attempt in 1912 only to find that the Norwegian Roald Amundsen had narrowly beaten him to it. Scott and his four companions perished on the return journey, creating one of the great 'heroic failures' of British exploration history.

Shackleton's second expedition - and his first as commander - in 1907-09 had failed to reach the Pole by the agonisingly short distance of just over 1.5 nautical miles (2.8km). With the 'Holy Grail' of the first to reach the Pole already taken, Shackleton's 1914 expedition set out to achieve another 'first' - to cross the Antarctic continent "from sea to sea", from the Weddell Sea to McMurdo Sound via the South Pole.

Irvine Gaze's involvement came about purely on a last-minute whim - the two ships of Shackleton's British Imperial Trans-Antarctic Expedition were about to sail from Sydney when it was discovered there was a man missing, so he signed on. The family was not impressed and he was subsequently largely ostracised as a result, especially since the Antarctic adventure meant he would not return to Australia until 1917 and even then he quickly left for Britain to do his bit in the war. Co-incidentally, Irvine was not the only member of the family on the expedition. His cousin, The Reverend Arnold Spencer-Smith, was its Padre.

The 1914 expedition proved to be yet another heroic failure and also provided Irvine Gaze with considerably more adventure than he'd bargained for. The expedition was split into two elements – Shackleton and his team aboard the *Endurance* went to the Weddell Sea on the western side of Antarctica with the intention of trekking across the continent via the South Pole.

Irvine Gaze was aboard the *Aurora* which went to Ross Island in McMurdo Sound. From there, the team planned to establish a base at Scott's hut and lay stores depots from Ross Island to the Beardmore Glacier, which Shackleton planned to traverse after reaching the Pole.

Of course, it all went wrong for Shackleton. His ship became entrapped in the Weddell Sea ice and had to be abandoned. Young Australian photographer Frank Hurley was aboard, his graphic images of the *Endurance* being gradually crushed to death by the relentless ice contributing greatly to the fame he would achieve as a leading light in his field.

After being stuck on a floating iceberg for five months, Shackleton and his men made it to uninhabited Elephant Island from which he and four others rowed 1300 kilometres to South Georgia, some 1500 kilometres south-east of the Falkland Islands in the South Atlantic. From there, the group was able to make its way to a Norwegian whaling station and rescue. After several attempts, the survivors of the group left behind on Elephant Island were also eventually rescued.

Meanwhile, the Ross Island party was completely unaware of all this and six including Irvine Gaze and Arnold Spencer-Smith had begun laying depots from September 1915 despite their ship having broken its moorings due to the wind and sustaining damage before it could be unloaded. The whole expedition was rapidly turning into a disaster.

Irvine Gaze's party ran into further trouble on the return journey from laying the depots. Spencer-Smith died from exhaustion and scurvy, a condition which afflicted everyone. Faced with impossibly difficult terrain, starvation and numerous other issues, things looked grim for Irvine and his friends.

Two of the party set out on foot in May 1916 and were never heard of again. Eventually, the *Aurora* was able to be repaired and sailed to safety after being stuck in the Antarctic for more than two years. Ernest Shackleton's obsession with the Antarctic continued, as did his run of failures. He tried again in 1922 but died aboard his ship, the *Quest*.

When Irvine Gaze returned to Australia he found the First World War in full swing. His need for adventure was obviously not satisfied because he almost immediately sailed to England to join the Royal Flying Corps, trained as a pilot and flew with 48 Squadron on Bristol Fighters over the Western Front. After training at Point Cook, his brother had also travelled to Britain and was an instructor with the RFC.

Irvine's adventures continued unabated during his service with the RFC. He was shot down twice, both times by Germany's JG.1 'Flying Circus' unit commanded by the legendary Manfred von Richtofen, the 'Red Baron'. By the time Irvine was shot down for the second time in 1918, von Richtofen had been killed and the squadron was commanded by a certain top German fighter pilot called Hermann Goering.

When he was captured after this incident the Germans noticed he was wearing a white medal ribbon on his flying tunic. They asked him what it was and he explained it was the Polar Medal, awarded for the Shackleton Antarctic expedition from which he'd only returned a year earlier. Irvine's German captors were mightily impressed, providing a dinner in his honour in the Officers' Mess before taking him to the prisoner-of-war camp!

. . . .

Irvine Gaze returned to England after the November 1918 Armistice and met Freda Sadler, whose grandfather owned the Westhampnett Mill in Sussex near Chichester and adjacent to the Duke of Richmond and Gordon's Goodwood estate. It was the start of an association with a part of the world that would later play a major role in Tony Gaze's life. Westhampnett airfield was his first posting as a newly-qualified Royal Air Force pilot in early 1941 and with Tony's input and encouragement it became the site of the Goodwood Park motor racing circuit after the war.

Freda had been a driver at the Royal Flying Corps station at nearby Tangmere, an airfield built by German prisoners-of-war during World War I and one which would assume importance as an RAF base in the next war. Little flying took place at Tangmere during the inter-war years and the site was used mainly as a storage facility. It underwent considerable development during the RAF's expansion period of the late 1930s and during the Battle of Britain was a major Fighter Command station.

That Freda was a driver was unusual enough for a woman in those days but she also indulged in a little competitive motoring. When she and Irvine Gaze were married in England before returning to Australia, the die was cast for their offspring – aircraft and cars were bound to play a part in their lives.

By then Irvine had lost his claim on the family property in Western Australia as both his brothers had survived the war and his father Frederick had divided the property in half, built himself another house and settled the brothers on their own places. Irvine returned to Victoria to resume helping run the local Ezywalkin' operation and establish his branch of the family as the only Gazes there – the rest of the family was in the west.

Tony Gaze's birth in February 1920 was followed by that of brother Scott two years later. The inevitable involvement with cars and aircraft didn't take long to occur. In early 1928, when Tony was eight and Scott six, their father took them to a motor race meeting at Safety Beach near Dromana on the Port Phillip Bay side of Victoria's Mornington Peninsula. The racing was around a couple of main and side roads with a paddock in the middle and in those days it was all done by 'proper' racing cars like Bugattis, Lombards and Ballots plus locally-built specials.

A Sopwith Gnu biplane was operating from the middle of the paddock, giving joyrides. The Gazes went for a ride in it, the experience rekindling Irvine's interest in flying and creating the boys' interest in both it and motor racing. Shortly afterwards – on 26 March 1928 – the first Australian Grand Prix was held at Phillip Island and the Gazes travelled there by car and ferry to watch the race.

In those days nearly all motor races in Australia and elsewhere were handicaps because there wasn't enough cars of similar performance to have today's emphasis on outright performance and finishing positions. It was all a bit amateurish compared to today with no such thing as crowd control with spectators walking around on the edge of the track and jumping out of the way of the racing cars as they came by.

The Gaze family saw Arthur Waite declared the winner of the inaugural Australian Grand Prix in his works supercharged Austin 7 after 16 laps and 105 miles of racing at an average speed of 56 miles per hour.

These motor races excited interest in all three of the Gaze males, young and old. Irvine began contesting trials – rallies these days – but he also started flying again, joining the aero club at Essendon. The boys also became involved with horse riding and found themselves in the happy situation where on one weekend they'd go flying – with the two them sharing the front cockpit of a Cirrus Moth while they were still small enough to do so – and the next weekend they'd be off to the Melbourne Hunt Kennels to ride their ponies.

This went on for quite a few years but the only motor sport they were involved with by then was hillclimbs because there wasn't much else in their part of the world apart from the dirt track at Aspendale Speedway on the shores of Port Phillip Bay. The Gazes went there several times to watch the action.

The Gaze brothers had a happy and interesting upbringing which some who might regard themselves as being less fortunate could have been tempted to describe as 'idyllic'. There were plenty of things happening to keep them amused, space to roam on the family property, good educational opportunities and parents who generally encouraged whatever activities they wanted to be involved in.

As for flying, Irvine entered aerial derbies, which were handicapped competitive events. Unfortunately, this activity came to a sudden halt when another pilot in a de Havilland DH.9 hit power lines and crashed in a sheet of flame while coming into land at Essendon during one such event. This prompted Tony's mother to put her foot down and ban Irvine from flying any more!

Tony went to Prep School in Melbourne and then to Geelong Grammar where he proved to be athletic, excelling at rowing in particular. From there, he went to England and Cambridge University (Queens' College) in 1938 to study Natural Sciences.

. . . .

Tony became more interested in cars and just before going to Cambridge he met wealthy young Englishman Peter Whitehead at Rob Roy hillclimb on 13 June 1938. Whitehead was visiting Australia for the first time to represent his family's wool business and had brought his supercharged ERA racing car with him to contest various events including the 1938 Australian Grand Prix at the famed – and unsurfaced at that stage – Mount Panorama circuit near Bathurst in New South Wales. Whitehead set a new record at Rob Roy the day he met Tony, his time of 31.46 seconds taking a very substantial four seconds off the previous mark.

The appearance of the 23-years-old Whitehead and his advanced ERA at the Grand Prix generated considerable excitement and interest and the combination did not disappoint, winning the handicap race against some serious local opposition. Tony got to know Whitehead then, starting a long-standing friendship and motor sport association which fully developed after the war and lasted until the Englishman was killed in a rally accident in France in 1958.

By the time he left Australia for Cambridge, Tony was very interested in motoring and motor sport so in England he joined the Junior Car Club. He had a letter of introduction from the Light Car Club of Australia and also the Cambridge University Automobile Club, but somewhat ironically he wasn't allowed to have a car while at Queens' College.

Tony decided to get into a bit of motor racing so he went to Brooklands "expecting it to be the members just having a jolly good time running around the track." He borrowed an English-bodied Hudson from his uncle, Bob Sadler, turned up on the practice day and found that everyone who was anyone was there with luminaries such as Peter Whitehead, Johnny Wakefield, Raymond Mays, 'B Bira' (Prince Birabongse Bhanuban of Siam) and many others lining up their cars for scrutineering. It was far from the 'jolly outing' Tony was expecting – this was serious motor racing.

Tony had to have a passenger with him because he was a beginner and managed to convince the Vacuum Oil Company's racing manager – who was a friend of the family – to ride with him. Tony considered this to be very brave of him! They went quite well for a while but then a common Hudson problem emerged – its fuel pipe ran very close to the exhaust, causing fuel vaporisation and therefore leading to a lack of continuing and appropriate noises from the engine.

In the clubhouse afterwards Tony met a lot of people and he was made feel very welcome. It was only later that he found out that both his car and the other Hudson competing were almost flagged off for dangerous driving – not because the drivers were a problem but because the cars appeared to be very unstable coming off the famed Brooklands banking.

The Brooklands debut would be the end of Tony's motor racing career for a while. His passion for rowing remained and he competed for Queens' College and the London Rowing Club, this taking up all his spare time. The London Rowing Club's black and white colours would later appear on the helmets of two Formula One world champions – Graham Hill (1962 and 1968) and his son Damon in 1996.

Tony had one more experience of motor sport in 1938 when he hired a Vauxhall to go to Donington Park in October to watch the Auto Unions and Mercedes contest the Grand Prix. Unfortunately he missed most of the race because the car broke down en route and he arrived late but was able to see Tazio Nuvolari win in his Auto Union followed by Hermann Lang's Mercedes-Benz W154, Dick Seaman's W154, Hermann Muller's Auto Union and Robert Mazaud's Delahaye.

But the world was changing. Three weeks earlier, British Prime Minister Neville Chamberlain had returned from a meeting in Munich, Germany with Adolf Hitler. The rise of Nazi Germany in the 1930s had cast a shadow over the world and most in Britain were convinced that war was inevitable. Tony Gaze was one of them and changed from a Natural Sciences to Mechanical Sciences degree at Cambridge so he could read Aeronautics because he thought it would be more useful in a time of war.

Chamberlain's policy of appeasement towards Germany and its ambitions was never going to succeed, despite the British PM's "peace in our time" assurances. Hitler was a liar and a cunning politician who was easily able to con the weak Chamberlain. The situation worsened during 1939 as Hitler's promises were eventually recognised as being meaningless by all but the most ardent appeasers.

On 1 September 1939 Germany invaded Poland, beginning its push westwards through the Low Countries towards France and eventually – it hoped – Britain. Two days later Britain declared war on Germany and the lives of countless millions of people around the world – including that of Tony Gaze – changed forever.

TWO

TYRO PILOT

WHEN WAR WAS declared on 3 September 1939, Tony Gaze was determined to emulate his father Irvine and join Britain's fight against Germany as a pilot in what was now the Royal Air Force. When the RAF Recruiting Service called at Cambridge he applied and after undergoing the necessary aptitude tests and interviews he was deemed suitable for pilot training and accepted as such on 10 October 1939.

Tony's younger brother Scott also decided to join the RAF and sent a message saying he was on his way, travelling to Britain with his aunt who had gone to Australia to help the boys' father Irvine when their mother Freda passed away shortly before the war started.

In Australia, Irvine Gaze also joined up to 'do his bit' and with the rank of Squadron Leader became the Commanding Officer of several Royal Australian Air Force training establishments including No 3 Elementary Flying Training School (EFTS) at Essendon, Victoria, No 8 EFTS at Narrandera, New South Wales and No 6 Initial Training School at Bradfield Park NSW. The latter was a non-flying unit at which trainee aircrews were tutored in subjects such as mathematics, navigation, law and administration, signals, science and armament before being sent off to flying training units.

When Scott arrived in Britain the Gaze brothers reported to Portsmouth Barracks with the intention and expectation of going straight into the RAF as cadets, only to be told there were no flying training places immediately available. They therefore had to bide their time until there was and filled their days with activities like taking evacuated children to the safety of the countryside. They officially joined up on 9 January 1940 with the rank of Aircraftman Second Class (AC2) - the lowest of the low! Initially based at Uxbridge, their duties included such things as dishwashing and other menial tasks.

Tony and his fellow new recruits came across some unexpected political activity at Uxbridge. They were given a hard time by Labour supporters and other left-wingers who abused them for joining an 'imperialist war' war against their hero, Joseph Stalin, and the Soviet Union.

Germany and the USSR were at that time allies, having signed a non-aggression pact just over a week before Germany invaded Poland and started the war. As Stalin was always mindful of his own ambitions, the agreement contained clauses about the partition of Poland. Soviet forces had taken part in its invasion, taking over the eastern part of the country. A partition agreement was formally signed in late September 1939.

It wasn't until Germany began its attempted invasion of Russia in June 1941 that Britain and the USSR became allies when they signed the Anglo-Soviet Treaty of Mutual Assistance. This gave communists within the British labour movement the chance they had been waiting for and allowed their influence within the trade unions to steadily grow - something Tony would discover in 1943 when he undertook Wings of Victory talks with factory workers.

At Uxbridge, the RAF discovered that Tony and Scott had been machine gunners in the school cadets so they were moved on to ground defence duties at Long Benton - a balloon repair station - then Dishforth in Yorkshire, the base of 10 Squadron's Armstrong Whitworth Whitley bombers. Hitching a ride in the Whitleys' rear turrets became a regular activity and as German intruders were around all this flying was done with loaded guns.

It was rather hoped that a German would have a go at the Whitleys because - as Tony notes - "The Lewis guns we had on the ground weren't much good against Heinkels coming over at 18,000 feet!" Perhaps this is an indication that one of his most notable attributes as a fighter pilot - the desire to always want to have a go at the enemy - was already starting to emerge.

But the Gaze brothers and their fellow 'new boys' also witnessed the realities of war for the first time at Dishforth. They often saw Whitleys that had returned from night leaflet-dropping 'raids' having their rear turrets washed out after what remained of an unfortunate air gunner had been taken away....

. . . .

Flying training places eventually became available and both Tony and Scott were sent to Cambridge for their initial, ground instruction. The brothers went through this and their entire flying training together, which was unusual because family members were normally separated. When the time came to be posted to their first operational squadron, they also went together.

Now with the rank of Leading Aircraftman (LAC) Tony and Scott found themselves as part of a 'mob' of people just like them - Australians, Canadians, New Zealanders, South Africans, Rhodesians and even a few Americans - who had tried to get into flying training as soon as war was declared but were put on hold. Having had six months in one uniform they were "as scruffy as hell" according to Tony but at the same time pretty 'military-wise' by then, having learnt most of the lurks.

This caused some concern for the instructors at Cambridge because up until then they'd had people who were all sergeants with bright new uniforms. Instead they had a bunch of scruffy and largely irreverent colonials who were mere LACs. The instructors thought they could really boss the new boys but of course this group made certain they didn't. Tony notes that the instructors "were very pleased to get rid of us and send us to the flying training schools."

Tony and Scott were posted to No 7 Elementary Flying Training School at Desford near Leicester. This had been the Reid & Sigrist company's pre-war training centre and was therefore run very much along civilian lines with every student having a room of his own.

Reid & Sigrist was contracted by the RAF to run five EFTSs during the war and was previously best known for its manufacture of aircraft instruments. The company also produced a couple of one-off light twin trainers of its own design - the remarkably-named Snargasher (1939) and Desford (1945). Apart from the flying schools, Reid & Sigrist's main activity during the war was as a member of the Civilian Repair Organsiation, responsible for the repair and modification of Boulton Paul Defiants, Bell Airacobras and North American Mitchells at its Desford Airfield facility.

Like tens of thousands of others, the Gaze brothers did their initial flying training on the ubiquitous de Havilland Tiger Moth and as they'd both previously done a bit of flying with their father in Cirrus and Gipsy Moths when they were young, they were used to those sorts of aeroplanes.

The big moment of Tony's first lesson occurred on 26 July 1940 in Tiger Moth N6481, a time when the Battle of Britain was just starting to get into full swing. That 30 minute first sortie was typical of anyone's first flying lesson - familiarity with cockpit layout, effects of controls and straight and level flying.

Tony's instructor at Desford was a Sgt Ramsey, who he regarded as being very good as he got his pupils to enjoy flying - always the sign of a good instructor. On that first flight he pulled a trick with which many military pilots are no doubt very familiar. Sgt Ramsey asked Tony if his straps were tight. "Yes sir" was the reply, at which point the Tiger Moth was immediately rolled inverted.

Tony dropped about half an inch but it felt like he was going to fall out of the aeroplane. Lesson learnt!

Two flights a day was standard procedure so the training was at a fairly intense level. Tony soloed just one week after his first lesson - on 2 August - in Tiger Moth T5700 after logging 8hrs 25min of dual instruction.

Like most newly solo pilots, Tony found the most worrying thing about flying alone was the possibility of getting lost. He notes that "the first time you cut the umbilical and left sight of the airfield it was a bit frightening because there was always a haze and you really had to watch it. The first time I left, thank God, Leicester was there and because it was big and easily seen I knew where I was!"

Halfway through Tony's basic training at Desford and at a time when an attempted invasion of Britain was regarded as a matter of 'when', not 'if', some of 7 EFTS's Tiger Moths were fitted with underwing racks capable of carrying eight 20lb (9kg) anti-personnel bombs, four on each side. The plan was that the armed Tigers flown by instructors would attack the German landing barges when they came.

The 'Tiger Moth Bomber' concept had been initiated by de Havilland, using the bomb racks fitted to DH.84 Dragons delivered to Iraq in 1932. The company made 1500 sets of racks for Tiger Moths and the idea was extensively tested, although there were some issues with spin recovery and centre-of-gravity.

The idea was never used in anger, which is probably just as well. As has been written elsewhere, "the thought of Tiger Moths without cover of any kind bombing well-armed troops on the beaches hardly bears thinking about." Nevertheless, 7 EFTS's instructors, leading groups of pupils, practised 'dry run' bombing techniques on the jetty of a reservoir just north of Desford, with the racks fitted to their aircraft but not bombs.

Another idea to turn the Tiger Moth into an offensive weapon is also worth mentioning because it involved 7 EFTS's Commanding Officer of the time, Squadron Leader George Lowdell. He had been responsible for opening up Desford Airfield for Reid & Sigrist in 1929 and had amassed considerable display and 'crazy flying' experience at air shows before the war. As such, he was considered the right person to test the Tiger Moth 'Paraslasher'!

The Paraslasher was another idea born of Britain's situation in 1940. Devised by inventor and industrialist George Reid (half of Reid & Sigrist), it comprised basically a farmer's hand scythe attached to the end of an 8 feet (2.4m) long tube which lay flush with the underside of the Tiger Moth's fuselage when not in use and therefore did not interfere with the aircraft's training role. It was lowered when being put to its intended purpose – to literally slash invading paratroopers' parachutes as they were making their way to the ground.

Cutting enemy paratroops who had just landed in open ground was another planned use for the Paraslasher and George Lowdell successfully demonstrated this initially using life-sized pictures of Hitler and Mussolini painted onto canvas and then sacks of straw simulating a man. Lowdell became extremely adept at this and proved capable of cutting these targets into shreds even when they were prone on the ground.

Despite Lowdell's demonstrations, the Air Ministry decided not to go ahead with the Paraslasher because it was thought that most pilots would not be able to successfully emulate his extremely accurate flying. There was also the fact that in real life the Tiger Moths would undoubtedly be fired on and that an enemy soldier on the ground would be able to move, unlike a sack of straw!

The summer and early autumn of 1940 was an interesting time to be in England. Germany already controlled most of Western Europe including France and the Battle of Britain was raging. Britain was fighting for its life but the outcome of the battle would have a far-reaching and profound effect on the rest of the world and indeed world history for decades to come. If Britain lost and was invaded, freedom everywhere would be threatened.

The importance of the Battle of Britain cannot be understated – it can be strongly argued that it was the most important single campaign of the entire war. If had Britain later been unavailable as the 'launching pad' for the retaking of Europe, it would have been almost impossible to dislodge the Nazis.

Brits kept a close eye on the progress of the battle. All over the country, both civilians and military personnel were keeping a daily score of how many enemy aircraft the RAF had shot down got and how many had been lost.

Tony remembers that the whole country was getting ready for invasion: "Even when we were at Cambridge we were digging trenches on the crossroads – they were just so certain that invasion was coming. Cambridge is a long way from the coast but we were sent out to dig slit trenches at every crossroad where they were going to defend. Everyone expected the invasion at any moment but the British didn't get frightened. Churchill [who had replaced Chamberlain as Prime Minister on 10 May] really got them feeling they would fight down to the last ditch. You can't beat inspirational leadership at a time like that and Churchill provided it."

Everyone was glued to the radio for news, listening to the BBC and hearing reassuring voices such as that of newsreader Alvar Liddell, who became very much of the voice of Britain during that period to listeners not only at home but also abroad. A typical broadcast would go something like: "This is the BBC Home Service and here is the 9 o'clock news with Alvar Liddell reading it. Today, 23 German aircraft were destroyed by the RAF in big raids on London and the Midlands [a cheer from the listeners]. We lost eight fighters but six of our pilots were saved...." A bigger cheer invariably followed.

Tony and Scott Gaze's basic flying training at Desford continued until the first week of September 1940 when the Battle of Britain was nearing its climax and the Luftwaffe, crucially, had switched the focus of its bombing from the RAF's airfields to London and other cities. By the time of Tony's last flight at 7 EFTS on 3 September he had 51 hours in his log book - exactly half of which were solo - and an 'above average' assessment. The next step was advanced training.

. . . .

For that, Tony and Scott were sent to No 5 Flying Training School (FTS) at Sealand, near Chester to fly the Miles Master. This was a very different kettle of fish to the Tiger Moths used for initial training - it was a modern low wing monoplane with such advanced features as retractable undercarriage, flaps and variable-pitch propeller.

The Master Mk.I in which Tony first flew at Sealand was powered by 715hp (533kW) Rolls-Royce Kestrel vee-12 engine so the performance difference between it and the Tiger was substantial - nearly six times the power, more than twice the speed and over three times the rate of climb and maximum weight.

Tony's first flight in a Master (N7428) was on 10 September 1940 with instructor Plt Off Howorth taking him through the basics again - effects of controls, taxying, straight and level flight and medium turns. His first solo in the Master was four days later, the day before one of the most momentous in British history.

15 September 1940 is now commemorated as Battle of Britain Day, a day that witnessed the Luftwaffe's last major daylight offensive of the campaign launched and repelled by RAF Fighter Command. After that, Germany had to concede it had not achieved the air superiority over Britain that had been promised to Hitler by Reichsmarschall Goering and invasion plans were indefinitely postponed. The raids nevertheless continued into the following month, the last day of the Battle of Britain officially recognised as 31 October. The Luftwaffe then switched to a new phase of raids on Britain, the night *blitz*.

Despite the relatively complex nature of the Master, Tony says "there was no big drama about it – there were few accidents and we enjoyed flying something we reckoned was modern. Anyway, it also gave the instructors the chance to fly a modern aircraft because they were in the same position as we were after the Tigers – they'd never had undercarriages that had to be retracted or anything like that. We rather looked down on those still flying Hawker Hinds and other biplane stuff!"

Of course Tony did manage to outsmart himself once. On 16 November 1940 he took Master N7701 to the training station at South Cerney as part of his cross-country training and thought he'd do a 'line shooting' takeoff. In other words, a bit of showing off. After takeoff, Tony noticed the aeroplane seemed reluctant to build up any decent speed. He thought there may have been something stuck up the airspeed indicator pitot to give a false reading, he checked everything noting that all the lights were "nice and green", tried diving steeply but all with no effect.

It was only when he was halfway home that he suddenly realised the "nice green lights" were those indicating the position of the undercarriage. Green means down and locked! A somewhat sheepish Gaze flew on to his next destination thinking how lucky he was that they weren't on radio because "if we were I'd probably have been calling for help – then I'd have been in real trouble!"

But Tony had already been in more serious trouble with officialdom and had faced the unpleasant prospect of a Court Martial. He managed to avoid that – something that would surely have ended his career before it started – but still received a dreaded 'Red Endorsement' in his log book. This was a note, hand-written in red ink by the 'big boss', the Air Vice Marshal commanding the RAF Group with which the transgressing pilot was flying at the time.

In Tony Gaze's case it reads: "Disobedience – unauthorised low flying, R T Willock AVM AOC 21 Group 26/11/40".

October 13th had witnessed the first accident on Tony's course and the pilot was killed. The next day had a low, 800 feet cloud base and Tony flew around to have a look at the wreckage. He found it and saw the people on the ground salvaging it.

Then he discovered he had another Master on his tail, one carrying Junior Course markings. Like any self-respecting would-be fighter pilot there was no way he was "going to let a Junior Course bloke get on my tail". A mock dogfight ensued, all conducted at low level. After a while and quite a bit of fun Tony waggled his Master's wings to signal the end of it and for the other pilot to come up into formation. But it was not a Junior Course pilot at all – it was the Chief Flying Instructor!"

The CFI had also gone up to have a look at the wreck. On returning to the airfield Tony was immediately put under arrest for unauthorised low flying. Tony remembers that the CFI "had steam coming out of his ears" he was so angry, although much of that was undoubtedly due to a bruised ego as much as anything else because Tony had succeeded in keeping the CFI off his tail during their mock dogfight, and in full view of many witnesses on the ground.

Tony was under open arrest while awaiting his Court Martial. One day he was ordered to fly to headquarters for an interview with the Air Vice Marshal, who gave him the Red Endorsement. He asked: "How much do you know about flying, Gaze?" to which the reply "very little sir" was given. The AVM then delivered a lecture and "rather smilingly" gave Tony the endorsement.

It was later discovered that Tony's Defending Officer had got the Court Martial cancelled on the technicality that as the cloud base had been 800 feet on the day in question (low flying was officially designated as being below 1,000 feet) and that as Tony *was* authorised to low fly, what he'd done was not a Court Martial offence. Of course everyone including the AVM knew what he'd really been up to so some kind of punishment had to be meted out.

The only real flying incident Tony had while at 5 FTS had been on 11 October (again in N7701) during another solo cross-country exercise when he flew to Hullavington in Wiltshire, the base for a Hawker Hind training squadron.

Halfway there he was indulging in a few rolls when the Master suddenly caught fire. He followed all the correct procedures in the event of a fire – switch the fuel off, open the throttle – and the fire went out. Everything was alright on the return flight and the fire probably resulted from Tony doing what he describes as "some rather ropey rolls". The hydraulic fluid tank had been overfilled and with the negative 'g' it built up and had overflowed onto the exhaust with spectacular but ultimately harmless results.

At Hullavington the instructors showed great interest in Tony's Master because they were all still flying Hind biplanes. Naturally, every instructor offered to take the Master for a test flight!

With the 'Red Endorsement' incident obviously forgiven, Tony completed his advanced training at 5 FTS in early January 1941, earning his 'wings'. He graduated with another 'above average' assessment and had added a further 71 flying hours to his tally, bringing the total to 122 hours. Scott also successfully completed his advanced training – the Gaze brothers were almost ready to take on Hitler's hordes.

Like the other pilots who had got that far, he was now reasonably proficient at most aspects of his craft including instrument, formation and low flying, aerobatics, precautionary and forced landings and navigation. Selected as a fighter pilot, Tony would now take the last step before joining his first operational squadron – a stint at an Operational Training Unit (OTU) and his first experiences of flying the aircraft in which he exclusively spent his operational career, the Supermarine Spitfire. As before, Scott and Tony stayed together for this part of their careers.

It seems strange with the benefit of hindsight, but Tony remembers that "most of us wanted to go onto Hurricanes because we felt it had done the work in the Battle of Britain and the Spit had been given the credit. When we were put on Spitfires it wasn't a let down but there was a slight feeling of disappointment. But when I eventually flew a Hurricane I was damn glad I'd been put on Spits because it was so slow!"

· · · · · · · · · ·

The purpose of an Operational Training Unit is to prepare new pilots for the rigours of squadron service that lie ahead. In wartime this was especially important because young pilots were immediately thrown into combat, so at least a modicum of proper operational training would seem to be appropriate.

Unfortunately, that's not what Tony Gaze found when he was posted to No 57 OTU at Hawarden near Chester from 3 February 1941. The airfield was under repair at the time so pilots travelled by bus to Speke (Liverpool) to fly their Spitfires, sometimes staying the night and joining the fire watchers on the hotel roof while the docks were being bombed.

Tony is scathing about what he found at 57 OTU: "There was nil instruction. There were some bored ex-Battle of Britain pilots there who weren't really instructors - all they did was send us off to fly around - I think we had one or two formation flights and that was it.

"We were sent to the squadron completely untrained except for being able to fly Spitfires. Even so, we had only 14-15 hours on Spits before going to a squadron with no proper training. We were a damned nuisance to the squadron because they had to come off what they were supposed to be doing to teach us a few things because we'd had no combat training.

"We were just sent off on flights - we'd beat up our girlfriends' houses - there was no gunnery except that just before we left the OTU we were sent to fire our guns at the sea to hear the noise they made. There wasn't even a target, it was absolutely crazy. No simulated combat, no anything.

"When I went back to the OTU after my first tour of operations some of those instructors were still there - they'd decided they'd had enough of war and were just happy to sit there bored. When I got a Flight I changed the whole system and started challenging the other Flights to interception practices, dogfights and so on because I didn't want to send people out in the same position I had been."

After three check flights with an instructor in a Master, Tony's big moment came on 6 February 1941 when he was let loose in a Spitfire for the first time. The OTU's Spitfires were all Mk.Is, many of them well-worn veterans of the Battle of Britain. There was no such thing as a two-seat Spitfire then - there wasn't until after the war when Supermarine produced a few converted from single-seaters - so it was familiarise yourself with the cockpit, read the pilot's notes, learn the numbers and off you go.

That first flight lasted one hour and went off without incident, Tony logging a grand total of 14 Spitfire flights and 15 hours between then and 8 March when he was signed off as fit to join an operational squadron. Two days later, he and Scott were with 610 Squadron.

THREE

BADER'S BUS SERVICE

AT THE GAZE brothers' request, their first operational squadron posting was with 610 'County of Chester' Squadron, commanded by Battle of Britain veteran Squadron Leader John Ellis. The squadron had been formed in 1936 as an Auxiliary Air Force unit as part of the early stages of the RAF's general expansion instigated at the time as the strength of Nazi Germany grew and the first the first thoughts of a possible war were being considered. Like the other AuxAF squadrons, 610 subsequently became a regular RAF unit.

The squadron operated mainly from Biggin Hill during the Battle of Britain equipped with Spitfire Is but from late 1940 was based at Westhampnett in West Sussex near Chichester on the South Coast of England as part of RAF Fighter Command's 11 Group Tangmere Wing. From 18 March 1941 – just a week after the Gaze brothers arrived – command of the Wing was taken over the legendary Wing Commander Douglas 'Tin Legs' Bader.

The Wing quickly became known as 'Bader's Bus Service' and its leader was one of the first to carry his initials on the side of his aircraft rather than the normal squadron codes. This was originally introduced to allow easier identification of the Wing Leader in large formations but subsequently became a matter of status afforded to those of Wing Commander or higher rank. Bader's 'DB' markings inspired the callsign 'Dogsbody' which soon became his official one.

The Gaze boys had requested a posting to Tangmere because of the previous family connection to the area. Another pilot who flew with the Tangmere Wing was Johnnie Johnson, who would subsequently achieve fame as the RAF's top scoring fighter pilot of the war. Another future ace, Hugh 'Cocky' Dundas, initially flew as Bader's number three with Sgt Alan Smith as his number two.

Westhampnett was acquired from the Duke of Richmond's Goodwood Estate in 1938 for use as an emergency landing ground for nearby Tangmere, at which stage it was little more than a cleared field. It was upgraded to the status of a satellite airfield in 1940, re-opening in July of that year just as the Battle of Britain was getting underway. Its first regular tenants were the Hawker Hurricanes of 145 Squadron.

Westhampnett had an ongoing problem with water-logging until the northern winter of 1940-41 when some hard aircraft stands were built followed by a sealed perimeter track for fuel tankers and other vehicles on the instigation of Douglas Bader. The Irish labourers who built the track quickly discovered the venom that could come from the Wing Commander's mouth if he considered they were not working hard enough - which was often.

Concerns about invasion were still in force in early 1941. Westhampnett had retractable machine gun pillboxes dug in around the perimeter and Bofors guns, light tanks and search lights in orchards and small fields around the airfield. Tony's trips to see his girlfriend on the coast meant braving the Home Guard checkpoint each way. Fuel was very short and even with Tony's economical little MG J2 it was a problem. One night he ran out of fuel at a railway crossing and had to help himself to the kerosene in the crossing gate lamps to get back to base.

No 610 Squadron had moved to Westhampnett in mid-December 1940, three months before the Gaze brothers arrived as new Pilot Officers. By then, the Tangmere Wing comprised 610 Squadron, 145 Squadron and 616 Squadron, all equipped with the Spitfire II.

11 Group had been formed in May 1936 and was responsible for the defence of the heavily populated south-east of England including London. As such, it took the lion's share of the workload during Battle of Britain and therefore had the greatest number of fighter squadrons allocated to it.

Brilliantly commanded by New Zealander Air Vice Marshal Keith Park during the battle - who worked closely and effectively with Fighter Command AOC Air Marshal Sir Hugh Dowding - 11 Group was home to many of the bases which subsequently went into the folklore due to their role in the battle - Biggin Hill, Croydon, Debden, Hornchurch, Kenley, Manston, North Weald and Tangmere among them.

One of Keith Park's many problems during the battle was the commander of 12 Group (covering the Midlands), AVM Trafford Leigh-Mallory. His cumbersome 'Big Wing' theory of assembling large numbers of fighters to attack German raids was anathema to Park, who needed his fighters up and fighting within a few minutes, not the considerable time it took to assemble a Big Wing. By the time all the aircraft had assembled and were ready to fight, the German bombers had done their damage - largely to 11 Group's airfields - and were on their way home.

One of Leigh-Mallory's supporters was also 12 Group's star pilot during the battle, Douglas Bader, then leader of the Duxford Wing. By the time the

Gaze brothers arrived at 11 Group in March 1941, Leigh–Mallory had taken over from Park as its chief and Bader was shortly to join him as leader of the Tangmere Wing. By now, the Big Wing idea had more relevance as Fighter Command was no longer fighting a purely defensive war.

Douglas Bader is probably the best-known of all the British fighter aces and has been the subject of books including the Paul Brickhill's famous *Reach For The Sky* and the movie of the same name that followed. A pre-war RAF 'hotshot', Bader had crashed a Bristol Bulldog in 1931 while showing off during an impromptu low level aerobatics display, lost both his legs (and very nearly his life) and was invalided out of the RAF.

Getting around on artificial 'tin legs', Bader persuaded the RAF to take him back in 1940 and went on to score 22 confirmed 'kills' in the Battle of Britain and afterwards – flying both Hurricanes and Spitfires – between June 1940 and August 1941 when he was himself shot down and taken prisoner. A dogmatic and often bloody-minded man, Bader was simultaneously an inspiration and an annoyance!

Tony and Scott Gaze first met Douglas Bader when he went to their farm house billet to introduce himself – and he kept talking about himself for 20 minutes! When he left the brothers were looking at each other wondering what they'd got!

It wasn't until Tony was cleared to join major operations that he flew his first sortie led by Bader and experienced his leadership skills, these complimented greatly by the ability of the Wing's Controller, Group Captain Woodhall, to pass on enemy positions and altitude. Bader tended to give a running commentary, cheered up the worriers and went back to help those in trouble. Tony flew 30 sorties into Europe led by Bader.

In January 1941 and with the threat of imminent German invasion gone, Fighter Command's squadrons began expanding their roles and started conducting offensive sweeps over Europe. At first these were little more than cheeky shows of defiance but they soon became organised and effective incursions into enemy occupied territory.

There were several variations on these offensive operations, each with a specific purpose and code name:
Circus: A bomber or fighter-bomber operation escorted by fighters and intended mainly to entice enemy fighters into the air.
Ramrod: Similar to a Circus but with the aim of destroying a specific target.

Rhubard: Freelance fighter operations on a small scale attacking targets of opportunity; often conducted in bad weather so as to introduce an element of surprise.

Rodeo: A fighter sweep over enemy territory without accompanying bombers.

Sweep: A general term covering fighters flying offensive missions over enemy territory or the sea, with or without accompanying bombers.

. . . .

Tony Gaze was allocated to 610 Squadron's 'A' Flight and Scott to 'B' Flight. They quickly discovered that life with an operational unit was very different to a training outfit. The whole attitude changed from sticking to the rules to 'to hell with the rules'. The first time he went up with his flight commander they did a battle climb to 30,000 feet and on the order to return home the commander just went vertical – downwards. They pulled out at 500 feet and went home.

This was never done in training – any pilot who did would have been in big trouble. Of course the flight commander did that sort of thing to make sure his new charge would be able to stick with him no matter what, a vitally important and necessary skill to have in combat.

The Spitfire II was the first model to come out of the new mass production facility at Castle Bromwich in Birmingham. It was armed with eight 0.303in machine guns like the Mk.I, the main difference being a slightly more powerful Merlin engine and a Coffman cartridge rather than electrical starting system.

After logging a dozen or so test, mock dogfight, aerobatics and formation practice flights, Tony's first operational sortie came on 19 March 1941, a minesweeper patrol in Spitfire DW-J. There was some relief that this first mission – albeit a relatively innocuous one – had been got out of the way.

Tony relates how things worked at the squadron: "You knew through the flight office – or tent, usually – that you're on the list to fly with whoever it was in Red Section, Blue Section or something or another and when you were selected you felt very excited.

"You put your parachute on the wingtip of the aircraft, helmet on the gunsight, went back to the rest of the gang and waited. In those days I used to just sit down and think or spend the time polishing my aeroplane – you had to do something. Some people played cards, some just tried to sleep.

"There were the two telephones – the normal telephone and the operational telephone and they had different rings. Every time either of them rang you'd jump. Mostly it was just the ordinary one and then the operational one would ring – the bloke would answer it and say, for example, 'Red Section scramble'.

"You'd just get up and run for whatever section you were and by the time you got to the aircraft the crew would have the engine started and be waiting to help put your parachute on and strap you in. Some people put their parachutes on the tail, but being tall I found it easier to grab it off the wingtip and just slip it over my shoulder.

"You just went off with your leader and from a grass airfield it was from wherever you were facing – there was no taxying – just open up and go. Your leader would call up and say you're airborne, get a vector and height to go to.

"The first one of these I went on we clambered up to 25,000 feet and they said 'the plot has faded, they've gone home'. So you'd just head back home and land. You always went straight to the Intelligence Officer and made your report – obviously if you hadn't had any combat you didn't have anything to fill in – and you just said 'we got to 25,000 and the Germans went'. I think the Germans used to call their blokes off when they saw we'd got to 25,000 on their radar, so you'd go back feeling a bit depressed because there was no fight."

Tragedy struck the Gaze family on 23 March when Scott was killed in his Spitfire not far from Goodwood. He was just two months past his 19th birthday and had been with the squadron for only two weeks.

Tony relates what happened: "We were all flying in very low cloud expecting Ju 88 and Do 217 intruders popping out of the cloud and bombing. I made sure I was over the sea before breaking cloud and found we had two aircraft missing after landing, including Scott's. One of them finally landed but it wasn't him.

"A cloud of smoke several miles away turned out to be from his aircraft. I flew over the next day and the aircraft was in one piece and the ground in front of it was torn to pieces by the guns firing through. I thought he must have spun in flat – had he flown into the ground there would have been nothing but bits of Spitfire everywhere. As his guns fired through he may have been in action, but we don't know."

Tony feels that Scott's 19-years-old over-confidence may have contributed to the accident and that it would have been quickly jumped on and sorted out by Bader had he arrived at the Wing earlier and had more time to exert his influence on the youngster. But he didn't, and Scott was lost before he could show what he could do.

There was little time to dwell on Scott's loss because the next couple of months were busy for all of 610 Squadron's pilots, mainly flying patrols around the south coast of England with but no direct contact with enemy aircraft. The closest Tony got was on 14 April when he saw some Ju 88s bombing shipping in the distance. Three days later while up doing a radio test a case of misidentification could have been interesting when the aircraft he thought was a Beaufighter turned out to be a Ju 88! No harm done.

Tony and his colleagues were regularly flying two or three sorties a day during this period. Things got a little more exciting on 21 April when he logged his first offensive operation to Occupied France, escorting 17 Bristol Blenheims that were bombing La Havre. He fired his Spitfire's guns in anger for the first time on 24 April during a Rhubarb to France when he had the opportunity to shoot up barges, trucks and gun crews. But there was still no contact with enemy aircraft, something he was becoming increasingly frustrated about.

On 7 May, Tony at last had what he thought was a chance to take on the enemy while escorting a Lysander performing an air-sea rescue sortie over the Channel: "The first time I ran into them was a complete fluke.... three [Messerschmitt] 109s suddenly appeared. I found to my dismay that all the blurb I'd been listening to about the Spitfire being faster than the 109 down low was nonsense. I did all the right things, went through the 'gate', pressed the button and emergency boost thinking I'll catch these blokes up.

"Did I hell! By the time we got to the French coast they were three trails of black smoke with dots on the end of them, they'd got so far ahead of me. I suddenly thought 'wait a minute, we're now on their side of the Channel and it's three to one - you'd better go home!'

"So I went home and I didn't have much fuel left because you forget that your fuel consumption goes up from about 35 gallons and hour to 150 at full bore. I landed and was greeted by the pilot of the Lysander who thanked me for chasing the 109s away from him with a pint of beer...."

Squadron Leader Ken Holden took over command of 610 Squadron in early June 1941, at the same time Tony began flying the Spitfire IIB with a pair of 20mm cannon and four machine guns in place of the standard eight machine guns. Only 150 Mk.IIBs were built as the first production expression of experiments conducted with cannon-armed Mk.Is during the Battle of Britain.

Stoppages were frequent on those aircraft rendering them next to useless, but some changes to the cannon's feed system and the way the guns were installed eventually solved the problems. This mixed cannon/machine gun armament became the standard Spitfire fitting until the very last models when four cannon were installed.

Initially, Tony and the others flying Spitfire IIBs had terrible trouble getting the guns to work properly. Something went wrong on half their cannon tests and pilots found they generated an enormous amount of inertia. If one cannon went down the aircraft couldn't be held straight; with both firing an enormous amount of speed was knocked off.

The need for the extra firepower created by the cannon became apparent during the Battle of Britain as the weight of fire offered by the Spitfire's (and Hurricane's) eight rifle calibre machine guns might have been substantial at the start of the war but became less effective as armour protection increased. The Messerschmitt Bf 109Es used by the Luftwaffe during the battle were generally armed with two cannon and two machine guns and it quickly became apparent that this was a more effective combination.

Douglas Bader was one who steadfastly refused to change from using eight machine guns. Even when his Wing began receiving the further updated Spitfire V in mid-1941 he flew one of only 94 machine gun-armed Mk.VAs built out of the total Mk.V production run of 6,487 aircraft.

Bader reasoned that the cannon were no good because they would tempt pilots into shooting from long range rather than getting in close. He was wrong, because regardless of the guns fitted, the good fighter pilots would always try to get close to their quarry before firing and the bad ones would always spray bullets around the sky from miles out. But Bader obstinately refused to countenance any argument in favour of the cannon, despite the evidence. He later conceded that he had perhaps been incorrect!

. . . .

Finally, on 21 June 1941, Tony had his first combat on a Circus to St Omer while flying Spitfire IIB DW-K. It was a very busy few minutes for the novice during which he chased a 109 while making the normal beginner's mistake of firing from much too far away (about 500 yards), chased another two and fired at them from both head-on and with deflection and probably damaged one of them, and then got jumped by another pair of 109s, got hit, and had to make an emergency landing at Lympne in Kent.

The action proved if nothing else that Tony Gaze still had an awful lot to learn! He noted in his log book that he was "very frightened" and says he was hopelessly carried away by the whole thing, shooting out of range and forgetting that people might be shooting back! It was only when he'd "run out of everything" and was heading for home and thought he seemed to going very fast that he noticed his airspeed indicator was showing nothing.

He says: "I thought 'that's funny' and looked at my wings and one of them was full of holes. I could count nine holes in one wing and found out when I landed - with no airspeed indicator - that one of the bullets had cut off the pipe. I said to the crew 'Sorry for that, there's nine holes to fix' and they said 'Nine holes? What are you talking about? There's at least 18 - one where it goes in and one where it comes out!' I was blissfully unaware."

As had always been the case, many new pilots were being lost because they didn't keep a proper lookout while they were fixated on a distant target, firing from too far away and not knowing what had hit them. There were even cases of experienced senior officers flying straight and level with everyone shouting at them over the radio to warn them and then getting shot down because they were looking at their quarry off in the distance and didn't realise they had become a target. According to Tony "there were very, very few people shot down in a real turning competition."

. . . .

The sortie rate was high during this period with Tony and the others flying operations daily, mostly on Circus missions to France. There was regular contact with enemy aircraft but Tony was getting frustrated by his failure to open his scoring tally. On 22 June after a Circus to St Omer he notes in his log book: "Bags of 109s. Could not engage due to oil covering windscreen."

The squadron's 100th confirmed kill was recorded on the same day and Tony began to question his abilities. During one engagement he seriously considered chewing the tail off a 109 with his Spitfire's propeller after he'd run out of ammunition, but on most occasions he barely fired his guns.

He explains: "When you're in a flight and three people had got claims and you'd hardly fired your guns, you begin to think there's something wrong. I thought what the hell was I doing? By then I wasn't always a number two – I'd occasionally started leading other people, in which case I should have been the bloke doing the shooting and he should have been the bloke watching my tail."

The breakthrough finally came on 26 June while flying Spitfire IIB DW-H on a Circus to Lille. During the air battle Tony picked one Bf 109E off his CO's tail and destroyed it, then attacked a group of 12 other 109s firing at the outside one and claiming it as a 'probable' kill. The other 109s then turned on Tony, who had to get down to sea level to make his escape. While down there he saw what was probably the second 109 go down into the sea, but it could not be confirmed as his.

For Tony, the relief was enormous. His log book entry for that day has the words 'AT LAST' in upper case and underlined!

The action continued unabated over the next three weeks as the sortie rate to France was maintained, Tony's activities typical of many other fighter pilots at the time. There was always something happening: on June 27 his squadron was providing high cover during a Circus to Lille and was fired on by another Spitfire; on 2 July he scored a 109E damaged which was last seen smoking as it flew away; on 5 July he escorted another Spitfire with a stopped prop until its pilot was forced to bail out – Tony reported his position for the rescue services – and so on.

On 6 July Tony scored a half share in a 109 during another Circus to Lille accompanying six Short Stirling heavy bombers: "Bags of 109s. Little flak. Target knocked for six, debris up to 1000ft. Shared one 109E destroyed with CO. Section attacked by 109s which cleared off when we turned. Landed Shoreham to refuel."

Tony had his first flights in the new Spitfire VB on 9 July, taking W3376 and W3382 up for low cannon tests. He notes that despite having over 200 horsepower more than the Mk.II, the Spitfire V "didn't seem much different". The Mk.IIs also got metal rather than fabric-covered ailerons at around the same time which made them better at high speed.

The next day – 10 July – was a big one for Tony Gaze because during a Circus to Lens in Spitfire IIB DW-G he scored a double – one Bf 109E and a 109F, once again picked off Squadron Leader Holden's tail. This was a relatively long sortie at 1hr 40min which stretched the Spitfire's endurance to the limit considering there was substantial combat and therefore high fuel consumption involved. Tony landed at Shoreham with just four gallons of fuel remaining out of eighty-five, not really enough for an overshoot and landing.

Tony recounts the action which led to the awarding of his first Distinguished Flying Cross: "I didn't know I'd even got the first [109] because I was shooting at it, hit it and it rolled over but I hit its slipstream and rolled right around.

"This was very lucky for me because when I went around his number two shot right past me. If I'd have gone on down after the first one he'd have got me. The last thing he'd expect me to do was a roll, so I let the first one go and went after him and he was the one that blew up.

"He started sending out smoke – not the black smoke that comes out of a Daimler-Benz engine with rich mixture, it had a sort of reddy-brown colour and I thought that was the 'ha-ha boost' [nitrous oxide] cleaning the engine out. It just got thicker and thicker and he was going very fast in a long turn and I was inside shooting at him. I thought I'd better look behind me in case there's another one, so I had a quick look and when I looked forward there was nothing in the sky except a puff of smoke!

"I didn't actually see it blow up, but it wasn't there. When I got back I told them about the one that had exploded and that I'd certainly damaged the first 109 but I hadn't seen what happened to it. Then someone waiting behind me in the queue for the Intelligence Officer said 'are you the bloke who did the roll?' I said 'yes' and he said 'well that one went straight in'. So I got two!"

Tony makes some interesting points about the attitude of the German pilots at the time taking into account the fact that these combats were taking place over their own territory and there were plenty of spare aircraft waiting for them back at base:

"You never really knew how many people bailed out early. All of our stuff was over the other side and the German attitude was that if you were hit, get out. You can get a new aeroplane tomorrow – don't wait until you're properly clobbered – if there's a big bang, get out.

"Look at their aces – shot down eight or nine times – whereas as we couldn't unless you wanted to be a prisoner-of-war. You had to stick with the thing and hope to hell it would get you back across the Channel, which is what the Germans had to do in the Battle of Britain. An awful lot of Germans bailed out. All those I've spoken to since have said they bailed out the moment they were hit – they hade plenty of aeroplanes."

Tony scored another 109F 'probable' on 17 July (in Spitfire IIB P8749) during a sweep to Boulogne, but on his return – and much to his horror – Douglas Bader sent him on leave for a week saying he thought he was tired. Tony argued that he wasn't but to no avail – the boss insisted. "Forced on leave. Didn't enjoy it", says the note in Tony's log book.

Bader also vetoed Tony's plan to stay with his grandfather in Chichester: "No you won't", he said, "you'll be in the pub every night with the pilots and that's what I don't want you to be doing. You're going to your College at Cambridge". So Tony complied, driving up to Cambridge and "having a bit of fun" with the academics because they believed the stories about the RAF aircraft being superior. He let them know that this wasn't always the case because the 109 was faster than the early Spitfires.

Then Tony got a telegram saying he'd been awarded the DFC. With typical modesty, he was embarrassed about it because only three DFCs were awarded to the Wing's pilots at that point and of those, he was the only junior officer to get one. Ken Holden and 'Cocky' Dundas got DFCs at around the same time, but Johnnie Johnson had to wait until September for his first 'gong'.

"Why they gave it to me as the only junior bloke I don't know," he says. "The citation says it was because I saved my CO from being shot down and by shooting up two aircraft off his tail, but then that's what I was supposed to be doing!"

Johnnie Johnson's account of the action was a little less modest – on Tony's behalf – than that of the man himself: "Ken had a close shave when his squadron was set upon by a determined bunch of 109s and his escape was largely due to the brilliant ability of his wingman, Tony Gaze, a young Australian who smacked down two Messerschmitts from Ken's tail...."

The DFC Citation reads: "P/O Frederick Antony Owen Gaze was born at Melbourne Australia. He enlisted in the RAF in January 1940 and has shown a persistent desire to engage the enemy on all occasions. Recently he undoubtedly saved his squadron commander from being shot down over enemy territory by destroying his two attackers. He has destroyed at least three enemy aircraft."

· · · · · · · · · ·

Tony returned to his squadron on 25 July after his leave and immediately went back on operations. From the beginning of August he began flying the new Spitfire V.

Disaster struck the Wing on 9 August when Douglas Bader was shot down during a Circus to Gosnay and taken prisoner. He then proceeded to give the German's hell for the remainder of the European war! These exploits are well known through the *Reach For The Sky* book and film, but they also perpetuated a myth that persisted for many years – that Bader went down as the result of a collision with a Messerschmitt Bf 109. He was in fact shot down by a non-commissioned officer pilot from the Luftwaffe fighter wing JG.26.

Tony Gaze was involved in this sortie and it's noted in his log book thus: "Bags of 109Fs below. We did not attack. 10/10ths cloud at 15,000ft. Swept Channel.... DB missing!"

Tony remembers that day going wrong from the start when a unit new to the Wing - 41 Squadron - and its Spitfires failed to join up as 'high cover', leaving him and the others in 610 Squadron with two jobs to do. He considers that the day could have been very different if 11 Group had not decided to break up the Wing and 145 Squadron had been there as usual to provide top cover. The three squadrons (145, 610 and 616) had been working together very well and as winter was coming the whole Wing could have been rested. Instead, 145 Squadron went on 28 July and 610 on 28 August.

Tony describes what happened: "Near the target, DB made a big mistake. We had seen some 109s below which he couldn't, and he told us not to attack. By the time he saw them he'd wasted a few minutes, conditions had changed [as they quickly do at 300mph] and he was caught in a trap.

"A large number of 109s came down from above but we were unable to cut them off owing to their speed, so I called: "Break for Christ's sake, break!" as I couldn't give call signs. These aircraft should have been engaged by 41 Squadron at high cover, had they been there. We were outnumbered by 109s and made an undignified retreat. The German controllers had pulled off a perfect bounce with bait aircraft which led DB into the trap. Some people said it was his greed for victories!

"We missed his leadership, keeping us together and looking after those in trouble. Mind you, the ground crew were pleased to see him go because he was very arrogant and rude towards them!

"DB looked after his pilots in many ways other than in the air including getting them out of awkward situations with the police – both service and civilian – and he occasionally took a party of pilots to the theatre in Brighton or the Old Ship Club in Bosham, and I was usually included. But most of his time was spent with 616 Squadron, even his golf.

"I only flew as his number two on one occasion, was told what would happen if I lost him, so I stuck like glue. On the way home he tested me, got out his pipe, kept grinning and pushing a wing at me to see if I'd flinch. It looked as though he would fly between the two halves of Brighton Pier, but – thank goodness – he pulled up at the last moment. He always flew with 616 Squadron and I think this was a mistake as it left its CO, Squadron Leader Billy Burton, without a chance to lead his own squadron and also meant that 145 Squadron never saw him.

"The only time he led 145 he was responsible for causing two aircraft to collide with both pilots killed. Instead of taking them back to Merston and then coming back to Westhampnett himself, he brought them all back to Westhampnett and broke away downwards [instead of the normal 'break' procedure before landing] which either surprised the following aircraft or his slipstream hit them and they collided. One rolled over and went straight in, the other went into a flat spin and came down just behind Westhampnett Mill. The pilot survived for a while but later died.

"The women from the millhouse went out to help – one of them was a nurse – she was helping the pilot who was having trouble breathing. Then some bossy woman with a Red Cross badge came along and ordered them away and by the time the doctor arrived the pilot was dead. The nurse would have helped him."

The official report into the incident says the two Spitfires collided over Tangmere, not Westhampnett, and doesn't mention Douglas Bader's involvement at all, let alone the unconventional manoeuvre that caused it. Anything that has subsequently been written about it follows the official line, something that rankles with Tony Gaze to this day: "For the memory of the two blokes – he killed them!"

Tony continued flying Circus operations with 610 Squadron but despite some more contact with German fighters on several of these, scored no more kills, the result, he says, of going on leave, losing 'match practice' and not seeing them in time.

He had a strange experience on 14 August during a Circus to Boulogne while mopping up after the Blenheim light bombers had done their thing. He flew inland to St Omer where the Spitfires were engaged by 109s. There was quite a long dogfight during which part of his Spitfire's canopy blew off. There was no result but at the end of it all several 109s formated on Tony's Spitfire before moving off!

There was a special aspect to the 19 August Circus to Gosnay. During the trip, a Blenheim carrying a spare artificial leg for Douglas Bader made a small diversion to St Omer where he was being held and dropped it with the knowledge and approval of the Germans. They had originally offered free passage for a Lysander to land at St Omer to deliver the leg, but the offer was declined by the British who knew it would present the Germans with a propaganda coup. It was decided the leg would be delivered during a normal operation, and it was.

610 Squadron's last mission as part of the disbanding Tangmere Wing was on 27 August 1941, another Circus to St Omer. Two days later the squadron would move to Leconfield, Yorkshire as part of 12 Group for a stint performing convoy patrols. It was the end of any chance of real combat for the squadron's pilots for the moment, Tony wondering it if was because the squadron was regarded as being war-weary after an intense period of operations over enemy territory. "Off on holiday!", he noted, then added "Perhaps."

Of course, it hadn't all been work while flying operationally with the squadron. Young men are young men and fighter pilots are fighter pilots so there were plenty of enjoyable things going on to help keep their minds of the fact that each day might be their last. Girlfriends, fast cars, the pub and other diversions were all part of squadron life's off duty hours.

Tony loved the camaraderie of the RAF and the *esprit de corps* that existed between members of his squadron and the wing. Firm and lasting friendships were made with colleagues along with usually rather more temporary ones with local girls.... it always was and always will be part of the deal in wartime.

. . . .

They say a change is as good as a holiday but one aspect of the 'change' part of the deal which didn't go down too well with 610's pilots was that for their new duties, they would be stepping back in time and flying machine gun-armed Spitfire Is and IIAs. Tony ferried a Mk.I from Westhampnett to Leconfield on 29 August.

Despite his desire to continue combat flying and the routine nature of his new duties, Tony rates the convoy patrols as being one of the most important things they did, because the convoys and the goods they carried were of vital importance to Britain's survival - weapons of all kinds (including aircraft from the USA), raw materials, fuel and oil, food and a thousand-and-one other things necessary for Britain to continue its fight. Merchant shipping losses to submarines and air attack were so high at one stage it appeared that the war against Germany might be lost for that reason alone.

Tony notes that in 610 Squadron's area of responsibility "if you didn't have a couple of Spitfires over the convoys the Ju 88s were there in about five minutes. They were flying at nought feet on their radio altimeters 25 miles away from the shipping lane and they didn't have to see the convoy itself because the convoy was flying barrage balloons they could see.

"The moment there wasn't any Spitfires flying around amongst the balloons they were in, and every night. The navy didn't want us in the air at night because they didn't want anything in the sky that they weren't able to shoot at, so we'd stay over the convoy until last light and then go home. By the time we got back to the coast there was flak going up from the convoy because the Eighty-Eights were in, or E-boats."

What worried the pilots was the good chance that a Ju 88 might the follow Spitfires home, because in the dark they weren't in a position to do much about it due to a lack of fuel. Some Spitfires were lost to intruders during training when they snuck in and got them in the flare path while landing.

A couple of times during these patrols floating mines were spotted, and fighter pilots being fighter pilots, Tony and the others were very keen to blow one up. Besides, it was the closest they were going to get to causing damage to anything while flying out of Leconfield.

When he spotted one, Tony would go back to the convoy and call up to report there's a mine and he'd be more than happy to go and blow it up for them. But permission was denied on the basis that as he was flying a Spitfire armed only with machine guns and that he'd have blown himself up as he'd have to get too close to the mine to bring effective fire onto it.

Tony was unconvinced: "I never believed that, because a machine gun was all the navy used to blow them up. With a machine gun you were bound to hit one of the detonators because they were sticking out everywhere. Anyway,

I didn't do it – if I'd have damaged an aeroplane I would have been up on a disobedience charge!"

Tony Gaze completed his first operational tour on 19 November 1941 when he was – in his own words – "made an official dead-beat" and posted to his old Operational Training Unit, No 57 at Hawarden as an instructor. His eagerness to engage the enemy was, if anything, greater than ever, and to say he wasn't happy about this new posting is somewhat understating the case. He could see no reason why he shouldn't be able to go back to flying 'proper' combat operations with an operational squadron.

In his first tour of operations with 610 Squadron, Tony had logged 342 flying hours of which 218 were on operations. His total flying time was now 484 hours and he had 3.5 confirmed kills to his credit plus two probables and one damaged along with a Distinguished Flying Cross.

Remembering his own experiences of its inadequacies when he was at 57 OTU as a student in late 1940, Tony found that a few changes for the better had been made but it was stilly pretty haphazard: "You've got people like the fellow who ran the gunnery flight – I won't mention his name because he's famous – who used to boast about how *little* flying he did! I did a lot of flying because I knew I needed to teach the students gunnery.

"Then the Group Captain who ran the place promoted me to Flight Lieutenant and gave me my own Flight, so I altered things and we did all these simulated interceptions, challenging people to dogfights and formation aerobatics with all the instructors to keep them keen. It seemed to work, it changed things quite a bit. The others seemed to get the idea and we used our Fairey Battles as bombers to 'attack' the airfield and the Spitfires to beat them off."

Tony *did* do a lot of flying at the OTU in the nearly seven months he was there, logging 305 hours and bringing his total up to 789 hours. He flew Spitfire Is and IIs plus the Miles Master a few times and the Miles Magister basic trainer once or twice. He also flew a Hawker Hurricane for the first time, logging one-and-a half hours of local flying and aerobatics in Mk.I W8225 on 8 April 1942.

There were a number of Australian students at the OTU along with a couple of names who would soon become famous, the American Don Gentile and the Canadian George 'Screwball' Beurling. The latter scored 31 confirmed victories between May 1942 and December 1943, 27 of them while flying with 249 Squadron from Malta.

Always a maverick, he was allowed to retire in 1944 following the latest in a long series of scrapes with those in authority, for whom he was a constant problem. Beurling was an enormously talented and skilled fighter pilot but a loner. Most regard his talent as being largely wasted due to his inability to come to terms with authority, or it with him. Even at the OTU he caused problems with his attitude and was disliked by most of his fellow pupils.

Don Gentile originally joined the Royal Canadian Air Force to help in the fight against Nazi Germany and was posted to Britain where he joined 133 'Eagle' Squadron, one of the three RAF Spitfire units manned by American pilots. He scored two kills with 133 before all three squadrons were transferred to the USAAF in September 1942 and added a further 20 to his tally in P-47 Thunderbolts and P-51 Mustangs. He was sent home in 1944 to help sell war bonds as a 'celebrity' ace and the USAAF's top-scoring fighter pilot at the time.

Gentile had a reputation for being troublesome when he was sent to 57 OTU but Tony found him to be someone he got on with well. Their paths would cross again in September 1942 when Tony led three squadrons - including the 'Eagles'- on the ill-fated B-17 escort mission which cost him his rank - as discussed in the following chapter.

Despite whatever improvements he introduced to 57 OTU during his time there and whatever satisfaction that brought, unlike some of his co-instructors, Tony Gaze only wanted to get back on operations. The closest he got to air-to-air combat while at Hawarden was during a flight when his Spitfire literally ran into a flock of seagulls. The final score: six confirmed destroyed and ten damaged!

Tony's day of liberation came on 3 June 1942 when he was posted as 'A' Flight Commander to 616 'South Yorkshire' Squadron at based at Kingscliffe in Northamptonshire, another of the former AuxAF units. His new mount at Kingscliffe would be the high altitude Spitfire VI and a note in his log book note sums up how he felt about this new posting: "SAVED FROM SUICIDE!!"

· · · · · · · · · ·

GAZE ON THE SPITFIRE

The Supermarine Spitfire is arguably the most famous fighter ever built, but some suggest the good 'PR' it has always attracted has more to do with its looks and the sound of its Rolls-Royce engine than its effectiveness as a fighter. The bottom line is simple – throughout almost all of World War II it was the best pure fighter of them all, able to at least hold its own with and usually better than anything else in a dogfight. Pilots of all nationalities who were fortunate enough to fly Spitfires and other types almost universally agree with this.

It was only for a brief period in 1941–42 that the Spitfire was outclassed by the Focke-Wulf Fw 190, and that situation was rectified with the introduction of the Mk.IX with its two-speed/two-stage supercharged Rolls-Royce Merlin engine.

It has been written elsewhere that if the Spitfire was a mere show pony they wouldn't have built 22,759 of them (including 2,408 naval Seafires) and it wouldn't have been the only Allied fighter to be in production before, during and after the war.

Tony Gaze flew most of the major Spitfire marks during the war and scored all of his victories in them. From the Mark I through the II, V, VI, IX and XIV he built up an enormous knowledge of and affection for the aircraft, but also had the chance to fly other types.

Of the Spitfire he says: "The things were foolproof. You could take terrific liberties with a Spitfire and it would get you out of it because it wouldn't drop a wing, it wouldn't do any of the nasty things. It gave you a lot of warning in the stall and was just terribly nice to fly. It felt as if the wings came out of your shoulders – it did what you wanted it to do.

"You had to get used to the very sensitive elevators. The first time I looped one I blacked myself out because I pulled the stick back and the next thing I knew I was looking at the sky through a haze of black smoke out of the exhaust while doing a tailslide! I found the way to loop a Spitfire was to just ease off the forward pressure on the stick and it would go around beautifully.

"Later, in the middle of the war, they modified the elevators so it wouldn't do that [in 1942 by introducing a stick bobweight which was also disliked by legendary Spitfire test pilot Alex Henshaw] so it wasn't always trying to come out of a dive, put it that way – and when some of us complained they said that with these half-trained people coming through we thought they might do themselves harm with the elevators. "I said 'half trained? We weren't trained at all!'

"There was a nice feeling that if you did grey out or black out in a turn with someone right behind you, the thing would keep turning, whereas with the new elevators it would come out of it. An American pilot said he was very sorry for anyone who hadn't flown a Spitfire because everything else had a snag. A Mustang would drop a wing on you and do all sorts of nasty things if you treated it badly but a Spit wouldn't.

"Most of the trouble we had with Spitfires was finger trouble.... overbraking and going up on the nose, not nasty spin-ins or that sort of thing. Using a Spitfire for what it was designed – as a defensive fighter – you can't find anything wrong with it. The relative lack of range was its major operational problem."

What about the issue of fitting into the Spitfire's relatively tight cockpit? Traditionally, fighter pilots have been of shortish stature but at 6ft 3in (1.90m) Tony Gaze was well above the average height. It wasn't a problem. The Spitfire had plenty of rudder pedal adjustment for longer legs but also the 'articulated' control column used by the RAF at the time. The stick moved fore and aft conventionally for elevator control but the top part including the grip was hinged and moved laterally for aileron control, meaning the main stick didn't get impeded by long legs because it didn't move sideways. There were numerous Spitfire pilots who were as tall or even taller than Tony.

One of the challenges facing British fighter pilots after the first year or so of war was coping with crosswind landings. Airfields were big grass paddocks with no runways, so takeoffs and landings could always be performed into wind. The prototype Spitfire (and Hurricane) both originally flew with a tail skid but they were subsequently fitted with a tail wheel following a then secret 1936 Air Ministry decision to start building sealed all-weather runways at RAF bases.

Tony Gaze notes that he "didn't fly off a runway until I'd done a tour of ops – it was grass airfields and of course they had a tremendous advantage because you took a whole squadron off together. We took off in twelves and landed in sixes – it saved time and you always landed into wind – crosswind came in with runways.

"That was a bit tricky at first but we didn't have any great trouble – it was in the mind, really. From runways we took off in pairs which wasted time and fuel getting into formation and going somewhere."

Contrary to conventional wisdom, Tony found the Spitfire's relatively narrow track undercarriage had some benefits over aircraft with wider tracks: "It was a great advantage in lots of ways because it didn't swing terribly as it didn't dig one wheel in much. If you got a flat tyre you didn't have a nasty accident.

"With the [wide-tracked] Mustang if you had a flat tyre you wrote the undercarriage off because there was no possible way you could hold the swing, or if you got the tail up too quickly or didn't lock the tailwheel. Landing was very fraught because with the slightest irregularity the thing would ground loop". And landing the Spitfire?: "Always a three-pointer after a curved glide approach."

Others agree with Tony Gaze on the subject of narrow versus wide track undercarriage. Among them is famed British military test pilot Captain Eric 'Winkle' Brown who has noted while comparing the ground handling characteristics of the Spitfire and wide-tracked Hawker Hurricane that the latter was "more sensitive to side wind than a Spit, and in this respect its wide track undercarriage could cause a wild swing with injudicious corrective braking."

Captain Brown – whose vast experience as a test pilot includes evaluating captured German and other enemy aircraft immediately after WWII – rated the Griffon-engined Spitfire XIV as "the best of any propeller fighter, Allied or enemy, in the war."

Tony Gaze flew Spitfire XIVs from mid-1944 until the last few days of the European war when he transferred to a Gloster Meteor jet unit. He scored his last six victories in the XIV including Me 262 and Ar 234 jets – both of which he was able to overtake at altitude, significantly – and also rates it as the best: "As a fighter it was better than anything.... the Mustang was 17 miles an hour slower, had relatively no climb and couldn't turn with it, as we found out in the Ardennes.

"As a fighter the Mustang wouldn't roll as fast as a Spit and wouldn't climb anything like as fast. I think that when you got used to a Spitfire it was difficult to adapt to anything else – you were part of the aeroplane. How anyone ever flew those bloody Thunderbolts I don't know. It was like being in a flying boat with all this space around you. The joke was that when the flak came up you ran around the cockpit to avoid it!"

FOUR

TRIUMPHS AND TRIBULATIONS

FLIGHT LIEUTENANT F A O Gaze DFC reported for duty with 616 'South Yorkshire' Squadron at Kingscliffe near Peterborough in Northamptonshire on 3 June 1942, thankful that he was finally be going back to 'proper' operational flying as the commander of 'A' Flight. Johnnie Johnson was already with the squadron when Tony joined and was leading 'B' Flight.

The squadron was equipped with the high altitude Spitfire VI, rapidly developed to counter the threat from high-flying German bombers and reconnaissance aircraft such as the Junkers Ju 86P which had been operating unmolested over Britain and elsewhere since early 1941. Flying at up to 40,000 feet, they had been virtually immune from interception and were proving a nuisance. 616 was the first squadron to equip with the new Spitfire variant – of which only 100 were built – in April 1942.

The Spitfire VI was based on the Mk.VB but modified to fight at high altitude. Changes included the installation of a Merlin 47 engine optimised through its supercharger to produce maximum power at a higher altitude, four-bladed propeller (the first production Spitfire variant with this feature), extended wingtips and a lightly pressurised cockpit courtesy an engine-driven Marshall blower which forced air into the sealed pressure cabin. The Spitfire VI's service ceiling was officially listed as 39,200 feet, about 3,000 feet more than the Mk.V.

A feature of the Mk.VI's cockpit setup was that the canopy was sealed shut and could not be slid open like conventional Spitfires. Once the pilot was strapped in, the canopy was bolted down but could be jettisoned in its entirety in an emergency.

The sealed canopy was unpopular with most pilots as previously, standard procedure was to taxy, takeoff and land with the canopy open. Efficient heating meant the aircraft could be flown in shirtsleeves at high altitude, but this kind of dress was not always practical in combat with the result that pilots often 'cooked' when wearing more usual kit, especially at lower altitudes where the air was warmer.

Tony didn't mind the arrangement so much as he found it was possible to fly through cloud without water leaking into the cockpit. There were also several cases of pilots whose Spitfire's fuel tank – located immediately forward of the cockpit and behind the engine – started to burn after being hit during a fight but who managed to bail out without being badly burnt because the pressure cabin's hefty forward bulkhead kept the flames out of the cockpit.

Normally in a Spitfire the pilot had his feet on the fuel tank and the moment the canopy was opened the flames came straight up if there was a fire. With the Mk.VI the bulkhead allowed pilots to sit in the cockpit and undo everything with relative ease. Tony says that the only time it got dangerous was "when you pulled the lever and the top blew off and you went with it."

He adds that "the big snag was when you were at low altitude crossing the Channel on a hot sunny day – the compressor was still heating the air and you couldn't slide the hood back for ventilation and you got very hot. The extended wing tips made them go very high – we had squadron formations at 41,000 feet and to stay in formation at those heights was difficult because the Spit got very sensitive. If you went that high in a Mk.V you'd be virtually out of control but we managed to stay in formation in the VI."

Tony flew mainly training, practice interceptions and test flights from Kingscliffe along with a handful of patrols until the squadron moved to Kenley south of London (as part of that base's Wing) on 7 July 1942. Operational flying started in earnest from then, missions including sweeps across the Channel to France, convoy patrols and 'flaps', which involved attempting to intercept enemy aircraft and chasing them across the Channel.

It was during this period that Tony's obsession with polishing his aircraft began to take hold. It became a real phobia with him and he was always at it, attempting to squeeze a few more precious miles per hour out of his Spitfire. He became notorious for this and while other pilots played cards or read while they were waiting for some action, Tony could invariably be found polishing his aircraft, often with 'borrowed' materials!

He started seriously trying to improve the speed, climb performance and fuel consumption of his Spitfire VI at 616 Squadron by 'cleaning up' the wing leading edges up to the main spar, filling gaps near the tail unit, and polishing the propeller and the rest of the wing's top surface (the underside was broken up by ammunition chutes and so on).

It paid off, testing proving that Tony's aircraft was at least 10 miles per hour faster at rated height than a 'standard' Spitfire VI. The gain was at least as much in faster Spitfire IXs and XIVs, to the extent that in the latter he found he could usually catch the theoretically much more rapid German jets.

One aspect of the flying with 616 surprised and shocked Tony. The squadron was still using line astern formations instead of the 'finger four' formation that had been introduced by Douglas Bader during the Battle of Britain and was – so Tony thought – now the standard procedure. Similar to the formation used by the Luftwaffe, the finger four provided cross-cover protection where line astern had virtually none. Many number fours had been picked off from line astern formations as they had no protection whatsoever. Finger four also provided better attacking options. Tony had no hesitation in putting his Flight into a finger four when enemy aircraft were around.

He added two kills, a probable and a 'damaged' to his tally while with 616 Squadron. The first was a probable Fw 190 on 13 July during a sweep to Abbeville. Flying his regular Spitfire VI (YQ-G), he saw the 190 spinning down. It was originally credited to him as a 'damaged' but upgraded to 'probable' when three other pilots stated they saw it still spinning some 9,000 feet below. More than half a century later, in 1994, the wreckage of this Fw 190 was found during excavation work although its discovery has not changed Tony's official score.

On 17 July Tony and some others from the squadron had landed at Friston near Beachy Head when the weather closed in. The following morning he contacted 11 Group and was told that all flying had been cancelled due to the very low cloud but that enemy aircraft were active along the coast. Always eager to engage the enemy, Tony informed his bosses that Friston was only just in cloud but that he could get off and drop below the level of the 200 feet high cliff at the end of the airfield.

The Spitfires were then scrambled and vectored after three enemy aircraft near the French coast and found two Fw 190s which were chased over the Channel. Tony destroyed one (the pilot, Helmut Ufer of 2/JG 26, bailed out at only 300 feet) and damaged the other. Tony's camera-gun footage showed hits from all his guns on Ufer's aircraft and he received some newspaper coverage after this action. He was quoted as saying: "I saw the pilot of the first Focke-Wulf bailing out off Le Touquet. His cockpit was enveloped in flames and his parachute had holes in four places."

After the action, Tony climbed to 2,000 feet and gave a position fix to the air-sea-rescue people so they could come and get the downed German pilot, who was being dragged along the water by his parachute. Despite an extensive search, he was never found.

The squadron moved to Great Sampford in Essex at the end of July but a week later Tony was temporarily transferred to something called the UP Flight at

Farnborough, for reasons unknown to him. He didn't even know what 'UP' was until it was explained it stood for 'unrotating projectile' - rockets, in other words. The powers-that-be had apparently decided that Tony was to undertake testing of the rockets and stay at Farnborough until he was given command of the first Hawker Typhoon squadron.

He wasn't overly enamoured of this idea and did his best to get out of it, arguing it was an Army job: "I didn't want to sit on my bum waiting for D-Day to get some action." Tony eventually succeeded in talking his bosses into appointing someone else to take over the first Typhoon squadron, someone who didn't mind waiting.

Tony stayed at the UP Flight for just over a week but despite his reservations found it interesting. He was impressed with the 'Boffins' (scientists) working there because no matter what idea someone came up with, they'd try it out. They were working on the gyroscopic gunsight at the time and had models of aircraft running down a wire across the hangar while they tried different ways of calculating the lead.

They were also putting the wrecks of aircraft together to find out what had gone wrong, testing the bouncing bomb concept that would be used in the 'Dam Busters' raid the following year, firing Hurricanes off catapults for use on merchant ships and many more tests and trials.

Tony returned to his squadron in the middle of August but his brief stay at Farnborough did produce one moment of excitement. On 8 August a Heinkel He 111 bomber with balloon cutters on its wing leading edges flew over in bad weather. All the aircraft at Farnborough took off when an intruder came in so they wouldn't be bombed on the ground, so Tony went up with them and as he had a fully-armed Spitfire VI under him, he decided to follow the Heinkel and have a crack at it.

The ground controllers gave him a vector so he followed in the cloud. They eventually said he should break off because a Beaufighter had been called in but instead of going back to Farnborough he was directed to Croydon. As he came out of the cloud he realised he was going south over Croydon which meant the controllers had sent him right through the middle of the barrage balloons. Somehow, he missed them and their cables but was very, very lucky.

During the squadron's time at Great Sampford it was decided on a non-flying day to have an escape exercise. A group including the CO, Squadron Leader Brown, was dressed in civilian clothes, ferried blindfolded to points ten miles or so from the airfield and dropped off one by one. They then had to try to get back to the airfield headquarters without being caught in what was one of the first exercises of its kind. For Tony, some of the lessons learnt would come in handy in just over a year's time!

Tony scored one more victory flying the Spitfire VI with 616 Squadron, a Dornier Do 217 and his first bomber during a patrol over Dieppe on 19 August during Operation Jubilee, the ill-fated Dieppe landings. Jubilee was a massive operation involving all three services and intended to test the defences of the German-held French port. The landing force was launched from five English ports with Canadians making up the bulk of the more than 6,000 troops involved. It completely failed and over 3,300 of the Canadians were either killed, wounded or taken prisoner compared to fewer than 600 German ground casualties.

The air battle was equally disastrous, the RAF losing 106 aircraft versus the Luftwaffe's 48. The operation involved no fewer than 48 Spitfire squadrons providing close air support and top cover. That day was more expensive in terms of Spitfire losses than any other of the war with 62 of them downed.

Happily, Tony Gaze was not in one of them, his log book recording his day and in terms of the German losses noted, reflecting what the people of Britain were told rather than what really happened: "Combined operation on Dieppe which was thoroughly plastered. RDF [radar] and gun emplacements destroyed. Over 90 huns destroyed, 34 probable and 117 damaged. Abbeville aerodrome made u/s by Fortresses. Bags of 190s. Attacked one but stopped chasing it.... one shooting at me! Destroyed a 217. Bits fell off everywhere. Attacked by 30+ 190s which we managed to outclimb! But they cleared off when we were in a position to attack."

Tony flew four sorties on 19 August, patrols over the Dieppe area from Hawkinge: "First sortie - found a huge battle going on with 190s and 109s trying to break up the umbrella of Spits protecting the invasion. Fired on a 190 diving in to strafe only to have tracer from behind make me break away. Fired on several 190s with no time to observe effect. Medium cloud enabled enemy aircraft to climb up and dive through to attack.

"Second sortie - same as first. Had told my number two to warn me if the same thing happened again and it did. I was firing at a 190 carrying a bomb and diving at the ships when I sensed something behind me and called 'get this thing off my tail!'. My number two answered 'it's me!'

"Do 217s began bombing so I went up through the cloud and found one – it was brand new, still in primer. Hit the port engine, fired and feathered then starboard the same followed by large panels and a big flopping dingy which nearly hit me. My number two saw it come through the cloud and crash – the Navy was shooting at everything."

"Third sortie – much less activity, evacuation proceeding. Kept enemy aircraft away from doing much damage. Fourth sortie – escorting convoy. Only one 217 broke through but missed and escaped into cloud." Four operational sorties totalling 6hr 15min of flying in one very big day for all involved and a disastrous one for the Allies.

The Dornier victory took Tony's total to 5.5 confirmed destroyed plus three probables. He was now an 'ace' and it appeared his star was well and truly in the ascendency.

· · · · · · · · · · ·

Tony Gaze completed his last operational mission with 616 Squadron on 29 August 1942, a diversionary sweep for a Circus on Lille which brought his total flying time up to 915 hours. Three days later the was promoted to Squadron Leader and posted to 64 Squadron as its Commanding Officer.

Based at Hornchurch west of London, the squadron was part of 11 Group commanded by AVM Trafford Leigh-Mallory and was equipped with the new and still-secret Spitfire IX, which had entered RAF service – with 64 Squadron – just over two months earlier.

The Spitfire IX was rapidly developed as a result of the appearance of the Focke-Wulf 190 in 1941. It clearly outclassed the Spitfire V as a dogfighter and the need to develop an upgraded model became a matter of urgency. Happily, this need coincided with Rolls-Royce developing the 60-series Merlin engine with two-speed/two-stage superchargers and the ability to run at higher boost pressures. The result was notably more power available to higher altitudes, a 40mph speed increase and considerably enhanced rate of climb.

Tony's first Spitfire IX flight was on 1 September and the following day he flew the aircraft that would become his 'personal' mount, BS439/SH-G. Pilots who switched to the Spitfire IX quickly discovered it was – to quote Tony – "a whole new ballgame in terms of performance."

He elaborates: "For once you could believe the figures – the figures they gave us for the Spit V and VI were about 1,400 horsepower which is nonsense because they certainly didn't perform that much better than the II with 1,200 horsepower.

"The IX was all over the V in every possible way. It could go over 400 miles an hour and the V about 360. There was also rate of climb and time to height and we had long range tanks. Well, I say long range but it was only 30 gallons then, but the main thing was that we had virtually equal performance to the Focke-Wulf 190 whereas beforehand it was all over us.

"We were scared of the 190 because we didn't know exactly what it could do until a German pilot got lost and landed in Wales by mistake [in June 1942 – the same month the IX entered service]. I went to Duxford when they had it there to have a look. We were impressed by the armament and the rate of roll when they demonstrated it, although we'd already seen that. You expected it to have all sorts of servos and things on the ailerons, but not on your life! They were just plain slab ailerons with, I think, a very stiff wing. If we hadn't got Spitfire IXs when we did, God knows what would have happened."

· · · · · · · · · · ·

Tony led 64 Squadron on several Circuses over France during September 1942, usually escorting USAAF B-17 Fortresses. He gained some first-hand experience of the American bomber on 7 and 8 September flew as second pilot on a B-17F for a trip from Hornchurch to Polebrook in Northamptonshire and back for – would you believe – a party! The skipper of the B-17 was noteworthy – it was a certain Major Paul Tibbetts, subsequently of atomic bomb fame.

But any lingering party mood ended abruptly on 26 September when Tony was directly involved in an operational disaster that cost lives and aircraft and had a profound effect on his own career – the so-called 'Eagle Squadron Disaster'.

The mission was a Circus escorting 24 USAAF B-17s on a raid to the German airfield at Morlaix near Brest. By default, Tony ended up leading the escorting Wing comprising three Spitfire squadrons – his own No 64, a Canadian unit operating Spitfire Vs and 133 'Eagle' Squadron, one of the three units manned by American pilots who had joined the RAF in 1940-41 to help fight Nazi Germany.

No 133 had only just re-equipped with the Spitfire IX and the Morlaix raid took place three days before all three of the American units were scheduled to be transferred to the USAAF where they would become the 334th, 335th and 336th Fighter Squadrons of the 4th Fighter Group. The raid was to be something of a showpiece for Eagle Squadron and its new Spitfire IXs before the transfer, which would be performed with due pomp and ceremony.

The mission went horribly wrong thanks to a combination of very high tailwinds of 100mph and poor control from the ground, the controllers knowing about the wind but not telling anyone. Flying over solid cloud with no ground reference, the Spitfires were blown miles past the target, far into the Bay of Biscay. The planned rendezvous with the B-17s didn't happen until the time to return came up and when the Eagle Squadron let down through the cloud over a port they thought was Plymouth but was actually Brest.

Disaster followed. All but one of the Eagle Squadron Spitfires were either shot down over Brest or ran out of fuel and crashed trying to get back to England. The exception was Bob Beaty, who had left the formation early due to a rough running engine and despite also running out of fuel, was able to glide over the English coast and crash land on friendly soil. But the cost for the Americans was high - eleven of the new and still secret Spitfire IXs lost over or near enemy territory, four pilots killed and seven taken prisoner.

Most of the Canadian unit's Spitfires and all of 64 Squadron's made it back - just - but the disaster prompted a Court of Enquiry and trouble for the man leading the Wing that day - Tony Gaze.

He tells the story: "With 64 Squadron and the first Spit IXs we did all the working up for the Americans with their Lightnings and B-17s and suddenly we were told to fly down to Harrowbeer - which is north of Plymouth - for a large show for the Eagle Squadron which had also got Spitfire IXs by now before they transferred to the American air force. They laid on a show to Morlaix with a small force of B-17s to give them a taste of their Spit IXs before they transferred to the American air force in a couple of days' time. It was basically a PR exercise for the Americans.

"Everything went wrong. Wing Commander Brian Kingcombe was going to lead the show but he burst a tailwheel or something and missed the briefing. He was leading the Canadian squadron so when he arrived he said to me 'I think you'd better lead, I'll look after our squadron and the Eagle Squadron will fly on top'.

"So that's what we did and we were working on a time factor, which is wrong. It's crazy to reckon that you're going to rendezvous with the bombers 150 miles away at a certain time, but that's what we were supposed to do. So we just climbed up and when we got to the French coast where we were supposed to meet them, there was nothing there. We were over cloud so we were flying navigationally blind on a compass course and timing to where we were meant to meet the Forts.

"When the rendezvous time came up and we still hadn't seen the Forts I was just turning around wondering what to do when we saw them in the distance – only a small number of them as some had already turned back. I thought 'I'm not going to turn back immediately because we've still got plenty of time according to our time to the target and distance navigational calculations' – we couldn't run away when we saw the Forts, they'll wonder what the hell's going on – so we'll escort them back to the coast.

"So we escorted them back and just as we got to the time when we should have been approaching the English coast, the cloud started to break up and there was a rugged coastline with waves and things breaking on it about where we thought we were, which was England.

"Up to now we'd been on radio silence but I didn't like the look of the coastline so I called up and was told 'you are 160 miles south of base'. So I called 'don't go down' to the others but the next thing we knew the Eagle Squadron had gone straight down through the cloud and come out over what they thought was the English coast, got into a nice formation and flew over a big city.

"The next thing we heard was 'stop these bastards shooting at us' and of course it was Brest they were over! They flew around completely bluffed over what was going on, they still thought it was England they were over. So they all ran out of fuel or got shot down, except for one [Bob Beaty] who had turned back earlier after some sort of problem.

"I had a bit of a think and obviously we'd got a screaming headwind now where we'd had a jetstream up behind us on the way out and unknown to us we'd been over the Bay of Biscay somewhere. The temptation was to dive down and get out of this wind, then I thought you can't throw away 20,000 feet – use it to get extra distance and extra speed.

"I'd done an engine handling course at Rolls-Royce at Derby and knew the best economy settings, so I called up and said '1,800 revs +2' [pounds of boost] and put my nose down until I was losing height at 1,000 feet a minute and got quite a bit of speed up. I looked around to see where everybody was and the Canadians had disappeared, the Eagle Squadron had disappeared, so I concentrated on our lot and I called up Beaty to find out where he was. He said 'I'm low over the sea and I don't know what to do and in trouble'.

"I told him to climb to 3,000 feet and go over to Button D for dinghy on his radio, which would alert the air–sea-rescue people. It didn't sound as if he was going to make it so I told him to get up to a height where he could get some radio range, get onto the rescue people and keep talking to them because they would send out a Walrus or something if he had to bail out.

"I called him every now and again to see how he was getting on and told him to go right back on the power because he was obviously out of the wind down there – just stay in the air as long as he could and hope to heck he could get to England. I found out later that despite his calls they never sent a rescue Walrus out. We crossed the English coast at about 1,200 feet and I saw a Spit crash land underneath us and I thought it was one of mine. We got into Harrowbeer – just – and I stayed up last, of course, because I had more fuel than anyone else. [Tony was in the air for 2hrs 20min, right at the limit of the Spitfire's endurance].

"We heard that most of the Canadians had got in at Bolt Head near Dartmouth but there was no sign of the Eagle Squadron – we knew we wouldn't see them because we heard what was going on. I didn't know that the one I'd seen go down was Beaty and it was only years later that I found out that his was the aircraft I saw crash land, the only Eagle Squadron bloke who got back. Brian Kingcombe's lot lost a few, I think, and he thought we'd all gone down with the Americans.

"As for the brand new and secret Spitfire IX, it came off the secret list the next day because the Germans had got a present of quite a lot of them! The remainder of the Eagle Squadron – the other pilots who'd been sent as spares – had to hand their IXs in and went back to Vs when they became part of the USAAF three days later. Apparently it was a very odd-looking ceremony when they were transferred because there weren't many people there! They called back everyone they could from leave and everywhere else to try and make it look like a squadron."

. . . .

Tony and Brian Kingcombe went together to Fighter Command to report this disaster and were greeted by Group Captain Harry Broadhurst. After the war he became Air Marshal Sir Harry Broadhurst and the Commander-in-Chief of RAF Bomber Command. It was while in this role in September 1956 that he attracted some unwanted publicity when the Avro Vulcan in which he was sharing the cockpit with Squadron Leader Donald Howard crashed on approach to London Heathrow airport in poor visibility during a Ground Control Approach (GCA).

The Vulcan was returning from an otherwise successful tour of Australia and New Zealand, the first time the new bomber had ventured overseas. It hit the ground half a mile short of the runway, wheels down, in a field of brussels sprouts. Don Howard applied full power and the aircraft veered up but immediately went out of control.

Like the RAF's other jet V-bombers – the Valiant and Victor – the Vulcan only had ejection seats for the two pilots, both of whom 'punched out' safely. The rest of the crew – three radio/navigation/radar operators – were located below and behind the pilots and only had the main entry hatch in the floor below them as a means of escape. In the Heathrow crash and several others they had no chance.

Broadhurst's attitude to Tony Gaze was immediately hostile, although he was undoubtedly also 'copping it' from those above him over what had happened. It certainly was a disaster and he decided that Tony would be held almost entirely responsible. It was not often that the RAF lost an entire squadron in a single operation.

But part of Broadhurst's attitude was odd and uncalled for. His opening remarks to Tony included: "Gaze you're an Australian – I don't like Australians." Why Broadhurst had a dislike of Australians generally and Tony Gaze in particular no-one really knows, but the issue would appear again shortly after the war had ended when Broadhurst announced in public that Tony would not be receiving the Distinguished Service Order (DSO) he'd been recommended for.... more of which later.

Tony was ticked off by Broadhurst for not doing exactly what he was told, to which the Australian replied: "What do you mean? I got everybody who stayed with me home safely." But it was to no avail. Broadhurst was obviously looking for a scapegoat and Tony Gaze would be it.

Tony says: "I felt bad about being blamed for the Eagle Squadron disaster because it was so avoidable. If the controllers had warned us when our ground speed was 100mph more than normal we'd have realised we had a huge tail wind and compensated." It's interesting to note some of the controllers received hasty postings to less than desirable locations in the Far East! The B-17s' navigators also got a roasting, apparently.

And the reasons for the disaster? "Complete disinterest by the controllers because they admitted afterwards that within a short time we'd gone completely off their map. You can't suddenly be seen to be cruising 100 miles an hour faster than normal. You'd think you'd call the leader and say, 'Hey, do you realise what you've got behind you?' They just let us disappear off the map.

"They were a weird group – mostly auxiliaries, amateurs. All it needed was a radio call. They didn't need to break security, just say something like: 'weather report to all aircraft – there is a jetstream at 20,000 feet, adjust your navigation'.

"The rendezvous was a long way out. Normally you'd rendezvous crossing the English coast, stay low until halfway across the Channel and then climb. In this case they came in high from wherever they were and we were supposed to meet them at 20,000 feet over the French coast."

The next day – 27 September – was also a bad one for Tony when he bent his favourite Spitfire (SH–G) on landing when returning to Hornchurch from Exeter. The brakes had failed: "Pranged my beautiful G. Pulled wheels up to avoid overshooting. No brakes."

The next big mission in which Tony was involved was on 9 October, a Circus to Lille with 115 USAAF B-17 Fortresses and B-24 Liberators. The Spitfires were there to provide support but overshot the target, partially due to some bloody-mindedness on the part of Squadron Leader Gaze.

Having been told off by Broadhurst for supposedly not doing exactly what he was told on the Morlaix raid, Tony decided he would now do just that, even though he knew he had been given incorrect vectors to fly by the ground controllers: "I don't think the squadron appreciated it, but I was in a bloody-minded mood and I flew *exactly* what I was given, the wrong bloody vector! I knew it, and I bloody flew it! We missed the big show over Lille because we went inland. That didn't help me I suppose because we missed the big battle over the target."

Two black marks in rapid succession, at least in the eyes of his superiors. Tony was summoned to see AVM Leigh-Mallory at Hornchurch and given two equally unpalatable career options – he could either keep his rank and go off flying – 'go on a rest', as they politely called it; or keep flying and drop rank. Tony was sufficiently angry to immediately think he'd rather drop rank than stop flying but told Leigh-Mallory he'd let him know.

Tony went back to his squadron and discussed the matter with his friend and colleague, the New Zealand ace Squadron Leader Colin Gray who ended the war with 28 confirmed kills. Gray strongly advised Tony not to drop rank because he'd never get it back, but Tony continued his bloody-minded attitude to the whole affair – not unreasonably because the disaster was certainly not his fault – and was demoted to Flight Lieutenant and posted back to 616 Squadron at Westhampnett.

Tony notes that "Colin Gray was absolutely right – the only reason I got back to Squadron Leader [just before the European War ended] was because I was put on Meteors and they had two engines, so up I went. So I was a Squadron Leader in 1942 and a Flight Lieutenant in 1945!"

He says he didn't mind so much, as long as he had enough rank to authorise his own flights, which Flight Lieutenants could. He'd have been "a bit upset" if he'd gone any lower down the pecking order and had to get someone else to do that. The situation created some anomalies, however, with most of Tony's contemporaries Wing Commanders and Group Captains by early 1945 while he was still a mere Flight Lieutenant – and by then a three times decorated double ace!

Tony's brief stay with 64 Squadron saw him log 61 hours flying time of which 39 were operational; his total flying time was now 977 hours. His only combat claim during this period was one Fw 190 damaged during a Rodeo to St Omer on 11 October. He got within 50 yards of the 190: "Bloody near rammed it! If I'd had a gun-camera it would probably have confirmed this as there were more than a dozen cannon strikes on the wing roots and fuselage, but I broke away too sharply to watch it go down as his number two was too near for comfort."

This wasn't quite the end of that particular story for Tony. As he had flown through the 190's condensation trail his Spitfire was covered with ice. He was completely blinded, was on instruments and in enemy skies. For all Tony knew, there could have been other 190s around him and he would never have known what had hit him if he was attacked. He climbed to 35,000 feet, weaving all the way and flew blind towards home before doing a fast and straight 'downhill' run until the ice melted. He says he had never been more frightened in his life.

FIVE

THE ITINERANT AIRMAN

THE NEWLY 'reduced in rank' Flight Lieutenant Tony Gaze returned to 616 Squadron and its Spitfire VIs at Westhampnett on 2 November 1942 for a two month stint of more convoy patrols, Rhubarbs and Circuses. It was during this posting that he recorded his 1000th flying hour (on 22 November during a Rodeo to Cherbourg escorting Boulton Paul Defiants) and his 100th offensive sortie, a Rodeo to Le Touquet on 4 December.

One week later, on 11 December, Tony and fellow pilot Bob Large were sent out to 'unobtrusively track' a German armed merchant raider which the Royal Navy had managed to lose in bad weather. The idea was to see if it had got into Cherbourg or Le Havre or was still somewhere in between the two ports. The pair set off at 200 feet under a thick cloud base of 800 feet, feeling nice and secure. About two-thirds of the way across the Channel they spotted some black dots low down that could have been aircraft but turned out to be only seagulls.... they both felt relieved.

But just as the French coast came into view the cloud suddenly cleared, leaving two Spitfire pilots very exposed in an area which would most likely be crawling with German fighters. They dropped down to sea level, did a sweep around the Cherbourg Peninsula, gritted their teeth and climbed to 3,000 feet in order get a good look at the harbour. The ship wasn't there, so it was back to sea level, onto Le Havre and repeat the exercise.

Another group of black dots was sighted and these were definitely aircraft, so Tony and Bob dropped lower, flying along the coast and passing minesweepers and patrol boats that would normally be shot at, but not today. Similarly, the ships didn't shoot at them, which was surprising.

At Le Havre they climbed again to have a look and didn't see the merchantman, although they did spot two 109s going low up the river. The two Spitfires dived low and finally attracted some flak - with no damage inflicted - before heading for home. Tony reckons the crews of the minesweepers and patrol boats must have thought they were Messerschmitts and didn't fire.

He added no more 'kills' to his tally during this period and direct contacts with German fighters were few despite regularly seeing them off in the distance. The closest Tony came to scoring another was on a Circus to Rouen on 12 December when the squadron was flying rear cover for B-17s. He had a quick 'squirt' at an Fw 190 from long range which rolled inverted and disappeared down into the cloud cover. His logbook notes: "Fw 190 probable? No!" ['probable' crossed out and replaced with] "Fw 190 frightened"!

616 Squadron began experimenting with using the Spitfire as a 'bomber', the intention being to stir up the Germans when there were no real bombers on a sweep into France. Various ways of annoying the Germans were thought up including taking the parachutes off flares and dropping them into France to start a few fires and bring the Luftwaffe up.

On training flights to show new pilots the French coast the squadron sometimes used fake radio calls while flying at 'dot' feet in order to tease the German fighters up. For example: "Elfin Leader from Red 1, I can't see the babies.... neither can I but they must be ahead of us..... shut up!" After having hopefully created a certain impression in the Germans' minds, the squadron spread out and climbed up.

On one occasion they got to 25,000 feet and their controller reported: "Bad luck, nothing about – wait a minute! Forty-plus climbing at 10,000 feet below you and more inland". With discretion definitely being the better part of valour in this case, they got away quickly to be told: "You just about got the whole bloody Luftwaffe up!"

Then the idea of bombs came up, dropping them from the very high altitudes the Spitfire VI was capable of flying at, although weighed down with a bomb their ceiling would be less than usual and accuracy would be non-existent. Someone realised that the 90 gallon long range tank which had been developed for the Spitfire weighed nearly as a much as a 1,000lb bomb when filled, manoeuvring with the loaded tank attached was okay, so why not hang a thousand pounder underneath the Spitfire?

616's 'B' Flight got to work on the idea and just before Tony left the squadron at the end of his tour of duty in early January 1943, they fitted a bomb rack to the long range tank fittings and the bomb could be released in the same way the tank was jettisoned. Tony's departure meant he never got to try the idea out, but in the European Theatre it was probably the first attempt to turn the Spitfire into a fighter-bomber.

The concept had already been tested in the Mediterranean in August 1942 when the first Spitfire ground attack mission carrying ordnance was flown by 126 Squadron's Mk.Vs based on Malta. A pair of underwing racks for 250-pounders were locally fabricated, the bombs attached and a target in Sicily attacked.

The idea was successful and in December 1942 Malta's Commander-in-Chief, AVM Sir Keith Park, wrote to the Air Ministry urging production of the underwing racks as a standard fitting. Meanwhile, his Spitfires had been extensively using the local conversion kits on sweeps over Sicily.

Tony flew his last operational sortie with 616 Squadron, a Rodeo to Le Touquet, on 31 December ("Fiasco – Huns always above, undignified retreat") after which it moved to Ibsley near Bournemouth as part of 10 Group. He flew some test flights from there over the next week before he ended his second tour of duty and was sent off on a four-month 'holiday'. This included a stint talking to factory workers as part of the campaign to keep them productive.

Tony now had 1,054 flying hours in his log book and at the same time he was awarded a Bar to his DFC, something that at first glance might seem a little odd considering the serious brush with officialdom that had taken place less than four months earlier. No official citation came with the award: "It just suddenly came through with no warning", Tony says. "I'd shot a few things down including a couple of 190s by that stage and that was well regarded, I suppose." Tony was indeed well regarded by most – except perhaps Harry Broadhurst – and someone on high had obviously recommended him for the second DFC.

This not only recognised his consistently proven bravery and skill in combat but could also be seen as a strong signal of support in the wake of the Eagle Squadron disaster, a message that said 'we know it was not your fault'.

· · · · · · · · · · ·

On 8 January 1943 Tony Gaze was posted to something called 'PR3' at the Air Ministry, this an organisation that sent appropriate people out to the factories to give the workers pep talks and help ensure they kept working.

Strikes had become a growing problem. Despite being technically illegal in wartime Britain, the growing influence of communist shop stewards in the factories and mines was taking a toll. Most of the strikes were short but their cumulative effect was costly. The peak was reached in 1944 when 2,194 separate stoppages took place and caused the loss of 3.7 million working days.

Tony and others in the Services knew nothing about the level of communist agitation going on through the shop stewards and the large number of strikes that were called. With hindsight it can be seen that this was the start of four decades of union domination of British industry, where the unions and their leaders' short-sightedness, greed and lust for power meant that inefficient work practices and strikes became standard procedure.

This had the inevitable effect of diminishing British industry's ability to effectively compete, which in turn has seen areas in which it was once immensely strong – like aircraft and car manufacturing and shipbuilding – decline to the point where they are today. The irony is that the unions have been responsible for putting large numbers of British workers out of work, and it all started during the war.

Tony mainly did factory tours and found the whole thing was well organised. There was a pool of people from various areas including some who'd been delivering aircraft to Russia along with those whom the Air Ministry thought the factories workers might be responsive to. Tony thinks he was sent because he was an Australian: "The Bolshie people would be more likely to listen to me than an Englishmen", he says.

"The first thing that happened to me when I reported was that I was shut up in a room with a dirty great sheet of paper and told to read it and sign it. It was full of things I couldn't do and I wasn't supposed to get involved in anything political. I thought 'what is going on?', so I asked and was told that one of the places I'd probably go to was Shorts where Sunderlands and Stirlings were being built but they were on strike. I might have to try and talk them into going back to work.

"I was sent to Shorts with a sort of instructor who told me how to talk to them. The whole firm was on strike, almost. We met the directors and they felt the whole thing was falling apart and couldn't understand why all this communist agitation was causing the strike because the workers were being paid about twice as much as the people who flew the aeroplanes! There was no real question about wages – they were just agitating for the sake of it and for their political 'ideals'.

"Anyway, we did what we could and they did go back eventually. Then Avro went out and there were no Lancasters being made so they had to bring aircraft back from the OTUs and things to keep the bombing going. They sent the Dam Busting teams and people like that to talk to the Avro people.

"The only thing I really enjoyed was when I found they needed someone to talk to Aston Martin which was making control columns for Spitfires and things. I had an Aston Martin so I quickly put my hand up for that and asked 'while I'm giving my speech, how about giving my car a service?' So they did that and showed me pictures of my car racing at Le Mans and so on – so that was good!

"I went to Napier and saw a Sabre engine and also Fairey where the first of the Fireflies was being tested with a Griffon engine which we hadn't yet heard of. And Blackpool, Squire's Gate, where they were making bits for fighters. That was the place where when I got to the end of my speech and said 'any questions?' One of the girls stood up and asked me when was my day off!

"The last one I had that really annoyed me was when I was on my way north to talk to the people making the jigs for the Supermarine Spiteful – the Spitfire's supposed successor – the prototypes of which had just been ordered. I'm halfway up there in the train – in a first class sleeper and all that stuff – when the police came on board and took me off. I asked why and they said 'they're on strike' and I said 'boy, just let me at them, I've been waiting for this'. And they said 'that's why we're taking you off – we don't want a general strike!' They obviously had my views on all this sussed...."

Tony was supposed to do a six-month stint with PR3 but managed to get himself out of it after less than four. Some of his speaking engagements were associated with the 'Wings for Victory' national savings campaign. He found the overall experience interesting – and eye-opening in many ways – but his desire was to get back to operational flying as soon as possible. He only flew twice during this period, local flights in Spitfire Vs from Tangmere and Kenley in February and March to stay current.

· · · · · · · · · · ·

On 24 May 1943 Tony was posted to No 453 Royal Australian Air Force Squadron based at Hornchurch on the outskirts of London. Hornchurch was one of the RAF's more famous bases, established as a Royal Flying Corps station in 1917, its proximity to London making it a central point for the air defence of the capital.

The site reverted to agricultural use after World War I but was reacquired in 1922 for development as an RAF base. It reopened in April 1928 as RAF Sutton Farm but was renamed Hornchurch two months later. Part of 11 Group, the airfield played a significant role in the Battle of Britain when three Spitfire squadrons made up the Hornchurch Wing.

453 was one the many Commonwealth squadrons that flew as part of the RAF in Europe, the Middle East and the Mediterranean. Equipped with Spitfire Vs and IXs, Tony was with the squadron for less than a month and managed to log a handful of operational sorties but with no success in engaging enemy aircraft. A couple of these sorties ended in chasing some German fighters but with no luck.

Probably Tony's most exciting moment with 453 was just three days after he arrived at the end of a Wing air–sea–rescue sortie which had to be abandoned due to poor weather. Flying a Spitfire IX, he suffered an engine failure over the Thames Estuary and headed for a golf course to land on – because there was nothing else – and got down to 1,000 feet before realising there were cables stretched across it to stop German gliders from landing. Instead, he found a little cornfield near East Tilbury that was just about big enough to accommodate the Spitfire, which as per standard procedure for this situation was landed wheels up.

Once safely down someone with a screwdriver had to be quickly found so the guns could be unloaded. If Tony – or any other pilot – had been alone in that situation he would have needed to leave the aircraft and go off to find a telephone. Then the inevitable would happen – the nearest bunch of school boys would race over to the Spitfire, climb into the cockpit and press the firing button with undoubtedly interesting results!

Luckily, there was a tractor driver nearby who had a screwdriver so Tony unloaded the guns and went to the nearest place with a phone – a pub. That was a mightily convenient co-incidence and of course it would have been impolite of him to refuse a drink – or two or three. The result was that by the time they came to collect him, Tony had a quite a few under his belt!

He notes that: "The 453 Squadron code was FU and the aircraft code was C – and that's exactly how I felt!"

Tony enjoyed the flying at 453 Squadron but makes the interesting point that there was one aspect of being in an all-Australian squadron he didn't like so much: "I probably shouldn't say this, but I was used to squadrons with Brits, Kiwis, Poles, Dutch and God knows what in them, and the best man got the job, regardless.

"But in 453 it was all Australians and there was a Sydney versus Melbourne mentality. As I was so much senior to them – I was on my third tour and they were on their first – I became a bit of a father confessor. They'd come to

A formal portrait of Tony Gaze taken when he was in his mid-30s. At this time - circa 1956 - Tony was nearing the end of his career as a racing driver.

Left & below left: Tony's parents, Irvine and Freda Gaze (*née* Sadler). Irvine served with the Royal Flying Corps in World War I and is photographed here during that time wearing his Polar Medal, awarded for his part in Ernest Shackleton's ill-fated 1914 Antarctic expedition. Freda's grandfather owned the Westhampnett Mill in Sussex near Chichester, adjacent to the Duke of Richmond and Gordon's Goodwood estate. It was the start of an association with a part of the world that would later play a major role in Tony Gaze's life.

Geelong Grammar School boy.
Tony Gaze aged 15 in 1935.

Tony Gaze (right) aged five with his cousin Owen Moore in 1925. Tony's younger brother Scott can be seen in the Hutmobile behind them.

Tony excelled at rowing when he was at high school and continued the sport in England at Cambridge University. He went there in 1938 when he was eighteen years old.

A poor quality shot but an interesting one showing the view from inside the Hudson borrowed by Tony Gaze from his uncle for his first motor race at Brooklands in 1938. He expected the meeting to be everyone "just having a jolly good time running around the track," but it was serious motor racing with some big names there.

The 'Gaze Stable' in 1940 - cars were already playing a significant part in Tony's life. His brother Scott also joined the Royal Air Force in 1940, the pair going through their flying training and to their first squadron together. Scott is photographed here in October 1940 with the Alvis Tony acquired for him, while Tony's MG J2 is on the right. The photo was taken by Tony.

A Miles Master Mk.I advanced trainer of No 5 Flying Training School at Sealand near Chester. This was the aircraft type in which Tony and Scott Gaze earned their RAF 'wings' in January 1941.

A significant event - the page from Tony Gaze's log book noting his first flight in a Spitfire on 6 February 1941.

YEAR 1941		AIRCRAFT		PILOT, OR	2ND PILOT, PUPIL	DUTY
MONTH	DATE	Type	No.	1ST PILOT	OR PASSENGER	(INCLUDING RESULTS AND REMARKS)
—	—	—	—		—	—
				57 O.T.U.	HAWARDEN	TOTALS BROUGHT FORWARD
2	3	MASTER	T8044	F/O CRIDLAND	SELF	GLIDE APPROACH + LANDING
2	3	MASTER	T8044	F/Lt BROTCHIE	SELF	GLIDE APPROACH + LANDINGS
2	6	MASTER	T8044	SELF	—	LOCAL
2	6	SPITFIRE I	CA	SELF	-	1ST SOLO ON TYPE.
2	8	SPITFIRE I	BF	SELF	—	HANDLING
2	10	MASTER	N7835	Sgt BLAND	SELF	I.F.
2	10	MASTER	N7835	SELF	Sgt BLAND	I.F.
2	10	SPITFIRE I	BX	SELF	—	HANDLING + FORMATION
2	13	SPITFIRE I	BZ	SELF	—	FORMATION
2	14	SPITFIRE I	AL	SELF	—	LOCAL
2	27	SPITFIRE I	BM	SELF	—	LOCAL

Above: Pilot Officer F A O Gaze in the cockpit of his Spitfire during his first operational posting with 610 Squadron RAF at Westhampnett near Chichester. It was with this squadron that he scored his first 'kill' in June 1941.

Left: Another portrait of Tony Gaze and Spitfire at Westhampnett. He joined 610 Squadron in March 1941 and by the end of his first tour with the unit the following November had 3.5 confirmed aerial victories plus two probables to his credit. He was also awarded his first Distinguished Flying Cross during this period.

Age shall not weary him. A posthumous sketch portrait by Olive Snell of Scott Gaze, killed in his Spitfire on 23 March 1941 at age 19 while flying with 610 Squadron. The Gaze brothers had joined the squadron only two weeks earlier as their first operational posting.

An excerpt from Tony Gaze's log book recording his first aerial victory - a confirmed Messerschmitt Bf 109E on 26 June 1941. The words 'AT LAST' reflect the relief he felt at breaking his 'duck' as he had been frustrated by his perceived lack of success. He needn't have worried....

SINGLE-ENGINE AIRCRAFT				MULTI-ENGINE AIRCRAFT						PASS-ENGER	INSTR/CLOUD FLYING [Incl. in cols. (1) to (10)]	
DAY		NIGHT		DAY			NIGHT					
DUAL	PILOT	DUAL	PILOT	DUAL	1ST PILOT	2ND PILOT	DUAL	1ST PILOT	2ND PILOT		DUAL	PILOT
(1)	(2)	(3)	(4)	(5)	(6)	(7)	(8)	(9)	(10)	(11)	(12)	(13)
102·35	225·00	1·45	3·20							9·45	11·30	7·10
GRAONG	·40		1 probable	C.O.	1 destroyed 109E Self : 1 109E destroyed - 1 probable ? P/Horner Sir Ballard did no leave Redhill						AT LAST.	
Circus	1·45											
T. Fredon	·20											
Sweep	1·30											
	1·20											
	1·40			C.O. HORNER	Sub. MAINS							
hampshire	·20	73·30·00										
	·45											
	·40											

Spitfire II DW-G of 610 Squadron at readiness at Westhampnett. Tony flew this aircraft on several occasions. Note the parachute on the Spitfire's wingtip. Some pilots put their parachutes on the horizontal tail but being tall, Tony found it easier to grab it off the wingtip and slip it over his shoulder when scrambled.

'Bader's Bus Company' family portrait 1941 with the man himself front and centre, arms crossed and pipe in mouth. Tony Gaze is immediately to the left of Douglas Bader in the row behind.

After completing his first operational tour in November 1941, Flight Lieutenant Tony Gaze DFC was posted to 57 Operational Training Unit at Hawarden as an instructor and stayed there until June 1942. Remembering his own time training at 57 OTU and the serious inadequacies it revealed, he introduced simulated interceptions, mock dogfights, formation aerobatics and simulated scrambles as a matter of routine. This group from 57 OTU's 'B' Flight seems happy enough about it. Pupils there at the time included two future aces: the Canadian maverick George 'Screwball' Beurling and American Don Gentile.

Pilots of 64 Squadron at Hornchurch in early September 1942. Tony Gaze was promoted to Squadron Leader when he was posted to this unit, but was reduced in rank to Flight Lieutenant after being the made the scapegoat for the disastrous Eagle Squadron mission later in the month. Tony hand wrote the names of the pilots on this photograph in his usual minuscule (and often indecipherable) hand. No 64 was the first RAF squadron to equip with the Spitfire IX - SH-L is in the background.

With its starter attached, Tony Gaze in 64 Squadron Spitfire IX SH-A about to get underway at Fairlop in October 1942. He flew this particular Spitfire on eight operational missions.

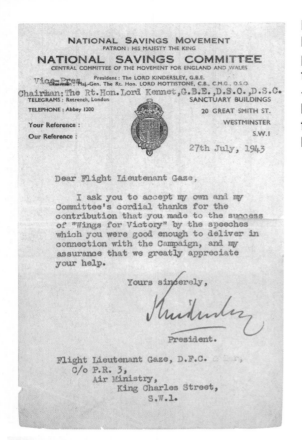

Between January and April 1943 Tony Gaze found himself visiting aircraft factories to give workers pep talks and delivering speeches for the 'Wings for Victory' campaign. He didn't want to be there - being taken off operational flying displeased him greatly - but at least he got a letter of thanks from National Savings Committee chairman, Lord Kindersley.

Tony Gaze flew with 453 Squadron RAAF and its Spitfire IXs out of Hornchurch in May and June 1943. An engine failure over the Thames Estuary on 26 May resulted in this forced landing in a field near East Tilbury: "The 453 Squadron code was FU and the aircraft code was C - and that's exactly how I felt!"

	30											
	1.40	operational										
	6.45	operational										
	1.15	operational		16.35 hr								
	missing	Dog fight with squadron 1 190 Destroyed. (And I'm sure 3 got another but no evidence) 8 190's. Got one in flames and another flicked inverted at 500' once it crashed. Hit in elevators at beginning of scrap, then in glycol after petrol down to 20 gals. Crash landed behind Le Tréport, escaped via Paris - Barcelona - Gibralter. Arrived England 28/10/43 - Admitted Halton Hospital with facial wounds from prang.									
49.35	1081.30	1.45	7.15									
(1)	(2)	(3)	(4)	(5)	(6)	(7)	(8)	(9)	(10)	(11)	(12)	(13)

165

Part of Tony Gaze's log book entry for 4 September 1943, the day he was shot down over France but escaped back to England with the help of the French Resistance. He didn't go down without a fight, taking at least one Focke-Wulf Fw 190 with him.

Mugshot of Tony Gaze taken at the British Consulate in Barcelona in October 1943 after having escaped from occupied France and walking over the Pyrenees into Spain. The patched-up damage to his right eye can be seen. From Barcelona it was on to Madrid, Gibralter and finally England on 28 October, nearly eight weeks after his 'bad day' over France.

The gun-cameras in fighters recorded the action, the film rolling whenever the guns were fired. From Tony Gaze's aircraft are shown one of the six Focke-Wulf 190s he was credited with destroying and the Messerschmitt Me 262 jet he downed near Munster on 14 February 1945. The 190 action was on 17 August 1943 near Antwerp while flying a Spitfire IX with 129 Squadron, the pilot bailing out just before the wing came off; the 262 victory was in a 610 Squadron Spitfire XIV. Tony Gaze was the first Australian to shoot down a jet aircraft in aerial combat.

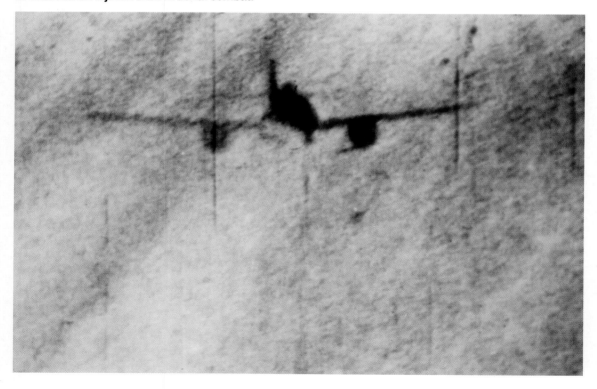

Tony Gaze's second stint with his original squadron - No 610 - began in July 1944 in England before the squadron moved to Belgium and then the Netherlands late in the year. Flying the powerful and fast Spitfire XIV, Tony added a V-1 'flying bomb', an Fw 190D and an Me 262 jet to his tally during this period with 610. This squadron photo was taken at Lympne in September 1944; Tony is in the front row, second from left.

Tony Gaze's last posting to a Spitfire operational squadron was with No 41 in March and April 1945 as the European war was in its final stages. The squadron flew Spitfire XIVs and MV260/EB-P with 'bubble' canopy was one of those on squadron strength at the time. He scored his final victory of the war on 30 April, downing an Fw 190D at the Elbe Bridgehead flying EB-E.

Tony Gaze joined 616 Squadron and its Gloster Meteor III jet fighters in Germany at the beginning of May 1945 and in doing so became the first Australian to fly a jet operationally and probably the first to fly a jet at all. Now a Squadron Leader again, he wasn't all that keen on the idea: "Farewell to Spits, bugger it!", he wrote. He made his first Meteor flight on 2 May.

Tony Gaze (in uniform under cockpit) with a 616 Squadron Meteor and assorted ground crew - many of them German - at Luneberg in May 1945, just after Germany surrendered.

Tony Gaze got to fly several captured German types after the surrender, and aircraft started arriving at airfields now occupied by the Allies even before the war in Europe officially ended on 8 May 1945. He flew Fw 190s seven times during that month including this example.

Tony with a Messerschmitt Me 262 at Lübeck. He went through the starting procedures with Germany's greatest night fighter ace, Kurt Welter, but the opportunity to fly one was denied, to the Australian's great disappointment. A Junkers Ju 88 is parked behind.

Squadron Leader Gaze commandeered a Siebel Si 204 light transport he found on an airfield near Copenhagen in late May 1945 and put it to useful purpose over the next couple of weeks. Vital missions performed included flying it to Paris to collect some champagne!

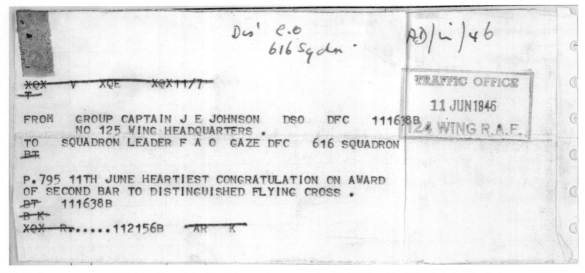

Tony Gaze was very highly thought of by his contemporaries including his friend Johnnie Johnson, the RAF's top-scoring fighter pilot of the war. Johnson sent Tony this congratulatory telegram on the awarding of his third DFC.

me and say things like 'I don't know why so-and-so got that job because I'm better than him' and so on. I didn't enjoy that side of it."

. . . .

Tony's next posting was short – just under three weeks – but interesting as it allowed him to add two new fighter types to his log book, the North American Mustang and Hawker Typhoon. The unit was No 268 Army-Co-operation Squadron at Odiham in Hampshire and he arrived there on 20 June 1943.

The squadron was now part of the RAF's newly-established 2nd Tactical Air Force, the substantial organisation that would provide the tactical air element supporting the planned invasion of Europe, now a year away. No 268 Squadron had its origins in August 1918, based at Malta and tasked with flying anti-submarine patrols over the Mediterranean using Shorts 184 and 310 floatplanes.

It was disbanded just over a year later but reformed in September 1940 as an Army Co-operation unit equipped with Westland Lysander short takeoff and landing aircraft. Able to operate from tiny fields, the Lysander achieved fame in WWII when it was used for clandestine operations, taking agents into and out of Occupied Europe, normally in the dead of night.

The squadron had re-equipped with the Mustang by the end of 1942 after also operating some Curtiss P-40 Tomahawks alongside the Lysanders. A poor fighter due to its lack of altitude performance, the Tomahawk was nevertheless useful for low-level tactical reconnaissance, the role for which the Mustangs would also be used.

These were early Allison-powered Mustangs which also lacked altitude performance but armed with guns and fitted with a camera, they were very fast down low and ideal for the tactical reconnaissance role. They brought back some remarkable photographs of the French coast, flying at low level and often facing intensive enemy ground fire.

The step up from the relatively slow, fixed undercarriage Lysander to the Mustang was a big one, and although some of the pilots had flown fighters before, many had not and most were inexperienced in the art of being a fighter pilot. Tony's job at 268 Squadron was to teach them air fighting skills and get them operational.

He recorded his first flight in a Mustang on the day of his arrival at the squadron and the Typhoon on 21 June in Mk.IB EJ953. A couple of Typhoons had been allocated to the squadron to simulate the Focke-Wulf 190 in mock combat as the squadron's pilots were put through their paces in the air. Tony flew almost daily during his time with 268 Squadron, sometimes twice a day as he took the pilots through a series of drills - dogfights, being bounced, attacking, formation flying and so on.

Tony comments on his first experience with the Mustang: "I found they were tricky on the ground because of the big wide undercarriage. You had to manually lock the tailwheel to keep them straight on takeoff and landing - it was another lever to pull.

"The Allison was a very smooth engine and for its day the aircraft was quick. It seemed to me that small things were important with the Allison. If you lost a couple of plugs or something it was serious, whereas with a Merlin if you lost a whole magneto you didn't know it until you tested the switches. We weren't quite certain how much the engine would stand running flat out for a long time and the general feeling was that it wouldn't be very reliable.

"Other than that, the Mustang wasn't much trouble apart from this business of the swing on takeoff if you got the tail the tail up too quickly or didn't lock the tailwheel. Landing was very fraught because with the slightest irregularity the thing would ground loop. I had it happen once but nobody saw it, luckily! I'd forgotten to lock the tailwheel and towards the end of the landing run it just went around no matter how much differential brake I put on to stop it. It didn't do any damage, so I didn't say anything about it. It was tricky. We had a couple of incidents with it."

As for the Typhoon, this was the most powerful aircraft Tony had flown so far with its 2,200hp and very complex 24-cylinder 'H' configuration Napier Sabre engine. First flown in 1940, the Typhoon was the first British fighter capable of exceeding 400mph in level flight. After some teething problems with the engine and airframe had been sorted out, it entered full operational service in 1942 and was subsequently used very effectively as a ground attack aircraft in Europe armed with guns, bombs and rockets.

The Typhoons allocated to 268 Squadron were early models with a heavily-framed cockpit and a car-type entry door. Later examples had a more conventional sliding 'bubble' canopy. This caused Tony some moderate grief: "The first time I looped one the door came open at the top of the loop and although I was firmly strapped in, I felt terribly naked sitting there with the door wide open. It shut again when I went down so it was no great worry, but I think in the middle of combat suddenly finding yourself with the doors open would be frightening. It tended to swing but nothing like as badly as the Mustang.

"Because the Typhoon engine's exhausts were level with your face in the middle you had to be on oxygen from start-up because of the carbon monoxide getting into the cockpit. That was the only thing that was impressed on me when they gave it to me and with instructions to pretend it's a 190."

The Napier Sabre was unreliable early in the Typhoon's career but eventually the problems were overcome. The engine had one potentially disastrous characteristic due to its sleeve valve design which Tony wasn't told about at the time and only found out about later when he flew the Sabre-powered Tempest V:

"They said that when you get to the end of the runway ready for takeoff, run it up until all the black smoke and bits of this, that and the other had come out of the exhaust or it will cut on you halfway down the runway. Someone should have told me that when I had the Typhoon, because it could have happened to me - I just treated it normally. That's the thing with sleeve valves - they obviously have to be lubricated with the sleeves moving. While you're taxying it builds up a pool of oil and will suck it in just when you need full power and the engine can cut." Happily, it didn't happen to him.

. . . .

After his brief stay with 268 Squadron, Tony was relieved to be sent back to operational flying on 26 July 1943, not as a part of a particular squadron but at Sectors Headquarters at Hornchurch as Supernumerary to the Station Flight where he was "floating, waiting for a job and whenever there was a squadron where somebody didn't turn up I'd go and fly". These were mainly with 129 Squadron along with a couple of sorties with 222 Squadron. Both were equipped with Spitfire IXs.

Tony may well have been "floating, waiting for a job" but he still flew regular operational missions including groups of several on successive days. During his four weeks' stint with the Hornchurch Station Flight he flew 12 Ramrods, two Rodeos and a Circus over Occupied Europe and added one confirmed destroyed, one probably destroyed and one damaged enemy aircraft to his tally.

Sorties flown in the first three weeks were generally frustrating, despite some contact with the enemy. On a Ramrod to Merville on 31 July while escorting 18 USAAF Martin B-26s, he notes there were "many 190s and 109s, general mill around, air pressure down so couldn't fire". With his Spitfire's guns pneumatically-operated, insufficient pressure in the system meant that Tony had no ability to fight.

A fighter sweep to Le Trait on 4 August also ended with no result despite attacking more than twenty 190s and 109s over Abbeville and again over Dieppe. Some sorties provoked no enemy aircraft activity at all while others did but they were too far away to deal with. In other words, typical of these missions but frustrating for pilots like Tony who were always looking to engage the enemy.

Most of Tony's serious action occurred during a busy four-day period between 16 and 19 August when he flew no fewer than 12 times including seven operational sorties. It was during this flurry of activity that he added to his tally, but not without some frustration due to his cannon consistently jamming. The increasing number of exclamation marks accompanying the 'cannon jammed again' notes in the following log book entries well illustrate his mounting frustration:

16/8/43 Rodeo to Knocke: "190 damaged. Robbed by cannon jam. Attacked gaggle of 109s and 190s. Damaged a 190. Cannons jammed so fired all mg [machine gun] at it. Strikes, black smoke, over-vertical dive...."

17/8/43 Ramrod (the first of two sorties that day): "190 destroyed – cannon jammed again! Forward support for Fortresses. Escorted down to Antwerp, dived from 28,000ft-4,000ft to attack EA. Destroyed a 190, pilot bailed out. Strikes all over."

18/8/43 Ramrod: "[DV-A's drop] tank fell off on takeoff so landed and scrambled in [DV]-E. Caught up with Wing just in time to turn back with them owing to cloud!!"

18/8/43: "Scramble to shoot down balloon at 23,000ft – cannon jammed again!!

19/8/43 Ramrod Brussels (Tony's second sortie of the day): "109G frightened [crossed out and replaced with] 'probable' from film. Dived to 500 [mph indicated]. Cannon jammed again!!! Fortresses, escorted them out.... attacked 109s. Fired alone – 350-150 yards & MISSED!!! No – film showed strikes."

This last encounter is interesting as subsequent analysis of the gun-camera film showed that the 109 would have been destroyed and was given to him as such at first, but because Tony never made a claim – he didn't see its ultimate fate because his Spitfire's windscreen was covered in oil – it was changed to a 'probable'.

This all happened two months later after Tony had returned from a little unplanned tour of Europe after having been shot down over occupied France, as described in the next chapter. When he got back to England he had a meeting with an Intelligence Officer who explained the bureaucratic process that not only proved it was a definite 'kill' but also prevented him from recording it as such.

Tony tells it: "The Intelligence Officer said 'we gave you that 109' and I told him I hadn't claimed it because I didn't see what happened to it. They said that from my camera-gun film they gave me a destroyed, but as I didn't claim it I could only have a probable! I found that a bit odd.

"They showed me the camera-gun film and I found out how they worked it out. They had this screen and knowing the wing span of the 109 they could calculate what the range was. Then they had these squares or circles that gave the pattern of your guns at that range and put them on the screen. And they said, 'Look – you hit with all the guns – every gun hit it, that's why we gave you a destroyed. But as you didn't make a claim you can only get a probable!'

"I read later that the 109 was followed down by two other blokes who couldn't catch it. They pulled out before they hit the ground and when they last saw it, it was in a vertical dive at 3,000 feet. Of course it must have gone straight in – absolutely no hope at all. So I officially got a probable."

That was Tony's final operational sortie with the Hornchurch Station Flight and 129 Squadron before moving to 66 Squadron at Kenley on 26 August to lead 'A' Flight. Nine days later he would find himself unwillingly embarking on what was arguably the most dangerous seven weeks of his life.

SIX

THE GREAT ESCAPE

LOG BOOK ENTRY 4/9/43: "Spitfire VB (LZ)A - Amiens - Escort cover to Bostons - Missing - 1 190 destroyed and I'm sure I got another but no evidence. Dogfight with squadron of 190s. Got one in flames and another flicked inverted at 500ft, sure it crashed. Hit in elevators beginning of scrap, then in glycol after petrol down to 20 gals. Crash landed behind Le Treport, escaped via Paris-Barcelona-Gibralter. Arrived England 28/10/43. Admitted Halton Hospital with facial wounds from prang."

There's a truism in aviation that states something like: 'a big mistake invariably results from a series of usually undetected or ignored small mistakes, the cumulative effect of which is often disaster.' So it proved to be in the case of Tony Gaze, who on 4 September 1943 was shot down over France by a Focke-Wulf 190A flown by Luftwaffe pilot Gerhard Vogt. Tony's scalp was the 14th of the 48 Vogt eventually claimed.

Just over a week earlier, Tony had arrived at RAF Kenley to lead 66 Squadron's 'A' Flight. The squadron was equipped with the Spitfire V, and this was the catalyst for Tony's series of 'small mistakes' on the fateful day. He flew seven operational sorties in his first week at 66 Squadron, mainly Ramrods escorting USAAF B-25 Mitchells and B-26 Marauders. He quickly became frustrated because his squadron's Spitfire Vs were being 'chopped off' by pilots flying Spitfire IXs, taking advantage of their superior speed and getting in first for potential kills.

Sometimes they would pop up in front of a 66 Squadron pilot just as he was about to fire, as happened to Tony the day before he was shot down: "I was just going to shoot and a IX chopped in front of me but I fired anyway I was so angry!" The mindset was in place - he was going to beat the Spitfire IXs to the punch come hell or high water. This was mistake number one in the sequence.

As the squadron was preparing to depart on its 4 September sortie, the young and inexperienced American number two Tony had been given approached him, upset that his Spitfire had gone unserviceable. He asked Tony what could he do, to which his leader replied: "Take mine and I'll get another one from the pool."

This was no great drama except that the aircraft Tony selected hadn't been air tested after maintenance and its serviceability state was unknown. Mistake number two. When he was taxying out he discovered the Spitfire's Merlin engine had no oil pressure but he decided to wait to see what happened during takeoff. Mistake number three.

Then, after takeoff, Tony noticed that although the oil pressure gauge did start to indicate, the needle appeared from the top of the gauge rather than the bottom and settled on a reading which was about double the maximum allowable. Tony decided to ignore it, thinking, "Oh what the hell, I'm not going to chicken out and go back," because there had been some pilots who had pulled out of missions claiming spurious oil pressure trouble. Mistake number four. He'd ignored two very strong messages – no oil pressure when taxying and double the maximum allowable in the air. "This was absolutely stupid on my part," he admits.

It was a case of 'pressonitis' despite the warnings signs. Tony had chosen to ignore them because he was hell-bent on getting into the action quickly before the Spitfire IXs had a chance to jump in and steal his and his fellow 66 Squadron pilots' thunder: "If we don't get going the moment we saw something we'd be chopped off again and be mere spectators as the IXs were so much faster than us."

During the sortie, Tony spotted about ten Fw 190s 2,000 feet below and called everyone to "get stuck in." He went down, hitting a 190 which started to burn. It seemed Tony's day was starting to get better but then he made his fifth and potentially fatal mistake – he assumed. After the action he started climbing back to height, assuming the aircraft he could just see in his peripheral vision was his number two following him. But it wasn't: "The next thing I was hit in the tail and had another look and saw my 'number two' was actually a 190 with a white spinner." And there was a second 190 with him.

Tony realised he was in serious trouble. He knew he could out-turn the 190s and so began a climbing turn which at least bought him some time to work out a plan. But he also knew he couldn't go around in circles forever. His options then became even more limited when another four Fw 190s joined in the hunt, like a pack of wolves closing in on their prey.

There was only one thing he could do and that was go down to the deck. He was still thinking reasonably clearly despite his dire situation: "In the earlier fight I had seen a 190 could stall and flick inverted at low level when turning tightly so I decided to pull a very tight turn when the time was right and hope they'd fall for it and spin in. I knew where they were in relation to me because I could see our shadows on the ground.

"I called on the radio saying 'I've got six 190s here and I could use some assistance' but nobody answered so I called 'don't bother, I've had it' and kept going. Unfortunately, I misjudged the turn and did it just a bit late and got hit in the radiator. I could see the shadow of my aircraft on the ground and there was a thick plume coming out of it, so I decided to climb and bail out. Then I thought 'don't be stupid because when you straighten up they'll blow you to pieces'. So I kept turning and looking for somewhere to park it."

Tony found one clear field so he decided to put his Spitfire down in it. There was no time to set the aircraft up for a proper forced landing - he drove it into the ground wheels up and at full flying speed, the Spitfire shedding bits as it careered across the ground towards the woods surrounding the field.

The Spitfire was wrecked but Tony was unaware of the extent of damage at first because he was knocked out when it hit the ground, the result of making his sixth mistake of the day - forgetting to lock his harness straps. His face hit the gunsight hard on impact and the whiplash effect forced the back of his head into armour plate 'headrest' behind it. Earlier Spitfires had padding there but now it was just bare metal.

Tony was unconscious for perhaps 30 seconds: "The 190s were flying around in formation and like an idiot instead of playing dead I got out. The wing was sitting behind me in the paddock with the undercarriage leg hanging down and the wheel spinning like mad. The nose was in the ditch at the end of it - it couldn't have gone any further. I thought I'd blow up the IFF [Identification Friend/Foe] equipment and pushed the buttons but there wasn't a bang - it had an inertia device so it'd probably blown itself up when I hit the ground.

"I got out the incendiary device to set fire to the Spit and then thought, 'What are you doing? Setting fire to an aeroplane in a forest you'll have the fire brigade and everyone else - let alone the Germans - come tearing in, so I just ran into the woods after putting my escape purse with money and photos in my pocket and throwing my jacket and tie under some nettles in the ditch. While running I passed this old man - at least he seemed old to me - near a hut and he shouted something at me but I just kept running to find a reasonable place to hide. I climbed a tree, sat in a fork of the tree and thought 'now what do I do?'

"Then a little dog came along and found me, followed by its owner, who led me back to the hut. The people there kept asking if I wanted to surrender - in French which I could understand having done it at school - and I said 'no'. They then produced a mirror so I could see the damage I'd done to my face.

There were two big cuts with the flesh hanging down – the right eye looked like a bit of steak with a pupil in it!"

. . . .

Tony was now about to discover the extent and high level of expertise of the French Resistance organisation and the bravery of many French people through the serious risks they took in their fight against Nazi Germany. Repatriating Allied airmen like Tony Gaze was just one part of their work along with espionage and sabotage. Being caught meant instant death for these people.

Their work was made doubly dangerous by the fact that a lot of the French population, while not necessarily sympathetic to the Germans, helped them. In many cases the simple need to survive provided the motivation, but in others a conscious decision to collaborate was made. For most ordinary French men and women it was a case of doing what they could to help fight the Germans, no matter how small. For many of those involved in the Resistance it was a full time job that didn't end until Germany was defeated.

The group was celebrating the crash of a 190 not far from where Tony had come down and he thought it must have been the one he saw flick. They kept asking Tony if he wanted to surrender, to which he continued to say 'no'. In hindsight it can be seen that this questioning was part of the process that led to his repatriation plan being devised and approved through the Resistance organisation. They had to be absolutely sure that he would not waver and therefore become a potential risk when things got moving.

One of the Frenchmen went back to the wrecked Spitfire to retrieve the first aid kit and did some repair work on Tony's mangled face, pushing all the bits that were hanging down back into place, disinfecting it and repairing it as best he could. Tony was then sent back to his hiding place in the tree after having exchanged his trousers for a French pair. A half an hour later another man came along and told him to walk in a certain direction until he came to a road where he'd find a bicycle leaning against a hedge. His instructions were to get on it and ride a few hundred metres down the road until he found another man on a bicycle, and then follow him.

Tony set off, although riding the bike was difficult because was very stiff as he'd hurt his back in the crash. He found the other fellow and off they went. Tony says it was a little strange because "we cycled on as if we were in England

- the Frenchman was saying 'hello' to everyone on the side of the road and they were taking no notice of me and my RAF bandages!"

The pair rode for about half an hour and came to a school in the village of Brunville-sur-Mer. The school was closed because it was the holidays and Tony was directed to the loft of the schoolmaster's residence where he stayed for a couple of weeks lying flat on his back most of the time. The local chemist came and dressed Tony's wounds and he eventually started coming down from the loft after dark. The requirements of the body's natural processes caused some discomfort because the toilet was in the garden and he had to wait until it was dark to emerge from his hiding place and use it otherwise he'd be spotted. It was a case of gritting his teeth and hanging on!

One night he was gingerly heading down the stairs and spotted a German rifle leaning against the bannisters. One of the Germans had called in for a chat because everyone in the village knew everyone else - whether French or German - so Tony had to quickly and quietly retreat upstairs and wait until the soldier had gone.

Towards the end of Tony's stay the kindness of his hosts was again demonstrated when the schoolmaster and his wife insisted he sleep in their comfortable bed. The schoolmaster was working for the Germans during the holidays building defences while at the same time sabotaging the work by bringing home important bits of wire and other materials he'd 'neglected' to include in the building works.

It was a small part of the sabotage campaign being waged against the occupying Germans by ordinary people right across France in the factories, the work gangs and the villages. Anything that hindered them, no matter how small, was good and helped make life that little more difficult for the 'Bosch'. As Tony correctly observes, they were "amazing people."

Members of the Resistance visited Tony at the school and various subjects were discussed including ways of converting the machine guns from crashed aircraft into ground weapons. They always had their radio switched on, listening to the BBC, which surprised Tony because it was often on while Germans were walking past outside.

Apart from being the main source of non-German controlled information, the BBC was an integral part of the Resistance's activities as the broadcasts were used to send coded messages to operatives in France and elsewhere. An innocuous phrase like 'Louise sends her love to Fred' could in reality be an instruction for the Resistance to perhaps blow up a certain bridge or prepare to receive an agent who was being dropped in.

When Tony's back had improved and his face had healed enough for him to be seen in public, he was told to be ready to depart at short notice. The message came through one night about three weeks after he'd arrived at the school, prompting a farewell party for the villagers' new Australian friend. The party even ended with a rousing rendition of 'God Save The King'!

. . . .

Tony left the relative safety of Brunville-sur-Mer the next day, setting off on a bicycle and following a young man. After about an hour they passed a group of German cadets being given a lecture with a flak gun guarding them. Tony's companion found the situation highly amusing because the Germans were looking everywhere for an RAF pilot when one had just passed by!

The pair kept going until they reached a railway station where train tickets were purchased. They travelled to Amiens and Arras and twice during the journey had to disembark and walk past derailed trains. By now, Tony's rescue plan had been put it motion - he was to be picked up by a Lysander and taken back to England. But things did not work out that way. On arrival at a house outside Arras they found a very frightened lady telling them to go and hide. The plan had been discovered and the people involved arrested.

Tony and his friend slept in a wood that night and the next day he was sent to Rouen where he spent the night with the commander of the local Resistance organisation, an Englishman. He gave Tony some interesting advice, telling him that he had become a bit of a celebrity and that he would find a lot of the local girls would want to sleep with him!

But there was a very serious side to this, Tony being warned to resist the temptation because "they'll wait until you're free and then they'll have to tell somebody and for sure one of the people they'll have to tell will be sleeping with a German. You'll be alright but we'll all get shot." Tony complied, somehow managing to resist the charms of hordes of young French women throwing themselves at him. Besides, he still had a crook back from the crash!

He was then sent to Paris by train where he met another contact who took him to stay in the Place de Breteuil with a charming elderly lady who had the famed French-Canadian spy 'Gaby' staying with her. Gaby changed the

Dutch and Belgian money in Tony's escape purse into French francs, allowing them to eat well in black market restaurants.

Great care was required in the Paris curfew because anyone breaking it would be picked up by the French Police. Tony's accent would have instantly given him away, quite apart from any other anomalies they may have noticed. Gaby had already been stopped by the police once. They asked him why he was out after the curfew so he put on the "but she was so beautiful and I could not leave her" routine – no doubt accompanied by lots of Gallic shoulder shrugs and innocent as a new-born lamb expressions – and got away with it. But he didn't try it again!

After the aborted first attempt to get back to England, the escape organisation contacted Tony and he was given the choice of either waiting nearly a month for a the next full moon and another pick-up by Lysander, or travelling immediately over the Pyrenees, a journey which would take four days. He chose the latter option, was given a real identity card and sent off by train on the long journey south to a town near Toulouse. He stayed there until a group of five fellow escapees had been assembled, enough to afford the services of a guide.

For a few moments it appeared they were going to be caught in Toulouse. Three of the group including Tony went by train and the other two by bus to Toulouse station. They met in the station restaurant and thought they'd been rumbled by Italian Alpine Guards who looked at them with a suspicious eye. The group's leader took everyone out of the restaurant as a train pulled up, led them alongside it and when they reached the station's entrance took them into the square on the other side.

There, they sat in a café to see if anyone came out looking for them. Nobody did, so everyone went back into the station and boarded their train when it arrived. It took them down to Foix at the foot of the Pyrenees and only about 75 kilometres from the Spanish border. In Foix they had their boots repaired and were given a pair of espadrilles – rope-soled sandals.

The group set off again the following night, each member accompanied by a 'girl friend'. Once clear of the town they met their guide who took them up a creek bed into the mountains. They climbed all night and hid in a stack of bedding by day for two days followed by night climbing, days in villages and the odd two-day climb on the highest peaks which topped 10,000 feet. They eventually crossed into Spain at dawn and reached the town of Andorra in the afternoon.

Halfway across the Pyrenees the group had came across some unaccompanied American airmen. They had been left behind by their guide because they were belligerent, difficult and refused to follow instructions, putting themselves and the guide in great danger as a result. They were all gunners from B-17s and had serious attitude problems with obviously no real understanding of the situation they and their guide were in.

The Americans joined Tony's group and everyone quickly discovered why they had been left to their own devices. The guide might say to them: "10 minutes rest, no smoking or talking" on the side of a mountain in the pitch dark. The Americans' attitude was that no-one was going to tell them what to do and if they wanted to have a smoke - or do anything else for that matter - they were damn well going to do it, regardless of the consequences. They completely failed to appreciate the fact that lighting a match under those circumstances was akin to turning on a searchlight. If they wanted to be caught, that was a good way of ensuring it happened.

It got to the point where everyone finally got sick of these 'septic tanks', the guide pulling out a revolver and explaining to them in no uncertain terms the reality of the situation. The worst of it was that the Americans seemed to have no concept of what would happen if the group was caught, and worse, no respect for the guide and the huge risk he was taking in helping them. If caught, he would have been shot there and then. "They were a bloody nuisance," Tony remembers, suggesting that everyone would have been much better off if the guide had used his revolver rather than merely brandishing it!

After a night in Andorra and a rest day, the group set off for Barcelona. On the last day of the journey several men were caught due to the sheer laziness of one. The group was planning to walk to a small railway station about 20 miles from Barcelona and catch a train from there to the city. The reasoning was that there wasn't much chance of getting caught going that way, but when the Americans found out it was an extra 10 miles walk compared with going direct to Manresa, one of Barcelona's main stations, one of them started complaining that he couldn't walk, claiming a sprained ankle.

His mates half carried him but it slowed the process down so much there was no hope of getting to the smaller railway station on time. Instead, they all had to go directly to the main station where two or three of them were caught by the Spanish Police. As it turned out, it didn't really matter because the rest of the group made it through and told the British Consul in Barcelona about them and he was able to negotiate their release. But the real point was that the whole operation was put at risk.

People on the run who usually quickly found themselves in real trouble were those travelling alone, without any backup or support. They were almost certain to be caught and unless they spoke Spanish they could be imprisoned for a long period of time. One of Tony's flight commanders had been caught on his own and he only got out of jail because they swapped him for a German. Without that he could have been there until the end of the war.

It was now important that everyone look as 'normal' as possible with clean clothes, combed hair and so on so they would blend into the crowd of commuters on the train. Tony was alright because he had kept a brand new pair of shoes in reserve, hanging them around his neck while he travelled and using his escape boots until they fell apart. He'd had a wash and shave and looked fairly respectable.

The ticket inspector on this final train journey only gave him a cursory glance, although Tony thinks he was indirectly helped by a very attractive girl sitting opposite. The inspector was obviously rather taken with the girl and quite reasonably much preferred to feast his eyes on her than Tony!

It's interesting how important the details of appearance could be. Those in Tony's group who were caught all had mud on their shoes. No self-respecting Spaniard would ever go to market or work in the morning with dirty shoes. To another Spaniard this was a dead giveaway.

The final hurdle was to get inside the British Consulate in Barcelona. It wasn't a simple matter of just walking up to the front door, knocking on it and waiting for someone to answer because there were two guards on duty and Tony and the others could be arrested right up to the moment they stepped inside.

Murphy's Law naturally kicked in at this point - the Consulate wasn't open. Tony had to walk around the square a few times waiting for that to happen. He eventually noticed the door was open, crept up on it and slipped inside past the guards. He'd made it!

· · · · · · · · · ·

Once the milestone of getting into the Consulate had been achieved, the rest was relatively easy. Tony was taken by car to Madrid where he stayed one night because of the need to go to hospital. He says there was a feeling that there would be no problem leaving Spain because the Spanish just wanted to be rid of him and others like him. In Madrid, Tony was given the false name of an army major who was to be deported and travelled by train to La Linea and Gibralter. He was accompanied by a guard to La Linea, there to make sure he did actually leave! In Gibralter he was given a uniform and then flown to England in an RAF Dakota.

Typically, Tony tried to get hold of a Spitfire in Gibralter so he could fly himself back. Not surprisingly, his request was declined by the powers-that-be, citing the potential dangers, the fact that he hadn't flown for a while, was still injured and so on. But it was a nice try!

Tony arrived in England on 28 October 1943, two days short of eight weeks after he had been shot down. It had been an amazing if fraught adventure, one which many Allied airmen were able to make during the course of the war thanks to the bravery of those who assisted them. Tony was fortunate in the sense that his escape was successful but many didn't make it. To this day he remains intensely grateful to the French men and women who risked everything in helping him get back to England so he could continue fighting the Nazis.

In England, Tony was intensely interrogated for two days by Intelligence Officers who went through every aspect of his escape in minuscule detail. The quizzing was intense and conducted as if he was some kind of criminal. He was admitted to Halton Hospital where his injuries were examined and then sent on leave with extra rations to prepare for surgery on his face. This involved much more than just patching up a few cuts and bruises, indicated by the fact that he was readmitted to Halton in November 1943 and not discharged until the first week of February 1944.

Tony's injuries would cause him ongoing problems. While in hospital, he was told he'd have to get rid of his beloved Aston Martin because it was an open sports car which left its driver exposed to the elements. The doctors said that cold air would aggravate the problems with his face, because half of it wasn't working, and suggested he obtain a sedan instead.

The Aston was still at Kenley, so he went back there to retrieve it and put it up for sale. An army major showed an interest and after a demonstration drive decided to buy the car. He and Tony went to the local pub to celebrate the sale but Tony somehow managed to spill his drink all over his face. The result was the onset of a chill and the discovery that suddenly, "half my face wasn't working."

He went to have it checked and after a session of having needles stuck in his face was told he wasn't paralysed as feared but had Bell's Palsy, the most common form of facial palsy named after the Scot surgeon Sir Charles Bell. It involves a weakness of the facial muscles due to inflammation of or damage to the facial nerve. It is usually temporary and affects only one side of the face causing the eyelid and corner of the mouth on that side to drop. Sufferers may also find it impossible to wrinkle the brow or close the eye.

Tony asked what this all meant and how long the condition would last. He wasn't exactly encouraged by the reply: "I was told 'probably six weeks, perhaps six months or maybe forever'. Thank you very much!" They eventually operated but Tony was left with a weepy right eye for the rest of his life, probably because of an artificial duct that was put in before the Palsy had completely gone – and all through spilling his drink after selling the Aston Martin.

Any thoughts of returning to flying in the near future were dashed and it wasn't until February 1944 that he again flew a Spitfire when he was posted to the Air Fighting Development Unit (AFDU) at Wittering, mainly flying fighter affiliation training sorties with bombers. Operational flying would have to wait until after D-Day in June 1944, nine months after his bad day over France. The medicos were concerned that he would lose binocular vision due to the tears from the weepy eye pooling up.

When he was approved to fly again it was with special permission to do so with the canopy of his Spitfire or whatever he was flying permanently shut because as soon as his face got caught in a draught or received a blast of air his right eye would close. RAF regulations stated that takeoffs and landings had to be performed with the canopy open and the door on half latch so the pilot had a chance of escaping if the aircraft turned upside down on the ground.

Tony would close the canopy before engine start and not open it again until the engine was shut down at the end of the flight. Apart from when climbing in and out of an aircraft, he never opened the canopy between then and the end of the war. But at least he was able to fly – and eventually fight – again.

SEVEN

WHO'S A NAUGHTY BOY, THEN?

WHAT MADE A GOOD fighter pilot during World War II, one whose skills marked him as being a notch or two above most of the rest in the era before missiles and computers? The obvious physical and intellectual qualities include a high level of pure flying skills, spatial awareness, the ability to instinctively and accurately calculate shooting deflection angles (at least before computing gunsights came along), the ability to constantly learn and of course, bravery.

Then there's the less easily measured qualities like determination, the ability to take calculated rather than reckless risks (at least most of the time), the desire to engage the enemy whenever the opportunity arose and look to creating such opportunities, and the ability to quickly reassess a given situation and adjust accordingly. There is also the matter of proper preparation – knowing your own and your enemy's aircraft and tactics, their strengths, weaknesses and limitations.

The fighter pilots who were able to combine all these qualities were the few who could be classed among the elite, the 'aces' from all nations who between them were responsible for most of the air combat victories recorded during the war. The vast majority of pilots were competent but lacked either the magical combination of skills and qualities required to move them up to the next level, or lacked the opportunity to prove themselves. Students of the air war are usually surprised to discover the high proportion of fighter pilots who never fired their guns in anger.

The fighter pilot's personality is often thought to be a factor in his success, but closer examination reveals that outward demeanor seems to be less important than what happens within. Very few good pilots were Biggles figures, the dashing, unflappable, indestructible and fictitious 'boys' own' characters many of us of a certain age read about when we were young.

Real pilots with that sort of 'devil-may-care' attitude tended not to live for very long. Real pilots were also often scared when they were in combat. The words "very frightened" appear several times in Tony Gaze's log book comments.

To take two examples of top pilots who feature in this book – Tony Gaze himself and Douglas Bader. Bader's personality was loud, domineering, demanding of all around him, critical and in many ways overbearing. He tested you, as this writer discovered in 1981 when he spent some time with the legendary pilot in both Australia and Britain.

From the first moment we met, Sir Douglas was on it – giving me a hard time, making demands and being difficult. But I quickly worked out he was testing me, looking for weaknesses he could exploit. I decided to fight back. Anything he threw at me was returned with interest, I let him know that I was quite knowledgeable and I gained his respect as a result. I got the feeling that he *wanted* me – or anyone else who was around – to stand up to him and as a result, booming laughter usually accompanied his remarks, my responses and then his counter. He seemed to enjoy taking the contrary view on a given subject just to provoke what might be called 'lively discussion'.

As a Knight of the Realm I had been addressing him as 'Sir Douglas' but it even got to the happy point where he said to me: "Drop the 'Sir' will you? Just call me 'Douglas' for Christ's sake!" I took this as being an order rather than a request, but one I was pleased to comply with. I felt I had been accepted by him.

And so it went on and we got on just fine, but the best part was that once that respect had been earned and he'd decided that you weren't a complete idiot, there was an enormous amount to be learnt from him. The same applies to most men and women who have achieved good and great things.

Tony Gaze is another from whom much can be learned, but his personality is quite different to Bader's. It is of a much more restrained man who gets his message across by much more subtle means. He says what he thinks and offers his opinions firmly and with conviction but quietly. He 'persuades' rather verbally bludgeoning you to make his point.

He's immediately friendly but you still have to earn his respect. Bader was an 'all or nothing man' in my experience. My feeling is with him you either gained his respect quickly or not at all, at least at the time I knew him which was in his later years.

My point goes back to the statement above that "closer examination reveals that outward demeanor seems to be less important than what happens within." The personalities of Gaze and Bader are very different on the surface but both exhibit exactly the same inner qualities, those noted above.

It's an attitude thing. In order to do their job properly, fighter pilots of that era had to have that impossible-to-define 'twinkle in the eye', the desire to push boundaries, maybe bend the rules and be naughty boys every now and again. No trainee fighter pilot worth his salt didn't sometimes do or at least think about doing some illegal low flying or aerobatics when the urge and opportunity arose, or to engage in an unauthorised mock dogfight if no-one in authority was watching.

Tony Gaze's October 1940 'Red Endorsement' at the Flying Training School for "disobedience – unauthorised low flying" can be regarded in some ways as a badge of honour. It was all part of learning to be a good fighter pilot and the same undoubtedly applies today, although it's now probably more difficult to get away with than it was back then!

Tony indulged in a bit of naughtiness in June 1944 immediately after the D-Day landings. Flying very unofficially – as he had not been cleared for operations following his adventures in France the previous September – he nevertheless made some history in becoming the first Allied pilot to land on French soil after the Invasion of Europe started. Trouble is, this could not be recognised and officially did not happen!

. . . .

But first there were some more mundane duties to perform, but at least he was cleared to fly again, albeit non-operationally. On 10 February 1944, Tony Gaze was posted to the Air Fighting Development Unit (AFDU) at Wittering, near Peterborough in Northamptonshire. On that day he flew again for the first time in five months, taking Spitfire II AF-B up for an hour of aerobatics and general "stooging around". It was good to be back in the cockpit.

Four days later he was sent on attachment to No 5 Group's Fighter Affiliation Unit (FAU) at Swinderby near Lincoln, flying mainly Spitfire IIs. Called 'The Circus', it was basically a Short Stirling Operational Training Unit so Tony and his fellow Spitfire pilots flew fighter affiliation sorties with them and also with the local Wellington and Lancaster squadrons. The idea was to get the bomber pilots and gunners trained in dealing with the enemy fighters they would face on operations.

Tony flew pretty much daily, sometimes twice a day on these sorties plus weather flights, formation practice, the inevitable air tests, army beat-ups, anti-submarine and shipping patrols and flights to other bases. Apart from the Spitfire II, he also flew the Miles Martinet (the target-towing version of the Master advanced trainer), Miles Magister, Percival Proctor and Hawker

Hurricane IID at Swinderby, the latter the 'tank buster' version of the famous fighter with a pair of 40mm cannon slung under the wings.

Tony had only one potentially serious 'moment' during his five months at Swinderby, on 8 April 1944 when the Spitfire II he was flying suffered an engine failure and resulted in a forced landing at Castle Donington.

One aspect of Tony's fighter affiliation duties is of particular interest because his opinion of the value of the 'corkscrew' manoeuvre used by bomber crews to evade enemy fighters differs markedly from conventional and popular wisdom. Basically, the 'corkscrew' was a tight, violent and fast-rotating descending spiral with changes of direction. Performing it was no mean feat in a big, heavy four-engined bomber like a Lancaster.

Playing the role of attacking fighter during the affiliation sorties, Tony concluded the corkscrew was wrong: "I thought that anything that involves reversing your direction is crazy because while you're reversing you're a dead shot. I thought it would be far better to go around in a very steep turn for 360 degrees because you'd be hard to follow at night, you'd end up facing the direction you started and all your gunners could shoot at the thing following you. Anyway, they didn't seem to like my view on this - they'd given someone a decoration for inventing it. .

"I was stupid in that I didn't get at it again when we started escorting them in daylight. It was more important in daylight as the enemy was coming down very fast because they were being escorted, which meant they would have to come down flat out because there'd be a whole bunch of Spitfires after them. This meant that if the bomber was going around in a steep turn, the German fighters would have to overshoot. But I forgot to write the letter I was intending to.

"After the war I was talking to some Messerschmitt 262 pilots who said they'd shot down some Lancasters because they'd done the corkscrew. They said the Lancs weaved like crazy but they could get them because of that, whereas if they'd just gone around the fighters would have overshot.

"At night, of course, there was no overtaking - the fighters were just creeping up on the bombers. But even then I still thought the corkscrew was silly because it put the gunners off. If you're going around in a turn and a fighter's following, the gunners can be on him the whole time."

. . . .

Tony had kept in touch with his old friend Johnnie Johnson, who was in mid-1944 a Wing Commander in charge of No 144 (Canadian) Wing based at Ford near Chichester, its three squadrons (Nos 441 'Silver Fox', 442 'Caribou' and 443 'Hornet') equipped with Spitfire IXs.

Johnson was well-established as one of the leading and most highly-decorated RAF fighter pilots and by June 1944 he had a DSO and Bar, DFC and Bar and two dozen confirmed solo kills to his credit plus seven shared. He would add another ten to this tally over the next three months and receive a second Bar to his DSO.

Knowing full well that Tony had not been cleared to return to operational flying, Johnson made the somewhat mischievous suggestion that he might like to get back into the swing of things and join the Canadian Wing for a sortie or two. Tony – who was as keen as ever to do the job he'd been trained for – took little time to agree to Johnson's suggestion and on 1 May 1944 'borrowed' a Martinet from the Fighter Affiliation Unit and flew it down to Funtingdon near Ford to fly an 'op' on the same day.

Despite the alacrity with which Tony accepted Johnson's invitation he says he was very worried about flying what amounted to an operation that was sailing very close to the wind in terms of its legality: "If anything had happened to me - if I'd shot something down or something had shot me down - it'd be a real problem." What he was doing was a Court Martial offence after all, and even Johnson might have found himself in a spot of bother if they'd been found out.

The mission was a Ramrod to the Paris area escorting USAAF B-26 Marauders, Tony flying Spitfire IX 9G-W with 441 Squadron. Perhaps luckily, it was straightforward affair with nothing untoward happening: "Good bombing, little flak, no enemy aircraft, swept around Paris, 190s on deck." Tony took his borrowed Martinet back to Swinderby the next morning to resume his fighter affiliation duties. He'd got away with it!

In the early morning of 6 June 1944 - D-Day - the greatest invasion force and armada ever assembled left England for the beaches of Normandy to start Operation Overlord, the Allied invasion of Europe and the beginning of the end for Nazi Germany. Five thousand ships, 60,000 troops, two parachute divisions and enormous numbers of aircraft were involved in the first wave to hit the beaches.

On that momentous day, Tony Gaze was not doing what he wanted to do and was not where he wanted to be. While his colleagues in the fighter squadrons were flying over France in support of the invasion, he was flying a Martinet from Swinderby to Digby to collect cannon ammunition. This activity did, however, have a meaningful purpose as part of Tony's plan to arm his unit's Spitfires to counter the expected wave of German intruders coming it at 'dot' feet to pick off RAF aircraft landing after operations over Normandy.

But relief was at hand. Johnnie Johnson had said to Tony that "when the balloon goes up, come down come down and join us after D-Day." So that's what he did, flying down to Tangmere and then Ford on 8 June and going out with the Canadian Wing again two days later. Flying Spitfire IX 9G-R with 441 Squadron, Tony logged two sorties that day, the first a patrol of the beachhead and a landing at airfield B2 near Caen, the second a sweep inland from Caen where he observed "good bombing by Marauders, bags of light flak, no enemy aircraft."

Then it was back to Ford, hop into the Spitfire II he'd brought down from Swinderby and return there - all in one day!

And it was a day that Flight Lieutenant Tony Gaze DFC and Bar made a piece of history that 'didn't happen'. At the end of the first sortie and on landing at airfield B2, he became the first Allied pilot to land and refuel in France after D-Day.

Tony explains: "My landing first at B2 wasn't planned at all - I was going to fly with Johnnie as I had previously when we went to Paris. We were going to do one trip with Marauders then refuel at B2 and do another trip with them. But as we were taxying out for the second show Johnnie radiod me and said that one of the Canadians had burst a tyre and would I stay with him and bring him over to France with the second show? So I waited for him and when they'd changed the tyre I took him over and we flew up and down the Normandy beachhead, but nothing was going on.

"I thought we were being rash with just the two of us so we went inland and got over the fighting and then the flak came up. I thought 'we can't go down and beat up the flak' because we don't know what the plans are so we retreated to the beachhead and flew up and down waiting for something to happen."

Tony heard the Wing coming back, heading to B2 to make history as the 'first in France'. It had all been carefully planned - there was a large public relations exercise associated with the event and the Canadians would be taking centre stage, along with their famous leader. Then a devilish thought came over him – he was a fighter pilot after all: "I looked down at the strip and saw it was very dirty and dusty and decided I didn't want to be the last one down – I'll be the first!"

The story unfolded, containing a healthy element of farce: "As soon as the Wing got within range I went down with my number two and landed. We taxied to the end of the strip and the crew was waiting with jerry cans along with a mass of media who'd been flown in by the Canadians to greet the first people to land and refuel. And it wasn't a bloody Canadian, it was me! It spoilt their day – they asked me where I came from in Canada and I had to tell them I didn't!

"So they grabbed my number two and he got all the attention. I don't know what Johnnie thought – he didn't say anything – but then I got really worried when Harry Broadhurst [then AOC 83 Group] turned up. I thought that if he sees me I'm for it because officially I was still non-operational. I hid behind the aeroplanes so he couldn't see me! We just hung around until we'd refuelled and did the second show.

"Johnny never admitted to any of this because officially it didn't happen! If it had got back to the Canadian powers-that-be they would have asked 'who's this bloke flying our aircraft?' It was much easier to just pretend it hadn't happened." When Tony got back to Ford he thought he'd better return to Swinderby straight away because he knew he'd been extremely lucky to get away with what was by any measure a serious breach of the rules.

There was still one potentially nasty hurdle to overcome at Swinderby, because apart from anything else, Tony had not asked for permission to go to 441 Squadron and had therefore been officially missing from his proper posting for three days – and he'd taken a Spitfire with him, albeit one he'd properly signed for.

But his luck held: "After asking me where the hell I'd been, my Air Commodore at Swinderby was sufficiently humorous to think the whole thing was rather funny, I think! But he knew as well as I did that if I'd asked permission to take a few days off to go down to Ford he'd have had to say 'no, you're non-operational'. So I got away with it He said my punishment would be announced at midday. It was a 20 minute talk over the Tannoy about my experiences over the beach head." Perhaps the Air Commodore couldn't face the paperwork that taking the matter further would have generated.....

Tony continued his duties at Swinderby but his desire to go back on to operations on Spitfires was looking as if it would be unfulfilled. He was told it probably wouldn't happen: "They really didn't want me back because of having been shot down before. If I'd been shot down again and captured they thought there was a danger it might compromise the Resistance." Instead, it was suggested he might like to go to the Pathfinder Force flying Mosquitos.

The PFF was part of 5 Group which was like a compact, self-contained air force in its own right doing special jobs like bombing dams, U–Boat pens and specific targets like the German battle cruiser *Tirpitz*. The famous 617 'Dam Busters' Squadron was part of it. Tony decided that even it the job meant he wasn't flying Spitfires, at least he would be operational. He agreed, and was on the verge of leaving the Fighter Affiliation Unit to convert to the Mosquito when a signal arrived saying he was report to 610 Squadron at Friston and its Spitfire XIVs.

Not surprisingly, this order was well received by Tony who had not flown operationally – at least not officially – since he had been shot down over France ten months earlier. He flew his last sortie with the FAU on 21 July 1944 and reported to 610 Squadron the next day. During his time at Swinderby he added 223 hours to his log book including 187 on Spitfires. His total flying time was now 1,364 hours and a new chapter of his career as an operational fighter pilot was about to begin.

EIGHT

DIVERS AND JETS

TONY GAZE JOINED 610 Squadron at Friston in Sussex on 22 July 1944, happy to be back on operations after an absence of ten months and also delighted to be rejoining the squadron with which he had begun his operational flying more than three years earlier.

The tool of the trade had changed considerably since then, 610 now equipped with the Rolls-Royce Griffon-powered Spitfire XIV with over 2,000 horsepower at its disposal, a maximum speed nearly 100mph faster than the Spitfire II Tony was flying in 1941, and nearly twice the rate of climb. As a pure fighter, the Spitfire XIV was regarded by many as the best of the war.

Tony first flew a Spitfire XIV on the day of his arrival at 610 Squadron, a 1hr 25min local and aerobatics flight to get the feel of this new mount. One characteristic he and other pilots who had come off Merlin-powered Spitfires had to get used to was that the propeller (now a five-blader) rotated in the opposite direction, necessitating revised rudder pedal footwork to counter the aircraft's swing on takeoff.

Tony didn't even know what a Spitfire XIV was until he went to Friston. After that first flight he noted that it was a "good kite but overpowered" and had a "terrific climb." He adds: "It was very surprising because I'd never really flown anything with so much power, apart from the Typhoon briefly. It wanted to fly sideways all the time and needed a lot of trimming and was not as nice as the Merlin versions. But as a fighter it was better than anything."

When Tony rejoined 610 Squadron its primary activity was 'anti-Diver' patrols, trying to intercept the V-1 'flying bombs' that had begun being launched against Britain the previous month. The V-1 was the Fieseler Fi 103, a small fixed-wing pilotless aircraft powered by a pulse jet engine mounted above the rear fuselage and incorporating a simple flight control system and an air log device which caused it to dive to the ground (thus the RAF 'Diver' code name) after travelling a calculated distance based on the amount of fuel carried.

Launched from ramps usually hidden in wooded areas in occupied France – principally in the Pas de Calais area – the V-1's forward fuselage was packed with 850 kilograms of Amatol high explosive. The engine cut when the calculated distance had been covered and the aircraft went down, exploding on impact. The V-1 became known as the 'buzz bomb' by those on the ground due to its distinct engine note. 'Doodlebug' was another popular name bestowed on the weapon. Whenever one approached it created considerable tension on the ground as people waited for the engine to cut, fervently hoping it would do so after it had passed over their heads.

More than 10,000 V-1s were launched against Britain – all but a few of them intended for London – of which 7,448 crossed the English Channel and 3,957 were shot down by either fighters or anti-aircraft guns. Just over 2,400 reached London, causing the deaths of 6,184 people and injuring a further 18,000. The first V-1s were launched on 13 June 1944.

The V-1 came in low and fast, typically below 2,000 feet and at or just under 400mph (640km/h). With a wing span of only 17 feet and a small, slim fuselage it was a difficult target to hit. Fighter pilots found that if they attacked from a reasonable distance out – say 400 yards – there were few hits. Bringing the firing range down to 200 yards produced much better results but also greatly increased the chances of the intercepting fighter being damaged or even destroyed if the bomb exploded in front of it. Many pilots were lost in this way and others had their guns resynchronised for the rounds to converge at 300 yards to provide a compromise between effective fire and safety.

A second method of dealing with the V-1 was 'invented' by Flying Officer MacLaren of 56 Squadron on 4 July 1944 when he placed the wingtip of his Hawker Tempest a few inches below that of his quarry and then gently flicked it upwards, toppling the V-1's gyros and sending it crashing to the ground, hopefully harmlessly in open countryside. This became a standard method of dealing with the V-1 but required very precise flying.

Tony Gaze relates how one of 610 Squadron's pilots had heard about this technique but came back from an anti-Diver sortie very shaken up "because instead of putting his wingtip under the V-1's wing he put it on top, so it rolled towards him and he had nearly a tonne of bomb coming at him!"

In order to shoot down a V-1, first you had to catch it. 610 Squadron's Spitfire XIVs were not quite ideal for the task because their performance peaked at medium–high altitudes, and the level at which the V-1s came in was too low for the XIV's speed and rate of climb to be properly exploited. Not that the aircraft was a slouch at low level. It was capable of about 380mph at 2,000 feet in level flight, about the same as a V-1 or fractionally slower.

The Hawker Tempest was better suited as it was the fastest fighter of them all down low, topping 400mph at V-1 altitudes and capable of overtaking most of them. Of the 1,771 V-1s claimed shot down by the RAF between June and September 1944, 638 were by Tempest pilots.

Tony describes operations against the V-1: "The chance of catching one in the short distance we had was low - by the time you caught the thing up you were in your own flak belt and then you'd look for the Tempests on the other side of the flak belt, just watching where the flak was and then diving down to clobber the V-1.

"When I joined the squadron they had us patrolling the French coast and you had very little chance because you were cruising up and down at about fifteen hundred feet doing a pattern and waiting for the radar blokes to say 'okay, there's one in such-and-such a place'. They were doing 400mph and by the time you got after them the thing was halfway across the Channel. By the time you got in shooting range you were in the flak belt." Tony's log book entry of 6 August notes that he chased a Diver for 15 miles but couldn't catch it.

But the day before he'd had success, shooting down a V-1 south of Beachy Head while flying Spitfire XIV DW-U: "I got a V-1 which tried to get me! I was directed onto this thing and I was getting near Beachy Head and they said 'you're very close' but I couldn't see it. I finally spotted it right behind me! I thought 'this is dead easy, I'll just pull up and wait for it pass and clobber it'. So I did!"

Friston was originally an emergency strip Douglas Bader had laid out near Beachy Head for refuelling. It had a quarry at one end before a cliff with about a 200 feet drop and a gully on one side with plenty of trees. It had been upgraded to an operational airfield as a base for aircraft being used for V-1 patrols.

Tony saw some unpleasant things at Friston including the demise of a Mustang and its pilot from a Polish Squadron. Tony was polishing his Spitfire when the Mustang taxied past, the pilot giving Tony a friendly wave. Then the characteristic of the Mustang that Tony always disliked so much came into play - its swing.

He remembers: "On takeoff the pilot failed to hold the swing and veered towards the gully, just getting airborne before the trees.. He clipped the tops of them and appeared to be getting away with it but hit the jib of a Coles crane that had been working there. That tipped the aircraft onto its back and it landed upside down past the trees. A small fire broke out. We all rushed and tried to lift the wing and get the pilot out but no matter how many we had, we couldn't get him out without a crane, but by the time we got one it was too late."

On another occasion, in the evening, Tony was driving to meet some people at a pub when he saw a Spitfire flying very low and slow alongside his car. It stalled, crashed and caught fire, Tony driving through a gate to get to it where he sprayed his fire extinguisher onto the cockpit. But when he got close enough to see what he was spraying he gave up and "went to the pub to get full...."

. . . .

By late August 1944 the number of Diver attacks against London had begun to diminish as the Allied Armies moved eastwards across Europe, capturing the V-1 launch sites as they went. As a result, 610 Squadron was moved from anti-Diver patrols to escorting bombers on daylight raids into occupied Europe and Germany. The RAF bombers, which had previously flown almost exclusively at night, were now performing an increasing number of daylight operations.

610 Squadron performed the first of its new missions on 26 August – a Rodeo to the Beaurais area – the first of some two dozen similar sorties Tony and his fellow pilots would fly over the next three months. At least these operations were flown at the higher altitudes at which the Spitfire XIV was at its best, but contacts with German fighters were virtually non-existent: "We escorted thousands of our bombers to the Ruhr and never saw any German aircraft ever," says Tony.

Everyone was keen to shoot at something but there were no opportunities. The closest Tony came was on 17 September (five days after the squadron had moved to Lympne in Kent) while escorting transports and gliders to Schouwen when 610's Spitfires strafed German flak ships in the harbour, setting one on fire.

This sortie was conducted on the first day of Operation Market Garden, conceived by Britain's General Montgomery and intended to outflank the German defensive line by establishing a bridgehead across the lower Rhine at the Dutch town of Arnhem. The aim was to place the Allied armies at the threshold of the Ruhr and help bring the war to an early end. 'Market' was the airborne assault element of the operation intended to seize eight bridges and comprising mainly British and Commonwealth troops; 'Garden' was the element involving US ground forces to cross them once they were secured.

Transport aircraft dropped 16,500 paratroops onto the area and gliders carried in a further 3,500 but the operation was a disaster, thwarted by strong, well organised and determined German resistance. Market Garden ran well behind schedule, Allied losses were heavy and the operation was finally abandoned when the it became clear that the primary objective - establishing the bridgehead at Arnhem - would not be achieved. The operation was later immortalised in the film *A Bridge Too Far*.

The crossing of the Rhine was obviously highly important to the Allies because it would ensure their advance through Germany. The Rhine represented both a geographical and psychological barrier for the Allies and Germans - to cross it virtually guaranteed victory for one side and defeat for the other. The Allies finally crossed the river in early 1945.

Tony Gaze survived another scrape on 19 September during a Market patrol while flying Spitfire XIV DW-P. The sortie was cancelled due to appalling weather after 610's aircraft were already airborne. While attempting to land at Lympne during extremely heavy rain Tony found himself about to run off the end of the runway so he pulled the undercarriage up to avoid this, still with the Spitfire's 90 gallon belly tank attached.

He describes the episode as being "very fraught" and notes that all three of the Spitfires that returned to Lympne "pranged". The others landed safety after diverting to Manston. There was an enquiry, of course, which absolved Tony of any blame - much to his surprise!

On 6 October Tony flew a Ramrod to Sterkrade (in DW-P) escorting 120 Halifaxes that were bombing a synthetic oil plant. No enemy aircraft were encountered but he saw three bombers go down to the heavy flak barrage. On the way home Tony escorted a damaged Halifax of 462 Squadron RAAF flown by Flt Lt Ted McGindle. Two of the bomber's crew members had bailed out and others aboard were wounded, but it wasn't until decades later that Tony learnt anything of the crew or the circumstances surrounding their plight.

Artist Robert Taylor was preparing a painting of the incident called 'Top Cover' showing the Halifax and Tony Gaze's Spitfire in formation on their way back from Sterkrade. Taylor's research - working with the Australian Halifax Association - revealed that McGindle and Gaze were living only 50 miles apart in Victoria. The Association got in touch with Taylor's Australian representative, Melbourne-based John Rayner, who in turn contacted Tony and the story behind the painting was fully revealed.

It's interesting that Tony remained not totally convinced that his was the Spitfire that escorted that particular Halifax, although he admits the chances are very high that it was: "I still look at it as a 'probable' rather than a certainty because it could have been someone else on the same day because there were 120 Halifaxes. They reckon the odds of that particular incident happening on that particular day at the particular time were such that it had to be me and it was worth making a painting of it. But neither he [McGindle] nor me noted our squadron codes so we can't be absolutely certain."

Perhaps Tony's lingering doubts were dispelled in September 2007 when he and Ted McGindle were both guests at a Royal Victorian Aero Club function. A print of Robert Taylor's 'Top Cover' painting was signed by both men and then raffled off at $10 a ticket!

A major step towards the ending of the European war occurred on 24 August 1944 when Paris was liberated. Exiled Free French leader General Charles de Gaulle returned to the French capital shortly afterwards and on 11 November – Armistice Day – Winston Churchill flew to Paris to meet him. This provided Tony with the opportunity to undertake an unusual sortie three days later – escorting Churchill's aircraft from France back to the RAF base at Northolt.

Unusual circumstances led to the flight and it ended with Tony going off on a small adventure of his own: "I wasn't meant to be on that. We got a signal that on landing one of our blokes had been led by the Americans in a jeep to a parking bay and the driver suddenly slammed on the jeep's brakes. The aircraft hit the jeep, chewing up its propellor and the bloke in the jeep.

"So I went to fill in. I flew on my own via Amiens to Javincourt and flew back escorting Churchill. His aircraft eventually went into cloud crossing the French coast and we lost him so I decided I'd go and have a look for my wreck from when I was shot down. I did see what looked like a wrecked aircraft in that area but I couldn't go down to confirm it was mine."

· · · · · · · · · · ·

As the Allied armies advanced across Europe, more of its cities and towns were liberated including Brussels on 3 September 1944. Three months later – on 4 December – 610 Squadron moved to Belgium, based at Brusselles Evere. On 15 December Tony took over command of 'B' flight and three days later Germany launched its last major offensive of the war, the Ardennes campaign in Belgium, popularly known as the Battle of the Bulge.

Germany's aim was to split the Allied armies and recapture Antwerp, their most important supply port in the region. Using armour, 30 army divisions and more than 1,000 supporting aircraft, the initial assault achieved the intended element of surprise and was conducted in poor weather, the German leadership correctly assuming that this would at least temporarily neutralise Allied air power.

In the end, the offensive was thwarted by mainly American forces and the battle was in effect over by the end of the first week of January 1945, although it continued for a week or so after that. Three factors gave the Allies victory – the US Army's superior lines of supply, its ability to quickly move men and armour from elsewhere to the Ardennes, and its ability to replace casualties where the Germans could not. And casualties were high on both sides, numbering about 100,000 killed and wounded each.

When the weather cleared on 23 December Allied air power was able to be unleashed, the USAAF's Ninth Air Force flying some 1,300 sorties on that day alone and on Christmas Eve 2,000 Allied aircraft attacked 31 separate targets. This day was critical to the battle as the raids mortally wounded the already struggling German supply organisation and seriously restricted the ability of the German armour to move due to a lack of fuel and spare parts.

610 Squadron's Spitfires supported the Americans through patrols and by providing area cover but as Tony notes: "All they did was try to shoot us down. We were shot at more by the Yanks than the Germans!"

His log book entries of 23-25 December covering a series of patrols in the Aachen-Malmedy area tell the story: "Supporting Yanks who were being pasted in Hun advance. Yanks called for help but proceeded to do their best to shoot us down with fighters and flak.... shot at by Mustangs.... shot at by Yank flak.... [and on one notable occasion] actually shot at by Hun flak!"

610 Squadron moved to Airfield Y.32 at Ophoven on 31 December, just in time for a massive German air offensive on New Year's Day 1945. The Luftwaffe celebrated the new year by putting up every available fighter in a last desperate attempt to gain air superiority by attacking 27 Allied airfields. Although 156 Allied aircraft were destroyed on the day, German losses exceeded 300, a blow from which the Luftwaffe never recovered. 610's new base was strafed, Tony remembering that "there was all these Yanks around us but they didn't fire at the 190s and things strafing the base, they all ran for cover."

Tony flew three sorties on 1 January, patrols in the Malmedy–Marche area, during which he "managed to avoid being shot down by Yank flak but lost section. Attacked eight long nose 190s [Fw 190Ds], destroyed one. Nearly shot down by Hun and friendly flak."

It was during Tony's first sortie of the day that he scored the 190D flying Spitfire XIV DW-T: "I chased the 190s and got one - they were probably out of ammunition - and could have got a couple more but I suddenly thought I was being silly to take on that number and went back. The German flak followed me to the river and the Yanks fired at me on the other side."

His Spitfire was hit by German flak during the second sortie: "It was very accurate. The one that wrote off my wing, the 88mm, that was the first shot. They had our angle of climb absolutely right. I was blown almost upside down and I looked over to the other four that were with us and they were climbing at a certain angle and the bursts were coming up at the same angle.

"I didn't know what had happened to my aircraft and I called my number two to have a look. He said there was a little hole in one of the wings - nothing to worry about - so I carried on and went home. I was met by the engineering officer and he said, 'Well, we won't see this one for a long time will we'? And I said 'Why? It's only got a hole in the wingtip'. He suggested I look at it from his point view and there was a ripple on the top of the wing where the metal had bent up."

The Ardennes campaign was well conceived and well executed by the Germans and caused the Allies considerable grief in its early stages. But it was Hitler's last throw of the dice and ultimately failed because of the Allies' vastly superior reserves, supply and support infrastructure.

After all the excitement of the Battle of the Bulge and the intense level of operational flying it entailed, Tony got a little very welcome relief courtesy ten days' skiing leave at Megeva in the French Alps towards the end of January - *trés bien*!

. . . .

Tony returned to 610 Squadron just in time for its move from Belgium to Eindhoven in the Netherlands at the beginning of February. Even though Nazi Germany was by now entering its death throes, there was still plenty of fighting to do. A series of armed reconnaissance and patrol sorties were flown over the next two weeks. Two of them - on 11 and 13 February - provided some reward when Tony shared in the destruction of a barge, four locomotives and 20 trucks. All good sport.

There was more serious sport to be had on 14 February, Tony celebrating St Valentine's Day with the destruction of a Messerschmitt Me 262 jet fighter. It was his first, the first for 125 Wing and the first time an Australian had shot down a jet in aerial combat. Flying Spitfire XIV DW-F, he encountered three Me 262s during a patrol in the Munster area but these were not the only Luftwaffe jets he came across during that sortie:

"It was a complete fluke because we were patrolling below cloud and Arado Ar 234 jets were coming down through the cloud and bombing. I had a shot at two of them trying to make them turn. I worked out what they were doing, coming in above the cloud flying on their radio beam and when they got to a certain point they'd dive through the cloud to bomb.

"So I went above the cloud to see their angle of dive or line of flight and called my number two and tell him to get going absolutely flat out on that vector so that when they came through he was on the same course. I went up through the cloud and iced up and was doing a turn in the sun to get the ice off when I saw three 262s were near me, into the sun. I chased them and found I was slowly catching them up. I didn't know what their wing span was so I didn't know what to set the gunsight on.

"We were going straight into the sun so all I had was silhouettes, and I suddenly realised I was close enough to shoot, so I did, hitting one of them in the side of an engine. I then turned away out of the sun so I could have a proper go at him. If we hadn't been going into the sun I reckon I could have got all three because they weren't looking. If I'd had a gyro sight I'm sure I'd have got them all because I could have sat back at 500 yards and picked them off.

"As it was I had to close in and the moment I fired they went into the cloud. I called my number two and said there's a 262 coming down on fire and he called back to say it had gone straight in. The beginning of the gun-camera film is interesting because it's got two shots of the 234 - I just got a quick squirt in. I'm pretty certain I hit it but you can't claim unless you see serious damage."

A few days later, 610 Squadron was sent back to Britain, based at Warmwell in Dorset for bombing training. The pilots practised high and low level bombing - with varying degrees of accuracy - but after only a week of this and nine flights it was suddenly announced that 610 Squadron would be disbanded (on

3 March) because the European war was starting to wind down and the RAF didn't need so many squadrons any more.

Tony flew 185 hours during this stint with 610 Squadron (including 125 operational) and had added one Fw 190D and an Me 262 confirmed destroyed (plus the V-1) to his tally, which now stood at 9.5 confirmed. He was nearly a 'double ace'.

On 13 March Tony achieved the rare distinction of being awarded a second Bar to his DFC, triggered by the Me 262 victory. "He has throughout displayed outstanding flying ability, a fine fighting spirit and unfailing devotion to duty," said the citation. Not bad for a pilot who was still a 'mere' Flight Lieutenant! Colin Gray's warnings of two-and-a-half years earlier about the dangers of losing rank had been well-founded.....

. . . .

With only a month of the European war remaining, Tony was posted to 41 Squadron in the Netherlands on 6 April 1945 as the commander of 'A' Flight. The squadron was also equipped with the Spitfire XIV and the posting provided Tony with a last flurry of operational activity which saw him add to his tally of air combat 'kills'.

The squadron was based at Eindhoven when Tony arrived and moved to Twente the following day before shifting to Celle in Germany on 16 April. Celle was the first 'proper' German airfield Tony and his colleagues had been to and they were amazed by standard of facilities they found – a mess which Tony describes as "palatial", swimming pool, beer cellar and workshops, all of which were undamaged.

Tony was with 41 Squadron for only three weeks but the level of operations was intensive. During that time he flew 42 operational sorties – an average of two per day – and flew 77 operational hours. Armed reconnaissance missions, sweeps and patrols were flown, resulting in the destruction of numerous trains, trucks and other bits and pieces on the ground. He had a chance to fire at Ar 234s and other types on a couple of occasions but several times combat was not possible because he came across enemy aircraft late in the sortie when fuel was low. Throughout these sorties, the German flak was consistently heavy and accurate

He downed a Junkers Ju 52 transport during a patrol in the Bremen area on 11 April, shared an Arado Ar 234 jet bomber with Flt Lt Rake the following day in the same area, and shared an Fw 190D Flt Lt Williamson near Schwerin airfield on 28 April during an armed reconnaissance sortie. They took on at least ten Fw 190s in this skirmish and Tony noted in his log book that "Wilky got one, cut me out dammit!".

Before that, on 20 April, Tony had what he describes as his "moment with Russians over Berlin", something that could have led to a serious diplomatic incident with Britain's and the USA's 'glorious ally'. Johnnie Johnson had organised a sweep to Berlin, the RAF's top ace leading the Wing on what turned out to be a one-off. Johnson took what he described as "our first team" with him, including Tony Gaze with whom he had not officially flown since the Bader days. Of course, there were those couple of sorties in May and June 1944, the ones that didn't happen! As an aside, it is well known that Johnnie Johnson didn't much like the Spitfire XIV - he much preferred his beloved Merlin-powered Mk.IX.

The sight of Berlin had a profound effect on many of the pilots who participated in this sweep - desolation, destruction, refugees, fires and the sight and sounds of the Red Army as it moved ever closer to the German capital. There was no 'race' to get to Berlin first between the Americans and British on one hand and the Russians on the other. The city's fate - and indeed that of the rest of Germany and Eastern Europe - had already been decided by US President Franklin Roosevelt, Winston Churchill and the Soviet Premier, Josef Stalin.

The Soviets would be allowed to get to Berlin first (they arrived on 2 May) and keep it, Germany would be partitioned and Stalin would be given a free hand in Eastern Europe. Both Roosevelt and Churchill abhorred communism as much as they did fascism, but they also recognised the Soviet Union's contribution to the defeat of Nazi Germany and the fact that post-war, it would be a major power. They also knew that the deal would cause problems in the years ahead.

As Winston Churchill said in a 1946 speech, delivered in the USA: "From Stettin in the Baltic to Trieste in the Adriatic, an iron curtain has descended across the Continent". Roosevelt never saw the post-war world as he died in April 1945, replaced by Harry Truman.

Tony Gaze recounts the 'incident over Berlin': "We arrived over Berlin with the Wing and I spotted well over 50 aircraft and called up Johnnie who asked what are they, and I said they don't look like Huns to me, they look like Russians. And they were, Yaks and others.

"He got a bit worried that we might get tangled with them. They came over us and a Petlyakov Pe-2 came down and started shooting at my number two! This made me angry, so I lined it up and was going to blow it out of the sky but it went into cloud just as I was going to press the firing button.

"Johnnie then led us away to the north, away from the Russians. They were an absolute mess – they were like a flock of birds, there was no pattern to their flying – they were just sort of flying around Berlin, going down to have a shot at whatever took their fancy and going up again.

"There were one or two of our people saying things like 'oh dear, you know I seem to have accidentally let light into my camera gun, do you think it'll do any harm?', so I think a couple of them did actually have a shot at them but didn't want it to be recorded on film. As for me, I seriously resented a bloody Russian shooting at me. I didn't shoot back at the Yanks when they did but I wasn't going to have a Russian do it. It could have got quite nasty but it didn't."

RAF fighter sweeps over Berlin were banned after that and it was probably just as well because there was a good chance of a 'misunderstanding' happening with unfortunate consequences. It's interesting how everybody – British, American and German – mistrusted or even hated the Russians. Many German soldiers and airmen who were interrogated immediately after the European war ended hoped or even assumed they would be joining up with the Brits and Americans to take on the Soviets and Stalin's regime, which was just as brutal as Hitler's had been.

Tony Gaze scored his last kill of the war on 30 April 1945, the same day Adolf Hitler committed suicide in his Berlin bunker. It was during a patrol in the Lauenberg area – his third of the day – flying Spitfire XIV EB-E. "Fw 190A destroyed, 8 Me 109s v. frightened!", it says in his log book. "Also me!"

. . . .

Tony flew his final sortie with 41 Squadron on 1 May, the same day he was transferred ("much to my dismay") to one of his previous units, 616 Squadron based at Fassberg in Germany and part of 10 Group's 122 Wing. The significance of this was initially lost on him because although 616 had pioneered the introduction to service of the Allies' first operational jet fighter, the Gloster Meteor, in July 1944, he didn't want to stop flying Spitfires and resisted the move. His objections naturally fell on deaf ears, so off he went to become a jet pilot and make a little history. "Farewell to Spits, bugger it!," he wrote.

There was some compensation, including promotion to Squadron Leader nearly three years after he'd lost that rank following the Eagle Squadron incident during his brief stint with 64 Squadron, and of course the making of more history by becoming the first Australian to fly a jet operationally. It's possible he was also the first Australian to fly a jet at all.

616 Squadron by then had the Meteor III on strength, the first major production version of the new fighter. The squadron had initially flown the Meteor I with Rolls-Royce Welland engines; the Mk.III had more powerful Rolls-Royce Derwents and considerably improved performance, although typical of British fighters, totally inadequate range and endurance. The Meteor also provided Tony with his first operational experience of a twin-engined aeroplane.

He was flown to Fassberg in a captured Siebel Si 204 eight-passenger light transport and crew training twin and told to do many flights in it to get used to flying an aircraft with two engines. It didn't quite work out that neatly because before Tony hopped into a Meteor for the first time he only had that single flight in the Si 204 under his belt and that was just 40 minutes as second pilot 'under instruction'.

On 2 May 1945, 616 Squadron moved to Luneberg and Tony flew the Meteor for the first time. As had been the case with previous new types there was no dual instruction and it was just a matter of cockpit familiarisation, read the pilot's notes, learn the numbers and go. By today's standards it seems astounding that this was the entire training for a pilot about to be let loose in an aircraft that represented the most advanced aviation technology of its time, but things were much simpler back then!

Tony celebrated his first 30 minute test flight in Meteor 'R' by beating up Celle airfield ("nice kite, bit heavy though") and on his return announced he was ready to go on operations and did so later in the same day. That was a sweep that lasted 45 minutes, the limit of the Meteor's endurance. "This range business is no joke," he noted . Tony flew six armed reconnaissance sorties in Meteors over a three day period in what proved to be the last week of the European War, and by the end of it had 4hrs 40min of jet time in his log book and one truck destroyed .

"The Meteor was not a real fighter like the 262. Everything was faster than before - climb 275, cruise 400 and watch the fuel. We never had enough to go around again on landing. We did practice attacks on Lancasters escorted by Mustangs and just played with them. I found that 45 minutes' endurance was it. The dive brakes were locked shut so we couldn't use them, so we used to come in fast because we reckoned that the same thing might happen to us as happened to the German jets, that we'd be picked off by a 190 or something while we were in the circuit.

"So we'd come in at normal cruise, shut right off and do a complete circuit with no power and land hot with no power. We reckoned we used more fuel taxying out in a Meteor than a Spit would use in an hour! The Germans refuelled their 262s at the end of the runway before going up and they had much bigger fuel tanks than we did.

"Right at the end of the European War they finally allowed us to unlock the Meteor's dive brakes so we wouldn't bend the aircraft when we went strafing because diving down from 15,000 feet - which we had to do to get any range at all - in a steep dive even with everything shut off you were still overspeeding and bending the aeroplane. Too late they let us use the dive brakes and also gave us another 180 gallons of fuel in a ventral tank which would have made a hell of a difference. We would have been able to shoot better because coming down at high speed the aircraft started snaking. I found the only way to shoot accurately was to deliberately put on a bit of skid to stop it snaking.

"Such was the firepower of the Meteor's four 20mm cannon grouped close together in the nose that if you hit a truck you'd break it in half. There was no tracer ammunition but you could follow the shells by the heat haze they generated."

Performance comparisons between the Meteor III and Spitfire XIV are interesting, the former representing the first generation of jet fighters and the latter the pinnacle of piston-engined fighter development. They show that in terms of speed, especially, the jets really did set new standards. At sea level the Meteor was about 100mph faster than the Spitfire and higher up nearly 50mph faster, but the Spitfire's maximum rate of climb was 15 per cent greater, the margin increasing with altitude, and the Spitfire was more agile. Service ceilings were similar but the Meteor's practical endurance without the ventral tank fitted was less than half that of the Spitfire. It wasn't often that a Spitfire's endurance figure looked good in comparison with another fighter!

The lack of 'proper' instruction on the Meteor caused Tony some grief on a flight out of Lübeck after hostilities had ceased: "I climbed north from Lübeck until engine surge problems caused a power reduction. I rolled over and aimed down, but violent shaking and buffeting caused me to pull off power and ease out of the dive, coming level at 25,000 feet and luckily pointing at Lübeck. I opened the throttles with no result and looking back saw two streams of unburnt kerosene trailing behind me.

"I tried all the relighting methods I could think of but stopped when I realised I would need all the battery power to clear the runway if I made the airfield. After playing around with different airspeeds I found Lübeck going down and not up in the windscreen so I reckoned I'd make it into there and not on the Russian side.

"I managed to get the airfield controller to stop a formation of Typhoons taking off and came into the circuit. The outside of the canopy then decided to completely freeze up so I had no visibility and had to land with the hood open looking sideways. I ran the aircraft to the end of the runway and told my welcoming party, 'look, the motors wouldn't relight' but when I tried to show them both engines started happily and I was able to taxy in. I hadn't read the bit in the book about not attempting to relight above 10,000 feet!"

Germany surrendered on 7 May 1945 and Victory in Europe (VE) Day was declared at one minute past midnight the following morning. After more than five-and-a-half years, the war which had been started by Germany was finally over and the Nazis vanquished, but at a terrible cost.

Like many other pilots, Tony Gaze's war had its ups and down but was successful in the sense that he had first and foremost survived and had also achieved much. Being awarded the Distinguished Flying Cross three times recognised those achievements.

As at VE Day he had logged 1,636 hours of which 613 were operational. He had flown 495 operational sorties, scored 12.5 confirmed aerial victories along with four probables and four damaged and also shot down a V-1. He had also shared in the destruction of over 20 locomotives and 20 trucks (plus another 140 damaged) along with flak ships, tugs, barges and tanks.

His 495 operational sorties comprised 103 patrols, 39 convoy patrols, 62 scrambles, 67 Circuses, 47 Rodeos, 60 Ramrods, 51 armed reconnaissance Rhubarbs, 18 shipping and anti-flak missions, seven air-sea-rescue sorties, nine sorties covering combined operations and 32 anti-Diver patrols.

Tony Gaze's war may well have ended on 8 May 1945, but there was still plenty of flying to come in peacetime.

NINE

FROM EUROPE TO AUSTRALIA

THE END OF THE WAR in Europe brought an end to Tony Gaze's combat flying career and also raises a point worthy of reflection. Like many thousands of others who had been through the war, he had crammed a normal person's lifetime of danger, adventure, responsibility, success and failure into less than five years. And – like many of them – he was still a youngster. Just 25 years of age when the fighting ended, he still had more than two-thirds of a lifetime ahead of him and a wealth of 'life experience' behind him.

For 616 Squadron's pilots in Germany, the cessation of hostilities brought with it a new activity. While continuing to fly training sorties in their Meteors, some of them also got the chance to fly Luftwaffe aircraft which were being brought down to Lübeck from Norway and surrendered to the Allies.

They started arriving on 5 May 1945 – three days before VE Day, interestingly – the crews at Lübeck greeting a mixture of types including Focke-Wulf Fw 190s, Junkers Ju 88s and Ju 388s. Their pilots were taken to the guardroom to complete the surrender formalities and to talk to them about their flying. Tony says the RAF ground crews wanted to kill them but the pilots wanted to pick their brains to find out what they knew! Some of the 190s had their fuel tanks removed because the ground crews discovered that the self-sealing material was made of beautiful leather, so they'd take the tanks out and strip off the leather.

As noted in the previous chapter, many of the German pilots expected to be helping the Brits and Americans to fight the Russians, but of course that wasn't going to happen, even if a lot of people thought it should. One of the Ju 88 pilots gave Tony a stopwatch he'd taken out of his aircraft. Perhaps he thought the gift would result in him being better treated.

The crew of a Junkers Ju 52 had an exciting arrival at Lübeck on the day the European war was declared over. The Bofors gunners at the base were celebrating victory by firing their guns into the air and as Tony remembers, "The poor bloke in the 52 didn't know what to do! Every time it approached some drunk would fire a red light and he'd go around again and in the end he ditched his German correctness, and went 'to hell with the red lights, I'm going to land' and did."

The Ju 52 was kept by the RAF for transport use because all available Dakotas were being collected to be sent to Japan because at that stage – before anyone knew about the atomic bomb – a massive invasion of the country was being planned. The British also kept one of the big German maintenance depots near Kastrup in Denmark open going in order to keep the Luftwaffe aircraft they were going to use serviceable.

Tony flew captured Focke-Wulf 190s seven times during May 1945, logging just under four hours in them including some aerobatics and generally 'playing' with them. His first flight in one was on 9 May when he ferried it from Luneberg to Lübeck. That one had been had been surrendered at Hanover a couple of weeks before the war had ended by a German test pilot whose wife lived there. He could see the war was rapidly coming to a close and decided to take the aircraft there so he would be near his wife.

The Wing Commander had it for his own use but when he was posted Tony took it over. He found it had been very roughly repaired and had a rough engine, although as he hadn't read the book he didn't realise that all 190s had quite rough engines.

On 18 May he decided to go to the Fw 190 assembly line at Travemunde to swap the aircraft he had for a brand new one. On the way he flew over the Ratzeburger Lake near the Lübeck airfield and found a boat with two people fishing in it and just for the hell of it beat them up at 'dot' feet. On arrival at Travemunde Tony landed the 190, went to the factory manager and blithely announced that he wanted to take a new one from the assembly line.

The manager said it was absolutely out of the question so Tony tried reasoning with him: "Look, here is a 190, we'll just swap this for a new one and you're left with the correct number." The manager still refused so Tony went to the end of the production line to help himself anyway! He discovered the oleo legs of the first one had been hacked through ("probably someone from our army, they did stupid things like that") so he pushed it out of the way with the help of one of the Germans and found the next one just had a nick in the leg which he quickly filed out.

Tony elaborates: "He pushed it forward and all I had to do was put in two big electrical plugs and do up two oil pipes and it was ready to go. I was running the engine up when out came the manager absolutely terrified about someone flying from the airfield, especially in a 190 and one that hadn't even undergone its first test flight yet."

A little bit of the Gaze bloody-mindedness kicked in at this point: "So I ignored him but he said 'there are 25 production tests that need to be done to this aircraft before it can fly'. I said 'get lost' and I got into the air only to find it was flying so left wing low I needed both hands and my knee on the stick to hold the wing up! Luckily Lübeck was only five minutes' flying time away and I landed safely.

"Of course the thing had still got black crosses and things on so they thought it was another one surrendering from Russia. So when I arrived I've got jeeps on either side of me with machine guns and God knows what. Anyway, they recognised me and we then got prisoners-of-war to paint RAF roundels on it - they did a marvellous job, really accurate. We used it until our Wing Commander landed a 262 with the nosewheel half down and it was decided they were dangerous because our ground crews weren't allowed to work on them. We were told we had to stop flying captured aircraft.

"So they took them all away and I think they scrapped them - I couldn't believe it - I thought they'd at least put them in a hangar somewhere for research. I think the only things they were really interested in were the 262s and the Ju 388 because it was pressurised and had remote control guns. Other than that they were just moved a corner of the airfield and left to rot."

Tony also flew a Messerschmitt Bf 108, Bücker Bestmann amd a couple of Siebel Si 204s, the latter the light transport twin he'd briefly experienced immediately before transferring to 616 Squadron and its Meteors. He found it in a field at Kastrup in Denmark after a flight from Copenhagen in the Bf 108 on 28 May. The propellers were off and the controls dismantled but it was put back together again and basically used as Tony Gaze's personal aircraft for a while. It was flown around Germany and Denmark.

Tony found another "very nice" Si 204 at Vaerlos airfield near Copenhagen in early June and decided to commandeer it: "I went into the crew room - typical German, everyone was at attention and clicked their heels - and I said 'that Siebel 204 out there, I want it cleaned and refuelled and I will fly it to Lübeck this afternoon'. 'No you won't', they said, so I tried the 'who won the bloody war?' line but that didn't work and they said I could have it in two days' time. I think it was full of schnapps which hadn't been removed or consumed yet!

"Then they said they would show me how to fly a Siebel 204, I explained that I already had flown one a fair bit but they insisted they would show me. So we went through it and I discovered I had been flying it with the fuel tanks selection completely wrong. I think they were relieved when I took off and disappeared over the horizon – if I crashed then it wouldn't be seen to be their fault!

"The 204 was very good. We used to take ground crews up in it and sometimes get a bit naughty by feathering a prop and watching them all panic. I flew the second one to Paris Le Bourget to collect some champagne because our catering officer had been one of the top people at the Savoy Hotel in London and he knew where to get champagne in Paris. So we flew him and a couple of others there, stayed overnight and went back to Lübeck the next day."

Tony had a close look at an Me 262 in late May when he flew to Schleswig in northern Germany and went through the starting, flying and handling drills with the CO of the unit based there, 10./NJG 11, the only jet night fighter unit to become operational before the end of the war. Oberleutnant Kurt Welter, Germany's greatest night fighter ace with 63 kills to his credit was Tony's 'instructor' and to the 25-years-old Australian the war-weary Welter seemed quite old – at 29!

Tony sat in the front cockpit of a two-seat Me 262B-1a/U1 night fighter and went through the starting procedure: start the two-stroke motor that got the jets spinning, rev it up, start on petrol and then change to jet fuel. He was taught the operating speeds and warned about the very slow retraction of the nosewheel and the very sensitive trim. There was also advice to fly only the single-seat Me 262 if the opportunity arose – which it didn't, to Tony's disappointment – not the two-seater as it was too dangerous. Welter had been flying them at night, landing and taking off from autostradas with only a single light at each end for guidance. This was done to avoid intruder Mosquitos.

On 26 June an air display was held at Kastrup in Denmark to help raise money for Danish children who had been disabled as a result of one of the RAF's most famous raids of the war, the attack by Mosquitos on the Gestapo headquarters in Copenhagen's Shell House with pinpoint accuracy from extremely low level.

What wasn't known at the time was that one of the Mosquitoes in the first wave had struck a flagpole and crashed into a school adjacent to the target. Tragically, the building caught fire and some of the following Mosquito crews saw the flames, thought it was the target and bombed the school instead of Shell House. Many children were killed and others permanently disabled.

It was Johnnie Johnson who cooked up the idea for the show after visiting Shell House and being told of the tragedy. The Danes had asked if it would be possible to have an open day at the airfield so people could look at the aircraft and from that the idea of a full air show grew with a number of aircraft flying and a small entry fee being charged for donation to the children. Even the Danish Royal Family became enthusiastically involved with the Queen and Crown Prince attending the show, which was a huge success.

Tony Gaze was asked to display a Meteor - which he did - but he had a couple of moments of doubt when his nemesis from the Eagle Squadron disaster, Harry Broadhurst (who was now an Air Vice Marshal and the boss of 83 Group), turned up for the dress rehearsal which included using live ammunition to sink German flying boats in the bay as part of the show. The rehearsal was completed and at the end of it Broadhurst went through a debrief with everyone, offering criticisms and suggestions.

He then turned to Tony: "And now you Gaze", he said. Tony thought, "Oh God, here we go, but he said my flying was fantastic - except of course that I had no idea about how to lay on a display - and that I had disappeared into the sun but the aerobatics were fantastic. He said 'come and see me afterwards and I'll tell you how to do it properly'.

"But he also said it was so good he was cancelling the Spitfire's display because it looked ordinary compared to the Meteor, which was bad luck for the Spitfire pilot who'd been practising hard. On the day, as I was walking out to the aircraft, Broadhurst came to me and said, 'Well Gaze, make sure they smell the paraffin' - in other words get really low. And I did too - I wasn't much above head height. But that was it. He didn't come up afterwards to say 'well done' or anything."

The crowd certainly appreciated Tony's display in the Meteor, as did Johnnie Johnson, who noted that "Tony Gaze belted a Meteor above the runway as only he could." Photographs of the Meteor's display show just how low Tony was on a couple of his passes - not much more than head height indeed - for a dwarf!

Tony stayed with 616 Squadron until it was disbanded on 29 August 1945 and renumbered as 263 Squadron. The squadron returned to England on 1 September, Tony completing the 450 miles journey in his Meteor in only 1hr 15min with a headwind, very impressive figures for 1945.

The squadron moved to its base at Acklington in Northumberland later in the month, Tony in the meantime having a spot of leave before rejoining the squadron as its Commanding Officer. This should have provided him with another promotion to Wing Commander but it didn't happen: "They suddenly decided before I could put my Wing Commander stripes on that Meteors didn't really have two engines – only one! – so I didn't go up a rank and stayed with them until they decided I'd done enough flying."

Tony's last flight with 263 Squadron was on 1 December 1945 in Meteor III HE–C and at that stage it appeared his flying days might be over because his next posting was supposed to be to Transport Command for general duties. "Finished with flying!", he wrote in his log book, although happily, that proved to be not the case. By then, Tony had logged 1,770 flying hours including just over 100 on Meteors.

· · · · · · · · · · ·

At the end of 1945, the 'Broadhurst factor' once again reared its ugly head in Tony's life in a public display which indicated a certain level of ignorance and lack of tact on the part of a man who was now a very senior RAF officer.

It was at a New Year's Eve party attended by Broadhurst and other senior officers plus a number of others including Tony Gaze. A reasonable amount of alcohol had been consumed, which may have influenced Broadhurst's behaviour. During the conversation he suddenly turned to Tony and said, "By the way Gaze, I've knocked back your DSO." Many people heard it including a number of other senior officers.

It was a very poor example of behaviour, nobody thought it was right bringing a thing like that up in public. Tony was extremely embarrassed, as were others. The awkwardness of the situation was exacerbated by the fact that he had no idea he'd even been put up for a Distinguished Service Order, which ranks second only to the Victoria Cross of the British military awards and medals (the George Cross is the civilian equivalent of the VC).

Tony couldn't think of anything to say except "I'm sorry you told me sir", to which Broadhurst replied "why?" – a question any reasonable person would surely see as completely unnecessary. Tony said that he'd feel embarrassed when he saw his CO because it's a black mark against him when he recommends an award for someone and it's not granted. Tony repeated that he wished he hadn't been told.

Tony continues: "He [Broadhurst] then got a bit 'so what?' about it but as it was a party I just shut up. Then Broadhurst told me a second Bar to my DFC was better than a DSO anyway, so I left it. It wasn't the proper way of doing things but when you're high-ranking you can't be answered back to. I thought that if he wanted to tell me he shouldn't have done it at a party with a whole lot of people listening, he should have waited to for a chance to take me aside and tell me.

"Or why tell me at all? The last thing you should do is go and tell someone who doesn't even know he's been put up for something that he's been knocked back. When you're at a party like that, what do you do - walk out? I was embarrassed and so was everyone else who heard it. I still believe it was simply because he didn't like me due to the Eagle Squadron shambles, but he probably copped it for that, being the boss of the show."

It was an unfortunate and unsavoury incident which did Air Vice Marshal Harry Broadhurst no credit at all.

· · · · · · · · · · ·

In early 1946 Tony was sent to Rolls-Royce as Commanding Officer of the engine handling school. He stayed there for only three weeks before managing to talk his way out of it after discovering they wanted him there for three years to make it worth their while after training him to lecture on all of Rolls-Royce's jet and piston engines.

He then "mooched around for a while" before being attached to RAF Bentwaters in Suffolk with 56 Squadron for a few days in May 1946 where he at least was able to get a handful of Meteor flights under his belt. Next was 691 Squadron at Exeter as Commanding Officer, working liaison with the Navy – towing targets for them, dive-bombing them and so on. He found it quite interesting except that he was in charge of a lot of fed-up pilots who'd had years of training and had just got to the stage of being ready to go into action but couldn't because the war had ended.

In order to keep the pilots busy and relatively happy, Tony came up with all sorts of exercises for them to do including mock invasions, practice armed reconnaissance sorties, air defence exercises and formation aerobatics to take their minds off the boredom of towing targets for the Navy. The squadron had Spitfire XVIs, Harvards, Vengeances to tow targets and Tony had use of a Meteor, although he flew all the types on strength including his beloved Spitfire.

Tony stayed at 691 Squadron for three months before taking up his last posting in the Royal Air Force - from 27 August 1946 - with 61 Operational Training

Unit at Keevil in Wiltshire near Bath as Officer Commanding the Test Flight and Chief Ground Instructor. He didn't do much of the latter but did do a lot of test flying in Spitfire XIVs, XVIs, XIXs and 21, some display flying in plus the occasional flights in Harvards, Martinets, Ansons and Oxfords.

By now, Tony's involvement in motor racing was increasing and taking up much of his spare time. He had purchased a supercharged 2-litre Alta racing car and was regularly competing in British club events and hillclimbs. When he returned to Australia in late 1947 Tony took the Alta with him and continued racing it there, including in the 1948 Australian Grand Prix at Point Cook in January. His motor racing career is covered in detail in the following chapters.

Tony and the Alta were entered in an event at the Shelsley Walsh Hillclimb over the weekend of 20-21 June 1947 but he was ordered to display a Spitfire 21 at the Derby International Air Rally on the Sunday. The Mk.21 was very nearly the end of the Spitfire line. Powered by a Griffon engine and fitted with an entirely new wing using a different aerofoil section, the prototype first flew in October 1942 but service entry wasn't until March 1945 following a number of development problems.

It suffered serious handling problems which took considerable time to sort out. When the Air Fighting Development Unit evaluated an early example it heavily criticised the Mk.21's instability in the yawing plane and recommended it be abandoned and replaced by the Hawker Tempest or Spitfire XVI. The AFDU even went as far as concluding in late 1944 that "no further attempts should be made to perpetuate the Spitfire family." Only 120 Spitfire 21s were built but the problems were solved and the new wing lived in on in the post-war Spitfire 22 and 24 and Seafire 45, 46 and 47.

Tony wasn't at all happy about giving up his motor sport in order to perform at Derby: "I tried to get out of that because I had my car entered in the hillclimb. They rang me up to tell me to pick up the Spitfire and display it. I said 'no I'm not, I'm entered in the hillclimb' and they said 'who pays you?' I said 'but it's the weekend!' They said 'no' – so I did!

"I couldn't really argue too hard but it was silly in a way because the day I went up there to do a test flight [on 20 June, the show was the next day] – I'd never flown a 21 before – there was an 800 feet cloud base so the only thing I could do was a few rolls to see what it felt like."

The Spitfire 21 Tony flew at Derby was borrowed from 41 Squadron and one of only a handful fitted with six-bladed contra-rotating propellers. The contra-props nullified the torque created by a conventional propeller behind the very powerful Griffon and therefore eliminated any swing on takeoff and the need to constantly retrim the aircraft in flight. Tony notes that "the contra-props would have driven me mad on a long flight because at low revs they flickered, creating a distracting strobe effect."

Despite being unhappy about having to do the event, Tony evidently 'wowed 'em' at Derby, *Flight* magazine reporting: "The Spit has never been better displayed. Especially attractive were the four point hesitation rolls."

The Derby event marked the nearing of the end of Tony's career in the RAF and as a Spitfire pilot. Less than four weeks later he flew a Spitfire for the last time, a few days before leaving 61 OTU and the RAF. The date was 15 July 1947, the place Keevil, the aircraft Spitfire XVI TD407 and the flight an 'air test' of 30 minutes' duration. Tony's total flying time in the RAF was 1,897 hours and 45 minutes.

His boss at Keevil, Wing Commander R H Thomas, gave Tony a glowing 'report card': "Assessment As Test Pilot – Squadron Leader Gaze has been at this Unit as Officer Commanding Test Flight for the past 12 months. He is an exceptional pilot and his knowledge of every phase of aeronautics, both theoretical and technical is very considerable. His keenness to be in the air at every conceivable opportunity is most refreshing."

. . . .

After returning to Australia in late 1947, Tony joined the Light Car Club and spent most of 1948 establishing his motor racing career. He was also preparing to become a married man. In England he had met Catherine ('Kay') Wakefield in Charles Follett's office at the Royal Automobile Club in London in 1944. Kay was the widow of former champion British racing driver Johnny Wakefield who had served as a Royal Navy Fleet Air Arm pilot during the war and was killed flying while testing a Supermarine Seafire, the naval version of the Spitfire.

Six years older than Tony, Kay came from a wealthy family. Her father, Colonel George Heywood, had built up a successful printing, publishing and newspaper delivery business in Manchester while her mother Evelyn was from the Platt Engineering family. During World War II Kay had worked as a French translator and as a driver for the Americans in England. One of her passengers had been General Dwight Eisenhower, Supreme Commander of the Allied Expeditionary Forces in Europe and subsequently US President.

When Tony asked her why she drove for the Americans rather than the British she replied: "Because the Yanks have much better uniforms!"

The relationship between Tony and Kay developed in the immediate post-war period while Tony was still serving in the RAF but getting more regularly involved in motor sport. Kay knew many of the racing drivers of the time and others involved in the sport in Britain through her late husband, providing Tony with a network of useful contacts in addition to those he had collected himself.

Tony and Kay were married at St John's Church of England in Toorak, Melbourne on 22 June 1949.

Despite Tony's increasing involvement on motor racing, which over the next decade would see him and Kay regularly travelling between Australia, Europe and New Zealand, he still had some military flying to do to round off that part of his career. He joined the Royal Australian Air Force in late 1948, looking to serve with No 21 (City of Melbourne) Squadron, one of the newly-established Citizen Air Force squadrons.

They came about as a result of a policy announced in 1948 by the Minister for Air, Mr Drakeford, that the RAAF would once again have active reserve squadrons from April of that year. Five such squadrons would be formed, each one based in a capital city and named after that city. All would be fighter units, all would initially be equipped with Australian-built CAC Mustangs and their personnel strength would comprise 40 per cent permanent RAAF and the remainder Citizen Air Force.

The first four squadrons formed (or more correctly reformed from units originally established in 1936-37) were 21 (City of Melbourne) based at Laverton, 22 (City of Sydney) at Bankstown, 23 (City of Brisbane) at Archerfield and 25 (City of Perth) at Pearce. The fifth squadron, No 24 (City of Adelaide) was not reformed until 1951 and was based at Mallala. Four of them had their Mustangs replaced by Vampires in 1952-55 and all were relegated to non-flying status in June 1960.

Tony didn't just walk into 21 Squadron despite his vast experience. Even though they were looking for recruits Tony remembers that they considered he didn't fit in because he was a bit too old – at 28! Air Commodore (later Air

Chief Marshal and Chief of the Air Staff) Frederick Scherger - who was then Deputy CAS - was a great friend of Tony's father Irvine and he helped smooth the way for Gaze the younger's return to the cockpit of a fighter.

Even then Tony's remarkable record in the RAF didn't seem to count for much. He went back to the rank of Flying Officer and had to start from scratch: "They put me back on Tiger Moths - only the Australian air force would do that - after having flown jets and things, and then it was on to Wirraways and Mustangs."

His first flight in an RAAF aircraft was in Tiger Moth A17-705 from Laverton on 23 January 1949, a 30 minute 'dual check' with Squadron Leader Springbett, who was hopefully suitably embarrassed! He flew the same Tiger Moth solo twice more on the same day and on 6 February did his first Wirraway flight (in A20-710), again with Squadron Leader Springbett checking him out. His first Wirraway solo followed later in the same day.

Tony logged about 22 hours on Tiger Moths and Wirraways in short bursts over the next couple of months - he was a part time flyer now, remember - before finally being let loose in Mustang A68-52 on 5 April for his 'conversion to type'. After that it was the assortment of training activities undertaken by the squadron including battle formations, low flying, battle attacks, instrument flying, cross country flights and so on. He also flew Wirraways a few times including on both 'dry' and 'live' dive bombing practice before doing that in Mustangs, from which he also got to fire rocket projectiles once or twice.

There was the occasional diversion, like formation displays over Melbourne and Adelaide, and aerobatic displays at Wangaratta and Hobart. Tony's attitude towards the Mustang softened a little during his time although the characteristics he didn't like when he flew them in England of course remained, like the prolific swing and heaviness of the controls. "But for the job we had it was ideal," he says, "because we just cruised around Australia doing demonstrations because the regular air force was in Japan and any time someone wanted a demonstration they called upon the Auxiliaries because we were the only ones with fighters."

While flying Mustangs with 21 Squadron Tony had a couple of moments due to engine problems. On 14 February 1950 he was flying A68-54 to Hobart for a display with the squadron on what was supposed to be a day trip. He noticed the oil pressure gauge was reading 'zero'. At first he thought it was a problem with the instrument but when the oil temperature also dropped to nothing he realised the engine had no lubricant in it.

Tony immediately turned back towards Laverton and didn't alter any of the power and propeller settings in case the lack of oil caused a runaway propeller. He considered putting the Mustang down at one of the airfields near Geelong but thought they would be too small for a successful landing and decided to stay aloft near the coast in case the aircraft caught fire. If it did, he could aim it out to sea and bail out. He'd been talking to the air-sea-rescue people on the radio through all this, who helpfully suggested he might delay doing anything until the ASR Dakota took off!

Somehow, the Mustang's Packard Merlin kept going and did so until Tony throttled back near Laverton's circuit when there was a bang and it stopped.... his decision not to change any of the settings had been a wise one. After dead-sticking onto the grass, Tony had a quick look at the oil covering the fuselage and ran to grab another Mustang so he could join the squadron and do the Hobart display. Tony wasn't told the reason for the engine failure but years later he heard it had thrown a conrod right through the crankcase.

Safely aboard the second Mustang, Tony got as far as the coast when he realised he'd left his all maps in the first aircraft. There was nothing to do but point the fighter due south and assume that Tasmania would eventually appear in the windscreen! A Convair airliner was spotted travelling in the same direction so Tony lined up on its course and eventually joined the rest of the squadron which was waiting for him at Wynyard. The display went well but the weather kept the aircraft in Hobart. No-one had a change of clothes but some parties compensated for the inconvenience!

Tony nearly ended up flying Meteors again: "Just as I decided to go motor racing I was supposed to fly Meteor F.4s with 600 Squadron [RAF] in England on exchange, and it was all arranged. If I hadn't gone motor racing I'd have ended up in Korea because I'd commanded a Meteor squadron and the RAAF was looking everywhere for people teach them to fly Meteors. They had to bring Englishmen over, and I was already in 21 Squadron."

A Meteor III was the first jet aircraft to be officially taken on RAAF charge in June 1946 when an ex-RAF example was sent to Australia by the British War Ministry, technically on loan to provide experience with this new type of aircraft for both air and ground crews. It was not until 1951 that the Meteor entered regular RAAF service as the second jet to do so (after the de Havilland Vampire), the 93 F.8s delivered directly to 77 Squadron in Japan for operations in the Korean War and replacing Mustangs.

Tony went to England for his planned period of flying Meteors – and for some motor racing – and met the 600 Squadron people, most of whom he already knew well. But before he got a chance to fly a signal was received from Melbourne saying that the RAF wanted too much money for him to fly a Meteor and that they were cancelling the arrangement.

Tony then decided to resign and concentrate on his motor racing career. His last flight with 21 Squadron had been on 2 July 1950 in Mustang A68-43, a 1hr 30min 'limit turn attacks' sortie. In the 18 months he'd been with the Citizen Air Force Tony had added 164 flying hours to his tally, bringing the total to 2,061hrs 25min.

Thus ended an illustrious military flying career to make way for a new one on four wheels. Although Tony did a couple of flights in a Chipmunk in 1955 and a considerable amount of gliding from 1958, it would be 11 years before he once again flew powered aeroplanes regularly.

TEN

FOUR WHEELS

THE TRANSITION FROM fighter pilot to racing driver was a natural one for Tony Gaze, as it was for a number of World War II pilots with an affinity with fast machinery. In Tony's case the connection was deeper than merely the desire to fill a 'need for speed' in the post-war world because his connection with motor sport started well before the conflict as a child through the influence of his father. He had also briefly tasted motor racing first hand with his maiden event at Brooklands in 1938 (as related in chapter one) but serious thoughts of further four-wheeled competition had to be put on hold for a few years. First, there was a war to be won!

The fascination with fast cars was always there and he was able to indulge his liking of them throughout his life. During the war he'd owned a succession of interesting vehicles starting with an MG and then an Alvis he'd bought for his younger brother Scott. When Scott was killed in March 1941 flying his Spitfire Tony used the Alvis until his sergeant burnt the clutch out. It was replaced with an Aston Martin that had raced twice at Le Mans, followed by an Alvis Speed 25. The open Aston was reluctantly disposed of and changed for "something with a lid on it" to keep cold air off his face following the injuries he received when shot down over France in September 1943.

Although the record books indicate that Tony Gaze's motor racing career didn't reach the dizzy heights of some of his contemporaries, it was nevertheless a significant one with some good results achieved in a number of interesting cars. Further, as a privateer he was more often than not competing at the highest levels against drivers and teams from the top shelf.

Equally important was the context of his motor racing - an Australian competing on the world stage at a time this was extremely rare. Apart from the 'headline' achievement of becoming Australia's first Formula One Grand Prix driver in 1952, Tony was a pioneer of bringing 'internationalism' to Australian motor sport.

He raced not only in Australia but also around the world in Britain, all over Europe, South Africa and New Zealand. He competed against and became friends with many of the very big names of the era - Australians Lex Davison, Stan Jones (father of 1980 World Champion, Alan), Tom Sulman, Alec Mildren, David McKay and Doug Whiteford along with international stars such as Stirling Moss, Mike Hawthorn, Alberto Ascari, Giuseppe Farina,

Roy Salvadori, Peter Collins, 'B. Bira', Phil Hill and many more including Australia's greatest international star, Jack Brabham.

A significant friendship and racing association was formed with wealthy British wool magnate and successful racing driver Peter Whitehead, and to a lesser extent with his half-brother Graham. It has been noted that 'three-quarter brother' is probably a more accurate description of Graham's place in the family tree because although both Whiteheads had the same mother, their fathers were brothers.

Tony had, of course, met Peter Whitehead in 1938 when the then 23-years-old Englishman brought his supercharged ERA racing car to Australia to contest various events including that year's Australian Grand Prix at Bathurst. Considered highly advanced for its time, the ERA and its driver created considerable interest, topped by the combination winning the handicap GP against some serious local opposition.

Another strong association was with four-times Australian Grand Prix winner Lex Davison and his wife Diana, herself a competitor of note. Apart from the friendship that developed between the couple and Tony and Kay, Lex made good use of several cars he acquired from Tony, notably the Ferrari Type 500 Formula One car in which he had substantial success including two Australian Grand Prix wins.

Tony owned and raced some of the top equipment of the time including HWM and Aston Martin sports cars plus the Ferrari previously driven by Alberto Ascari to consecutive world championships. Tony was also part of the all-Australian 'Kangaroo Stable' with three Aston Martin DB3Ss and intended to take on the international sports car racing scene in 1955.

Tony's romance with Kay Wakefield had a major bearing on his motor sport aspirations in the immediate post-war years, especially while he was still in Britain. The widow of former British champion driver Johnny Wakefield introduced him to virtually all the drivers through clubs and meetings. For a time after the war, the only thing readily available to drivers was hillclimbs, Tony and Kay going to many of them at Shelsley Walsh and Prescott where he got to know people even more.

"With her I got to meet all the drivers. We started going to watch them in hillclimbs and so on and when I started racing around the airfields I started to get the hang of it," says Tony.

There was a certain freedom associated with getting more heavily involved in motor racing after the fighting had finished but while still serving in the Royal Air Force. "It's the whole war thing, isn't it?", notes Tony. "Five and a half years of doing what you're told and suddenly finding you haven't got a great boss looming over you. Everything you did in the Services was controlled in some way or another. I rather liked breaking away from it occasionally but the snag was they really had you – if you did break enough rules they'd got you."

Remembering his 1942 demotion and subsequent denial of being awarded the Distinguished Service Order, Tony adds: "And they got me – well and truly!"

At the risk of stating the obvious, motor racing was very different in the late 1940s and throughout the 1950s than it is today. Then, it was very much the domain of the 'gentleman racer', the talented amateur with sufficient financial wherewithal to compete against the relatively small number of professionals fully funded by car manufacturers and other companies involved in motoring.

These days we are used to seeing racing cars of all types and classes plastered in the liveries of their sponsors. Half a century ago cars competing in international events appeared in their national racing colours – British racing green, the red of Italy, the silver of Germany and so on – while advertising was limited to the odd small sticker carrying the logo of perhaps a tyre or spark plug manufacturer and a fuel supplier.

It would be a full decade after Tony Gaze's retirement from the sport that the modern era of overt commercial sponsorship began, pioneered in Formula One in 1968 by Colin Chapman's Team Lotus and its Gold Leaf Type 49s wearing the red and gold livery of the tobacco company.

Even though Tony could be regarded as one of the talented 'gentleman racers' with sufficient private income to allow him to buy racing cars, nice road cars and aeroplanes over the years, he wasn't by any means in the extremely wealthy category enjoyed by some of his contemporaries. In those days, the starting money paid by race promoters to some teams and drivers was an important part of their budgets and for many of the privateers it was vital.

These days we're used to the term 'appearance money' which is paid to stars in many fields of sport and entertainment just to turn up. Then, starting money meant literally that. Teams and drivers were often contracted to race but they only got paid the agreed amount if they actually started the race. A crash or mechanical failure in practice which prevented them from taking their place on the grid meant no money was paid, so such a misadventure could be a doubly expensive exercise.

Australian motor racing in the immediate post-war years was not too dissimilar to that of the 1930s with lots of hillclimbs and mainly handicap circuit races due to the limited number of cars available of similar performance. With one exception, the Australian Grand Prix remained a handicap until the 1952 event at Bathurst.

The exception was the 1949 race at Leyburn in Queensland and the decision to stage a massed-start scratch race caused some controversy because handicap racing had become almost universal throughout Australia, especially for longer races like the AGP. It was what the public had become used to as it had formed the basis for the 'style' of Australian racing in the 1930s.

Most of the cars used in the premier classes of racing in Australia immediately after World War II – pure racing and sports – were the same as had been seen before 1939 but new cars from Australia and thoroughbreds from Europe gradually began to appear in the late 1940s and early 1950s. Many of the local marques were the classic 'Australian Specials' – racing cars built up using the engines, drivetrains and dynamic components from proprietary brands, especially the Ford V8 and MG. With the ready availability of major components and spares, Holdens also subsequently became a popular basis for competition cars in Australia.

. . . .

As noted in the previous chapter, Tony Gaze's final RAF posting before returning to Australia in late 1947 was with 61 Operational Training Unit at Keevil near Bath between August 1946 and July 1947 as Officer Commanding the Test Flight and Chief Ground Instructor. He did a lot of test flying of various Spitfires plus some displays and recorded his last Spitfire and RAF flight on 15 July 1947.

While still in England, motor sport took up much of his spare time. He had purchased a supercharged 2-litre Alta racing car and was regularly competing in British club events and hillclimbs. He also acquired a Sports Alta, the result of becoming friendly with George Abecassis, the co-founder of another small British competition car manufacturer, HWM. He had been a bomber pilot in the war and he had two cars for sale, an Alfa Romeo and the 2.0-litre Sports

Alta. "I had a drive of the 2/6 Alfa on a wet night and ended up in a ditch, so I didn't buy that!", remembers Tony, "I bought the Alta instead."

Alta was a small-production sports/racing car and engine manufacturer established in 1928 by Geoffrey Taylor, its cars achieving some competition success both before and after World War II in the hands of drivers such as George Abecassis, Johnny Wakefield and the Whitehead brothers.

Geoffrey Taylor's original activity in 1926 was designing and building a light alloy, twin overhead camshaft four-cylinder engine. A self-taught engineer, his first and subsequent engines (and cars) were built by hand. The first 1.1-litre engine was installed in a car also designed and built by Taylor and he received so many offers to buy it he decided to build replicas and sell them. The Alta Car and Engineering Company was established as a result.

The engine subsequently grew into 1.5-litre and 2.0-litre versions, most of them supercharged, while the cars were built in both monoposto and sports forms utilising the same basic chassis design. The 1.5-litre engine could be readily converted to and from 2.0-litre form by changing the bolted-in cylinder barrels and pistons. Tony Gaze's Sports Alta was originally built in December 1935 for a Dr Williams from Wales and was delivered in 2.0-litre form. Alta cars didn't have chassis numbers as such but were identified by the number of the engine originally installed, in this case 54S.

Tony's Racing Alta (engine number 56S) had originally been delivered to Johnny Wakefield in supercharged 1.5-litre form in April 1936. Wakefield then sold it to Dorothy Turner who set a ladies' record at Shelsley Walsh hillclimb that stood for many years.

The car was repurchased by Alta at the outbreak of World War II where it was eventually fitted with a 2.0-litre engine and a Rootes supercharger operating at a hefty 22psi. The result was quite a weapon for its day – up to 285 horsepower was available in a car weighing just 740 kilograms giving a top speed of about 130 miles per hour (210km/h), acceleration from a standing start to 100mph (161km/h) in ten seconds and a standing quarter mile figure of about 14 seconds.

The car's gearbox was interesting. It had a four-speed pre-selector ENV and the clutch pedal was not used in the conventional way. The same gearbox was fitted to Tony's Sports Alta. The desired ratio could be selected in advance but there was no change to the new gear until the 'clutch' pedal was depressed. It was in this form that Tony Gaze purchased the car, but he quickly discovered that although it had exceptional performance, reliability was not its strong point.

This was 1947, a time that Tony's Royal Air Force career was winding down and he was planning a return to Australia to go motor racing: "I got an entry at Prescott [hillclimb] for both Altas. I was on my way back to Australia in my mind and I decided to have the Sports Alta overhauled at the factory before I shipped it over. Geoffrey Taylor had talked me into buying Johnny Wakefield's old supercharged Racing Alta and sell the sports car. But at Prescott I raced both of them because I hadn't sold the sports car yet. I came third in the sports car and fifth, I think, in the racing one which fired me with enthusiasm!

"I tried to get an entry at Shelsley Walsh Hillclimb. That was like gold then because they were the only things that people could run their cars in. I eventually got an entry [in June 1947] and it was all ready to go when I was told I had to give an air display at Derby flying a Spitfire." As related in the previous chapter, Tony objected but was reminded by the RAF as to who paid his salary! As a result, he never drove at Shelsley.

In the meantime, Tony and some of his colleagues at RAF Keevil had started racing around the airfield's perimeter track for something to do. It all became pretty well organised and led to plans to stage a proper race meeting there, but this was thwarted by officialdom: "At the time I was getting ready to leave the RAF and go home to Australia. We started looking for something to do with weekends because after five-and-a half years of war you don't know what to do with weekends because you hadn't had one for that long. On top of that they gave us a half day off on Wednesdays.

"So we started motor racing around our airfield and everyone was in it. We got handicapping organised, we had the Station Commander's Humber Super Snipe and the handicapping was so good that after a couple of laps of the perimeter track we ended up going up the main runway and we'd get four or five cars over the line only a couple of seconds apart.

"We had the idea of getting in touch with all our friends in the motor racing game and offering them a race around our airfield. We could lay it on - we had our own police, we had everything. It wouldn't have been very big but we'd have had everybody there because we were all mad keen to race cars around a track, not just up a hill.

"To do it we had to find a good reason so we got onto the Royal Air Force Benevolent Fund and said we'll lay on the whole show – we don't need to bring anybody in – it'll probably be about 20 cars and there'll be nothing official, they'll just pay an entry fee which will provide a bit of prize money for the winner and everyone will have the fun of racing. What money we get from the spectators will go to the RAF Benevolent Fund.

"And they just flatly turned it down! They didn't have to do anything except collect money as Keevil was in a mad keen motor racing part of the world. I think that would have been the first motor race in England after the war."

. . . .

After that, Tony resigned from the Royal Air Force and prepared to return to Australia. By now he was engaged to Kay Wakefield and they would be married nearly two years later at St John's Church of England in Toorak, Melbourne on 22 June 1949. Tony took the Racing Alta to Australia along with a 1.5-litre HRG sports/racer. The Sports Alta would follow later. In Australia, he worked with his father on his property 'Highlands' at Coleraine in Victoria's Western Districts.

Motor racing would now become his main activity, although the lure of the air was still strong and he joined the Royal Australian Air Force in January 1949 (see previous chapter) flying Mustangs with No 21 (City of Melbourne) Squadron, a reserve Citizen Air Force Unit. He remained in the RAAF until February 1950, in the meantime balancing that with his motor racing and his responsibilities on the family property.

HRG was another small volume British sports car manufacturer, its cars built between 1935 and 1966 "to the time-honoured formula of stiff springs and light weight", according to one description and using mainly Meadows and Singer engines. HRGs competed at Le Mans and Spa with some success in their class.

Tony's HRG was fitted with a streamlined 'aero' body when it arrived in Australia and it made its local debut at Lobethal in South Australia on New Year's Day 1948. Exactly one year later, Tony appeared in the HRG with new bodywork, the original all-enveloping streamliner body replaced by a new design with cycle guards over the wheels. The idea was to have a car which could run as either a sports car or an openwheeler, depending on the event, simply by removing or replacing the guards.

In its new configuration the car first appeared at Woodside in South Australia in a 30 mile handicap race which Tony won. Appropriately, the car was dubbed the 'Woodside' model in this guise. In both its original and Woodside forms, the HRG was extensively raced and hillclimbed with some success at Point Cook, Bathurst, Nurioopta, Fishermen's Bend, Woodside and elsewhere before it was sold in late 1949.

Tony scored a race win at Woodside in October 1949 and a class victory in the Australian Hillclimb Championship at Rob Roy in November. New owner Norman Steele purchased the car in Woodside form and finished seventh on handicap in the 1950 Australian Grand Prix at Nurioopta (South Australia) the following January.

Tony reflects on those early post–war racing days in Australia: "As far as racing was concerned, Australia was much the same as England then – it was mainly hillclimbs you could do because you couldn't close the roads for racing. I drove the HRG in a couple of Rob Roy hillclimbs – I think I came about third in class – and then the racing car arrived.

"At the same time as that I came down ill with jaundice after drinking from someone else's water bottle on the property and as soon as I was fit enough to drive I took the Alta to Rob Roy and broke the record [on 14 March 1948, a time of 28.88 seconds) – that got me quite keen again.

"I entered the two cars for everything I could and did reasonably well. The Alta was never really reliable. We raced quite a bit in South Australia because you could still close the roads there – at Lobethal and Woodside – and I won a few races at Woodside."

Tony's association with the HRG marque went beyond merely racing his own car, he was also involved in the importation of five more of them to Australia through Melbourne import company Brown & Dureau.

Things had not been going well for Tony working for his father ("everything I did was wrong") so he started looking for something else to do. He approached family friend Keith Dureau of Brown & Dureau who gave him a job. Tony remembers: "They imported everything from aircraft to cars and tractors, they made spark plus and razor blades. You name it, they were into everything, even pearl fishing. I got a job on the automobile side and one of the things we did was bring in some HRGs because up until then MGs had the 1.5–litre class virtually to themselves but the HRGs were beating them in England."

The HRGs were imported into Australia in chassis form and buyers had the choice of fitting either of the two body styles that had been applied to Tony's car - Woodside or Streamliner - or have them completed in so-called single-seat 'Bathurst' form as pure openwheeler racers. Buyers also had the option of completing their cars with special body styles of their own design.

Of the five chassis imported between 1949 and 1951, the first three had Bathurst bodies fitted and the final two special bodies. The first customer car went to Melbourne car dealer Stan Jones who went on to become one of Australia's leading racing drivers, winning the 1958 Australian Driver's Championship and the following year's Australian Grand Prix in a Maserati 250F.

Jones was a bit of a lad: "One of the people I sold one to was Stan Jones, the first single-seater," recalls Tony. "He was a used car dealer who made a lot of money and did reasonably well in the car in hillclimbs and was third at Bathurst. He also raced it at Woodside in the first [post-war] road race in South Australia and I was in my HRG. I beat him in the first race - just - and in the next one he rolled it over. I think something happened in the suspension, not quite sure - so I went to commiserate with him after the race to expecting to find him miserable, but he was excited!

"I said 'why are you excited, you rolled the thing!' He said 'oh but it was fascinating - one minute the sky was in its usual place and the next minute it was underneath me and then the sky went back to its ordinary place - it was thrilling!' I thought then that we had here someone who was willing to have a go, and of course he did. He put a supercharger on it which made it way the fastest 1.5-litre but it wouldn't last [the car failed to finish several of its early races]."

Brown & Dureau decided to end their automotive activities in 1951 after Tony had left Australia to race in Europe. The entire HRG stock of parts and equipment was sold and the last unsold chassis went to Stillwell Motors. This business was owned by another Australian racing driver who went on to greater things including winning four consecutive Australian Driver's Championships between 1962 and 1965 driving Brabham cars. Bib Stillwell was also involved in aviation and later became a senior executive with Learjet in the USA.

. . . .

The Racing Alta's career in Tony Gaze's hands could be regarded as a bittersweet experience for him. It was capable of beating just about anything when reliable, something that didn't happen anywhere near often enough. The problem was finding an acceptable level of reliability in what was a highly-stressed pure racing machine.

Along with the HRG, Tony's Alta made its Australian debut at Lobethal on New Year's Day 1948 but had suffered engine troubles, a sign of things to come. A bigger test came just over three weeks later on Australia Day - 26 January - when the car and its driver contested the Australian Grand Prix. Great things were expected of the car in the 42 lap, 100 miles handicap race at the Royal Australian Air Force base at Point Cook on the shores of Victoria's Port Phillip Bay.

This base has a very significant place in Australia's aviation history as it was the birthplace of military flying in the country. In March 1914 a Bristol Boxkite and Deperdussin were test flown there by the newly-established Australian Flying Corps, antecedent of the RAAF.

Because of the problems the Alta suffered at Lobethal there was some doubt the car would appear at Point Cook but it did and its potential pace was recognised when it was allocated the scratch starting position in the handicap race.

There was some serious opposition including Charlie Dean's locally-built Maybach Special powered by an engine from a captured German scout car, Lex Davison's large SSK 38/250 Mercedes (the same car he had driven to third place in the 1947 Grand Prix, replacing his planned Alfa Romeo which hadn't arrived in Australia in time), Alf Barrett's Alfa Romeo Monza, Frank Pratt's BMW 328 and John Crouch's Delahaye. A mixture of mainly pre-war specials and smaller capacity British cars like MGs made up the bulk of the remaining entry of 37 cars of which 26 faced the starter.

The handicappers saw fit to handicap Tony and the Alta by three minutes to what they reckoned was the second fastest car - Alf Barrett's Alfa - then there was a group of three including Crouch's Delahaye on 6min 30sec. Lex Davison was on 8min 30sec. There was a wide spread of starting times with Cec Warren's Morgan first away, no less than 18 minutes before Tony Gaze in a race that lasted about an hour and a half.

It was a very hot day - over 100 degrees in the old measurement - and several of the more fancied runners were in trouble early. The retirement list was long with only ten cars classified as finishers but unfortunately, the Gaze Alta was not among them. The car had been running 'off song' since the start of the race and Tony retired it after just five laps with magneto problems caused by overheating. The heat caused many of the cars and their drivers problems and three of them, including Alf Barrett, retired due to heat exhaustion.

The winner of the only Australian Grand Prix Tony Gaze contested was Frank Pratt in his BMW, a remarkable performance considering this was his first and only race on four wheels. He was a champion motorcycle racer and enjoyed a long and successful career on two wheels. Tony also drove his HRG at that meeting in a 10 lap supporting scratch race for under 1.5-litre cars, an event which according to one report was "enlivened by Gaze's near spin in midfield with his aerodynamic HRG...."

Tony and several other leading Victoria-based drivers including Lex Davison did not enter the 1949 Australian Grand Prix run at the Leyburn airfield in rural Queensland for political and logistical reasons. The race was run as a scratch rather than handicap event which divided opinion, while for some Leyburn was simply too far away.

They were back for the 1950 race at Nurioopta in South Australia on 2 January, Tony entering the Alta but failing to start. As had been in the case in 1948 the Alta was designated as the scratch car by the handicappers, "the acceleration of which perhaps justified its handicapping, although its finishing record made it all hypothetical," noted historian Graham Howard, a comment that perhaps well summed up the car's history.

Engine troubles continued to plague the Alta at Nurioopta, starting in practice and continuing through a short preliminary race. As a result, Tony withdrew from the main event and took the car home, disappointed again.

The Alta's reliability problems and therefore inability to realise its potential was a source of great frustration for Tony and those who prepared the car, Gib Barrett and Alan Ashton. There were some successes including setting a new outright record of 28.8 seconds at Rob Roy hillclimb (where the car was fitted with dual rear wheels), an Australian Hillclimb Championship in 1949 and some minor race wins. Tony also inverted the car once at Rob Roy after the front axle broke, ending up in a ditch which immediately became known as 'Gaze's Gully'.

The Racing Alta was offered for sale in 1951 ("best offer over £1,500") complete with Victorian registration OG 395 and 12 wheels including the dual rears. It was purchased by Wally Feltham in 1951 before passing to Bill Pitt who later achieved fame by winning the second Australian Touring Car

Championship in 1961 driving a Jaguar. He solved the engine problem simply by getting rid of it, using the basic chassis to build a much-modified Austin-engined special. In this form the car was acquired in 1963 by Graham Lowe, who set about a decade-long restoration to its former glory.

Tony had meanwhile brought his Sports Alta to Australia in 1949, this much less highly stressed than the monoposto and therefore considerably more reliable. Registered NC 015, the car provided Tony with some good racing and hillclimbing results at a time he was entering just about everything available to him in Victoria and South Australia.

After having left the RAAF in 1950, Tony turned his attention to moving back to England from where he could launch an assault on European racing generally and Formula 2 in particular. His last race in Australia was at Balcombe on Victoria's Mornington Peninsula on 12 June 1950 in the Sports Alta. He won, while Stan Jones was third in the ex-Gaze HRG.

Then it was "off to England to do some real racing" in 1951.

. . . .

THE GOODWOOD CONNECTION

Tony Gaze has one lasting monument to his motor racing career, the fact that he was instrumental in the establishment of the famous Goodwood circuit near Chichester in Surrey. He has a long connection with the place, starting with his mother Freda, whose grandfather owned the Westhampnett Mill adjacent to the Duke of Richmond and Gordon's Goodwood estate.

Westhampnett airfield was Tony's first Royal Air Force posting in early 1941, the land having been compulsorily acquired from the Goodwood Estate in 1938 for use as an emergency landing ground for nearby Tangmere. It was upgraded to the status of a satellite airfield in 1940, re-opening in July of that year just as the Battle of Britain was getting underway.

The Duke - Frederick Lennox, known to his friends as Freddie Richmond - ensured that the land remained the property of the Goodwood Estate and would be returned after the war. He was a great fan of motoring generally and a talented bike and car racer, achieving several significant wins in the 1920s and '30s before concentrating on managing his team of MGs and later coachbuilding.

Tony Gaze late in the war with the Alvis Speed 25 sedan he acquired after returning from his unplanned adventure in France.

He had to sell his beloved Aston Martin open sports car and replace it with a closed car to protect his damaged face from the elements. Blasts of cold air could have aggravated his injuries.

A spot of skiing for Tony at Davos, Switzerland shortly after the war.

On 26 June 1945 Tony flew Meteor YQ-X at an air display at Kastrup in Denmark, the event successfully raising money to help children who had been disabled during the famed raid on the Gestapo headquarters in Copenhagen's Shell House. He was instructed by AVM Harry Broadhurst to "make sure they smell the paraffin" - in other words fly very low. Tony obliged. This shot shows one of his passes - the next one was barely above head height!

After the end of the war in Europe, Tony Gaze remained with 616 Squadron on Meteors based in Germany. The squadron was renumbered No 263 at the end of August 1945 and returned to England. He remained with the squadron until the end of 1945.

One of Tony's last duties in the RAF was to display this Spitfire 21 (EB-D, borrowed from 41 Squadron) at the Derby International Air Rally on 21 June 1947. Note the six-bladed contra-rotating propellers, these fitted to a few Mk.21s in place of the normal five-blader. His last RAF flight (in a Spitfire XVI) occurred the following month. By now, Tony was starting to develop his motor racing career and would return to Australia at the end of the year.

Pilot's-eye view of Meteors in formation in 1945. Tony Gaze logged more than 100 hours in the jet fighter.

When stationed at RAF Keevil in 1946-47, Tony Gaze and some of his colleagues began racing round the airfield's perimeter track on weekends. It became well organised and gave Tony the ideas which subsequently led to the establishment of the Goodwood circuit. This 1946 shot shows some of the cars participating in those Keevil races.

Tony's 1.5-litre HRG Streamliner sport/racer which he purchased in England and took with him to Australia in late 1947 along with his Racing Alta. The HRG is shown here at its debut at Lobethal, South Australia on New Year's Day 1948.

The HRG appeared in modified form in 1949, its Streamliner body replaced by a more utilitarian shape. It was dubbed the 'Woodside' because it made its debut at that South Australian circuit, as here. It normally had cycle guards over the wheels but it is seen here in 'racing' trim without them.

Tony Gaze takes the HRG Woodside in sports car trim to victory in the Sports 1500 class at Rob Roy hillclimb in 1949.

Rare colour of the HRG getting away from the start line at Rob Roy. Tony was involved with the importation of five additional HRGs from 1949, customers including future Australian Grand Prix winner Stan Jones.

Tony married the former Catherine (Kay) Wakefield at St John's Church of England in Toorak, Melbourne on 22 June 1949. The widow of British racing driver and fighter pilot Johnny Wakefield (who died in a crash during the war), Kay was six years Tony's senior and came from a wealthy English family. Her extensive contacts in the British motor racing scene were helpful to Tony.

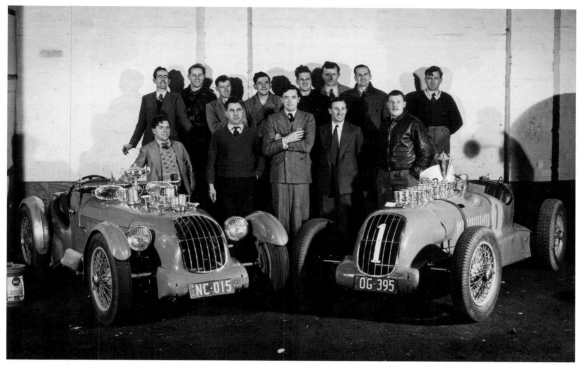

Tony (centre), the Sports Alta, Racing Alta with friends and associates at Tony's farewell party before he left Australia to tackle European Formula Two in 1951.

Tony had two Altas during his first stint racing in Australia 1947-50; a highly supercharged 2-litre Monoposto racing car and a 2-litre Sports model (illustrated). The Monoposto was very fast but also unreliable and consistently let Tony down; the less highly-stressed Sports Alta provided him with some good results in racing and hillclimbs. It is photographed here on its way to setting a class record at Rob Roy. The car also gave Tony a win in his last Australian race before heading off to Europe, at Balcombe, Victoria on 12 June 1950.

Tony Gaze purchased a new Alta 2-litre Formula Two car for his 1951 British and European campaign. The competition was intense and included some big names, but some reasonable results were achieved in what was not a top-notch car. This shot - taken at Silverstone - well illustrates a problem Tony always faced during his racing career - his height. With so much of his body sticking high out of the car he had built-in drag which cost him top speed at most circuits.

Tony in the F2 Alta at Monza in May 1951, in earnest discussion with officials "trying to get another practice lap." He finished the main race 12th - the winner was a certain Alberto Ascari who would become World Champion in 1952 and 1953.

On the banking at Berlin's Avus track in July 1951 during the race that effectively ended Tony's F2 campaign. The engine blew during the race and could not be quickly repaired due to a number of other Alta engines with broken crankshafts waiting at the factory to be fixed.

With his F2 Alta out of action, Tony drove this 1934-vintage 2.9-litre Maserati 8CM in Formula Libre races with some success. Notoriously difficult to drive, the car had a famous history, owners including luminaries such as Whitney Straight, Richard Seaman and Bira. The Maserati is photographed here at Silverstone in a support event for the British Grand Prix, Tony finishing fourth behind three modern Ferraris.

'Celebrity' race at Silverstone in May 1952, the International Race of Champions with Tony invited to start alongside stars such as Bira and Stirling Moss, all in left-hand-drive Jaguar XK120s. Tony's car is on the front row, furthest from the camera. Unfortunately, it blew its clutch at the start, just as this photograph was taken. Moss won - of course!

Australian motorsport history at Spa-Francorchamps and the Belgian Grand Prix on 22 June 1952
- Tony Gaze becomes the first Australian to contest a World Championship GP. Driving his HWM-Alta
he finished 15th.

Tony Gaze entered four World Championship Grand Prix races in 1952 and started three, using
a 2-litre HWM-Alta F2 ex-works car previously driven by Stirling Moss. It was decided to
contest the 1952 and 1953 World Championships with F2 cars due to the withdrawal of Alfa
Romeo from F1 and the resultant lack of competitive cars to challenge Ferrari.

Two shots of Tony Gaze and his HWM-Alta in the German Grand Prix at the old Nürburgring in July 1952. This was the last World Championship GP he started but was put out with a broken rear axle.

Motor racing hospitality 1952 style: Stirling Moss on the left with his latest girlfriend, Mike Hawthorne (second from right), Tony Gaze (right) and a couple of others grab a cuppa at the Ferodo truck.

'Australia's Own' on the international stage: Tony Gaze, Lex Davison and Stan Jones contested the 1953 Monte Carlo Rally in this Holden 48/215, finishing a creditable 64th against serious opposition. Unlike many of the other teams, the Australians lacked a spare car to allow them to recce the route of the final stages in advance.

Movie camera in hand, Tony Gaze grabs a bite to eat during a stop in the 1953 Monte Carlo while Stan Jones looks on.

Tony Gaze at the wheel, Stan Jones next to him and Lex Davison asleep in the back of the Holden as it is driven onto the boat to cross the English Channel during the 1953 Monte Carlo. The rally started in Scotland on 20 January and travelled to Monte Carlo via Wales, England, Belgium, Holland and France.

The Davisons and Gazes spent a considerable amount of time together, this shot of Diana Davison (left) and Kay Gaze taken in New Zealand in the mid-1950s. The premature deaths of Kay and Lex Davison led Tony and Diana to each other two decades later.

Tony Gaze decided that sports car racing was the way to go in 1953 and purchased Aston Martin DB3 chassis number DB3/9 from the factory. Its third event was the Grand Prix of Portugal at Oporto in June 1953, the car pictured here before the race with Tony and Kay Gaze standing behind it. The race didn't quite go to plan....

The remains of Tony's DB3 after its enormous accident at Oporto, the car catapulted into a tree at high speed by an errant driver in another car. The Aston burst into flames and Tony was left lying semi-conscious in the middle of the road. Remarkably, he suffered only cuts, bruises and scrapes but was very lucky to survive.

After the war Freddie Richmond became president of the Junior Car Club and then of the British Automobile Racing Club (a 1949 amalgamation of the JCC and Brooklands Automobile Racing Club) and was looking for a replacement for the Brooklands circuit which had closed at the outbreak of war, never to reopen.

Tony Gaze had, of course, spent a fair bit of time driving his MG around Westhampnett's perimeter track and heard of the Duke's quest in 1946 while visiting the Royal Automobile Club's premises in London. According to Tony, the resulting conversation went something like: "Someone said, 'Freddie's the president of the JCC and they're looking everywhere for replacement for Brooklands'. I said, 'Don't be bloody silly, he owns one!' And I went over and said, 'You've got an airfield, when are we going to have a sports car race at Westhampnett?'" It grew from there.

The first meeting at the new 2.4 miles (3.9km) Goodwood circuit was held on 18 September 1948, the 500cc race won by a certain youngster called Stirling Moss who had celebrated his 19th birthday the day before. It was also the future legend's first race.

Although Goodwood's length was regarded as being too short for a World Championship Formula One race, many non-championship F1 events were held there over the years along with sports cars, touring cars and all categories of openwheelers. The first F1 race at Goodwood on that inaugural day was won by Reg Parnell in his Maserati 4CLT.

These were the days that even the biggest Grand Prix stars often raced in several categories and the F1 teams contested a number of non-championship events at circuits like Goodwood. This lasted through the 1950s, '60s and to a lesser extent into the early '70s, after which it all started to become very serious due to becoming a multi-million dollar business. Much of the camaraderie between drivers and teams in different forms of racing was lost as the money factor increased.

Goodwood had that difficult-to-define nice 'feel' to it and teams enjoyed going there. The traditional Easter Monday meeting was an annual highlight. The circuit also had its dramas, however, and was the scene of two significant and very serious accidents: one that ended Stirling Moss's career on Easter Monday 1962 and another that claimed the life of Bruce McLaren in 1970 while testing, four years after regular race meetings there had ended.

It was Freddy Richmond who decided to close Goodwood as a full-time racing circuit in 1966 for safety reasons as he became concerned about the speeds contemporary top level F1 and sports cars were able to attain. There was also the issue of ever-encroaching suburbia, noise complaints and other related issues. Easter 1965 saw the last Formula One race at Goodwood, won by Jim Clark in his Lotus 25.

The final Goodwood meeting was held a year later, by which time all cars of over 3-litres engine capacity had been banned. Formula Two was the meeting's headline category and many of the Grand Prix stars of the time turned out to compete including Jack Brabham, Jim Clark, Denny Hulme, Jackie Stewart, Graham Hill and Jochen Rindt, all of them past, present or future world champions.

Goodwood continued as a test venue and for club racing events with Formula One teams taking advantage of it before gradually drifting off to Paul Ricard in France where there were no problems with noise.

Then, in 1991, the current era of Goodwood began when the first Festival of Speed hillclimb up the driveway of Goodwood House was held. This was an enormous success and the current Earl of March - grandson of Freddie Richmond - began campaigning to start a regular historic meeting at Goodwood. The Festival of Speed and Goodwood Revival meetings are regarded as two of the world's great motor racing events, bringing together a mouth-watering collection of cars and many of the world's greatest racing drivers - thanks largely to Tony Gaze.

ELEVEN

GRAND PRIX DRIVER

AND SO IT WAS back to England for Tony Gaze with the intention of going racing full time in 1951 and beyond. It was a move that in 1952 would see him make history by becoming the first Australian to contest the Formula One World Championship.

Tony had been in touch with people like George Abecassis and John Heath – the owners of small racing car manufacturer HWM – and others who were interested in running teams. Among the people HWM had driving for them in Formula Two were two up-and-comers, Stirling Moss and Peter Collins. Moss's star was very much on the ascendancy at the time while Collins went on to win three Grands Prix and place third overall in the 1956 World Championship behind Fangio and Moss. He was killed during the German Grand Prix at the Nürburgring in August 1958 while driving a Ferrari, just two weeks after his final victory.

It seemed to Tony that the racing he needed to get into was Formula Two because there were plenty of events to contest in Britain and throughout Europe. It was competitive and well supported, although Tony admits that he had the idea in his mind that it was "reasonably amateur, but I was dead wrong there." In fact it was just the opposite with plenty of big names and professional teams involved.

Formula Two had been created in 1948 as a support category to Formula One and was between then and 1953 for normally aspirated 2000cc or supercharged 500cc cars. In the early days, Grand Prix drivers often competed in F2 but with the establishment of the European F2 Championship in 1967 it was decided the category should be for less experienced drivers as a stepping stone to F1. Some 'graded' F1 drivers did compete, but were ineligible for points.

Interestingly, although all the European F2 Championship winners between the first series in 1967 and the last in 1984 when it was replaced by Formula 3000 went on to make names for themselves in F1 and win many races, none became World Champion. But in 1951 it was very different with no international F2 championship although there were some national titles. However – and for reasons explained later – the 1952 and 1953 World Championships were contested by F2 cars!

Tony Gaze ordered a new Alta F2 car for 1951: "I ordered a new Alta and engine because I got sick of the unreliable Alta and got in touch with the manufacturer, Geoffrey Taylor, and said leave the supercharger off and I've got a Formula Two car. I went over to England on the ship and took delivery of that and we had our first go at Goodwood where we didn't go very well because of gearbox trouble. At the washed-out Silverstone race I was in front of a couple of Alfa Romeos for a bit and then a thunderstorm came and the spark plug holes filled with water and stopped me. Anyway, the car got me through a season of racing all over Europe in 1951."

The Silverstone race Tony refers to was the BRDC International Trophy on 5 May 1951 in which he was classified 13th in the heat while the final was stopped due to the torrential rain. The names of some of the participants gives an indication of the quality of the field not just in that race but in many other F2 events of the time – Reg Parnell, Duncan Hamilton, Graham Whitehead, Stirling Moss, reigning World Champion Giuseppe Farina, Juan Manuel Fangio and Prince Birabongse Bhanuban of Siam, who raced under the *non-de-plume* 'B Bira'.

Geoffrey Taylor had developed a Formula One car and engine but his limited resources were stretched, thus thwarting development. He had become trapped in the 'no money equals poor results equals less money equals worse results' spiral that has always been a problem for motor sport's smaller teams and manufacturers. Alta engines had achieved some success installed in HWM chassis and Taylor made the decision to concentrate on F2, building both chassis and powerplant, using the same basic engine but without the supercharger.

His first Formula Two car (numbered F2/1, appropriately) was for Tony Gaze. Its chassis differed little from previous cars but was now clad in smart new bodywork. The engine followed usual Alta practice in having twin overhead camshafts driven by roller chains but its capacity was slightly different at 1970cc instead of the previous 1960cc.

Feeding the engine were four SU carburettors but power output was only about 130 horsepower. The car was also quite heavy so performance was not as good as some of its rivals. It did, however, have one tangible advantage and that was its eligibility to attract starting money in European racing. Geoffrey Taylor built four other examples of this F2 car for Gordon Watson, Anthony Stokes, Oliver Simpson and Peter Whitehead, the latter probably achieving the marque's best, if modest, results.

Tony had a good mechanic with him for the 1951 F2 season in Jim Gullan who was an engineer and racer. He had contested the 1937 and 1939 Australian Grands Prix and knew his way around motor racing well. Tony made him an unusual employment offer: he could either be paid the normal mechanic's wages and take care of his own living arrangements, or he and his wife could live with the Gazes on their English estate and stay in first class hotels while travelling but with no wages. He took the second option.

The Alta was never really competitive but did achieve a couple of decent results in Europe, especially considering the high calibre of much of the competition. At Monza on 13 May 1951 Tony finished 16th in the first heat, 13th in the second and 12th in the final. Alberto Ascari – who would be the 1952 and 1953 World Champion – won in his Ferrari while Stirling Moss was third in the HWM-Alta that would pass into Tony's hands in 1952.

The next two races at Genoa a week later and the Eifelrennen on 3 June gave Tony his best F2 results when he finished eighth in both events. At Genoa, carburettor troubles cost him some places. The track was a seaside promenade, two straights connected by hairpin bends at either end. Braking from flat out to only 30 or 40km/h caused the big methanol carburettor bowls to surge and flood two cylinders.

It took several seconds to clear each time and the penalty was obvious when he was following an HWM with the same engine. Tony had no trouble staying with it until the hairpins when the Alta faltered and dropped back. HWM used Weber carburettors, Tony changed to them and there were no further problems.

The Eifelrennen race was the second round of the West German Formula Two Championship and Tony was the first non–German home. Tony went well in practice around the 22 kilometre circuit and started from the front row.

The race was a "good chance missed," remembers Tony. "Unfortunately we had to change to a colder plug before the race as the ones used looked a bit near the limit and cut out after the long straight. All went well after the start and I made a couple of passes when we came down to Adenau and it went on to three cylinders. I set off for the pits after being repassed until near the straight it cleared onto four cylinders so I didn't go into the pits. I repassed a couple until it went back on three, then cleared again but then I went into the pits for a plug change. After that, all was well and we finished eighth after losing eight or nine minutes."

Three consecutive DNFs (did not finish) followed at Rome, Naples and Berlin's Avus, the latter (on 1 July) ending Tony's 1951 F2 campaign when the engine blew. Avus was a famous and most unusual track with two very long straights running closely parallel and joined by a hairpin at one end and semicircular bit of banking at the other. Its original length was about 19 kilometres but in 1951 this was halved because one end of the circuit encroached into Soviet-controlled East Berlin.

The blowup created a problem for Tony: "We raced all over Europe until eventually at Avus it threw a rod. At the same time Stirling Moss and Lance Macklin in HWMs with the same engine broke crankshafts. When we got back to England Geoffrey Taylor was so overwhelmed with repairs our season virtually ended. F2 was a great thing with races all over Europe but with F1 drivers and works teams involved there was no hope of winning. About eighth was good and it was all very enjoyable."

The European exercise was useful for Tony in several ways. He now had the experience of some racing on the highly competitive European scene and in several countries behind him; he had established or re-established contact with many of the important drivers, managers, teams and administrators involved in British and European racing; and having done a season of Formula Two, he was eligible for Formula One should the opportunity arise. It did – thanks to a change in rules for the 1952 Grand Prix season.

. . . .

Meanwhile, Tony was left without anything to drive due to Geoffrey Taylor's inability to repair the broken Alta engine which had a hole in its block thanks to the thrown conrod. He was at one of the racing drivers' favourite watering holes – the Steering Wheel Club in London – when a gentleman called Leslie Boyce asked Tony what he was doing in England, pointing out that he should be in Europe racing. Tony explained the situation and was offered Boyce's pre-war Maserati 8CM to drive at a meeting at Snetterton.

Boyce had only recently purchased the car and admitted he had been frightened by it when he first took it out at a meeting at Goodwood. The straight-eight, 3.9-litre 8CM was notoriously unpredictable when driven at speed. Nearly six decades later this car (chassis no 3011) is still being campaigned in historic racing by owner Peter Giddings who has also commented about driving it: "…. the most difficult car I have ever driven…. a series of quick violent reactions to whatever happens on a particular corner…."

3011 is a very famous 8CM originally built in 1934 for American millionaire Whitney Straight in whose hands it scored a number of victories including the South African Grand Prix, British International Trophy Race, JCC International Trophy at Brooklands and the Donington Park Trophy.

Subsequent drivers included Richard Seaman and Bira, whom Tony had watched taking the car to victory in the Campbell Trophy at Brooklands before the war. It had naturally never occurred to him at the time that 13 years and a World War later he would get to drive the Maserati himself, even though by then the car was obsolete but still eligible to race in Formula Libre events. It was also still capable of giving a good account of itself if driven well.

Tony mastered the Maserati quickly and drove it to some good results. His debut in the car at Snetterton was looking good until right near the end: "We had the race won until the last lap when a bird hit the windscreen. Everything then went wrong. The car went onto seven cylinders a couple of miles from the finish and I got beaten by a fifth of a second. Very annoying."

The problem was caused by an overheated magneto, an issue which re-emerged during the Formula Libre Trophy Race at Silverstone, a support event for the British Grand Prix. Some 'bush engineering' was applied by obtaining a coil and using the distributor as a magneto "stuffing the 6 volt coil and battery down the side of the seat," recalls Tony.

"But the engine wouldn't rev out, so I did the desperate thing and put 12 volts through the 6 volt coil and the car went almost as well as normal. The race was, I think, only 100 miles and I came fourth ahead of one of the 4.5-litre Ferraris. Interestingly I finished ahead of Ron Flockhart in the Raymond Mays 2-litre ERA which used to beat the Maserati before the war."

Famed motor racing journalist Denis Jenkinson witnessed this race and wrote: "Tony Gaze had an inspired drive in 3011 when he finished fourth behind three modern Ferraris...." Tony had several other drives in the Maserati and usually finished in the top two or three including a win at Goodwood.

. . . .

Even though Grand Prix racing had been in existence since the earliest days of motoring itself, it wasn't until 1950 that a World Drivers' Championship was instigated and 1958 before the Constructors' Cup was first awarded. The first Formula One World Championship regulations used in 1950 and 1951 allowed monoposto racing cars powered by either up to 4.5-litre naturally aspirated or 1.5-litre supercharged engines.

Italy's Giuseppe Farina was the inaugural World Champion driving Alfa Romeo 158 and 159 'Alfetta' 1.5-litre cars ahead of Juan Manual Fangio's Alfa after the six rounds. Fangio won the first of his five titles in 1951 in an Alfa Romeo 159. Technically, there was an additional round of the World

Championship between 1950 and 1960 – the Indianapolis 500 – but only one of the top European drivers ever contested it during that time so it had little relevance to the championship as a whole. Alberto Ascari was the one who went to the 'Brickyard' in 1952 but with no success.

The 1952 season generated controversy even before it started, resulting in a major change. Alfa Romeo decided to withdraw from Grand Prix racing, a threat it had made the previous year but failed to follow through. This left Ferrari and British newcomer BRM as the only serious contenders as neither Talbot nor Maserati were expected to offer much opposition.

The BRM had debuted in 1951 and thus far had proved disappointing. Faced with the probability of an uninteresting Grand Prix season due to the almost inevitable dominance of Ferrari, the race organisers all decided to make the World Championship Grand Prix races for Formula Two cars instead of Formula One, in the hope of getting some decent fields and competition.

The Grand Prix circus was very different then to the highly structured series of events we see today where a prescribed number of teams, cars and drivers contest the entire series with no newcomer or 'casual' teams able to join. Half a century or more ago individual races would usually host very different entry lists with a core of drivers contesting all the events and many others entering only some of them or perhaps only their local event. Entry was normally by invitation.

It was against this background that Tony Gaze found himself a Grand Prix driver in 1952, entering four of the seven World Championship races and making history as the first Australian to compete in the highest level of motor sport: "Just as I was thinking of returning [to Australia], the F1 rules were changed with F2 cars now eligible. I received invitations to F1 races, so I stayed, exchanging the Alta for an HWM.

"The agent who was going around negotiating for us with starting money and things said he was having problems with Altas because Peter Whitehead had apparently done something naughty – I'm not entirely sure what it was. The agent said that if I get an HWM I'd find it easier to get entries.

"There was a fellow called [Phil] Scragg who did a lot of hillclimbing and had turned a Jaguar-engined Alta into a hillclimb car and it was going so well that a friend of his wanted another one. They said they would be happy to take my F2 Alta, put a Jaguar engine into it and sell it to Scragg and do a swap for an HWM.. So that's what I did which didn't make me very popular with Geoffrey Taylor!"

The HWM Tony acquired was also powered by a 2-litre Alta engine and had been raced by Stirling Moss in 1951 during his time as a works driver for the team. Some have subsequently disputed this, but Tony has no doubts: "I know it was Stirling's because when I took delivery of it he turned up and took his special steering wheel away. So I was left with an HWM for F1. We did hopelessly but we expected that because we were up against professionals and we knew we were only there to make up the numbers."

Hersham Walton Motors (HWM) was established by George Abecassis and John Heath in 1949 initially to build Formula Two cars, both men having already made names for themselves as drivers, often in Altas. Stirling Moss and Peter Collins were early HWM F2 works drivers while the company later got into sports-racing cars, one of which was used by Tony Gaze. The marque had some successes but suffered a serious blow in 1956 when John Heath was killed while competing in the famous Mille Miglia sports car race.

World Championship Grand Prix races in the 1950s were typically 400–500 kilometres in length (or three hours maximum, whichever came first) and required refuelling stops and tyre changes. Tony Gaze engaged the services of HWM's head mechanic Frank Nagle to help him in his campaign but he knew it would be very difficult as a privateer in that company. There was even competition from within the HWM brand with works cars for Abecassis, Peter Collins, Duncan Hamilton and Lance Macklin appearing during the season.

Before contesting the 1952 World Championship races, Tony competed in three non-championship events in the HWM with some success. In the Lavant Cup at Goodwood on 14 April he finished fifth; the BRDC International Trophy at Silverstone on 10 May saw him 16th in the final (the works HWMs of Mike Hawthorn and Lance Macklin were first and second); and the Monza Grand Prix on 8 June held over two 35 lap heats resulted in an official 'not classified' albeit ninth best ahead of many others.

By way of diversion, Tony also got a drive in the International Race of Champions support event for the International Trophy race at Silverstone on 10 May, with the invited starters all in new left hand drive Jaguar XK120s provided by the manufacturer. Apart from Tony there was 'Bira', Stirling Moss, Baron de Graffenreid, Johnny Claes and the German Paul Pietsch. He would inadvertently cause Tony a problem due to the fact that he hadn't been given the silver Jaguar - Germany's racing colour - and that Tony had!

"There was about six of us," remembers Tony. "I have a photo of the start - I think the moment my clutch disintegrated! After practice Paul Pietsch came to me and asked if he could have the silver car. He had a brown one, so we swapped. I was on the front row with Stirling on pole in a green one which we knew had been worked on and was faster than the others.

"At the start the clutch went - completely seized - and at every gearchange up somebody went past, so after about five laps I'm running last. I think there was a rude note in the press about being last. At the end of the race I thought 'what am I going to do with this thing as it's in gear and if I get it out of gear I'd be stuck because I couldn't get it back in again.'

"So I crept into the paddock, got into the middle and switched the thing off and went to find [Jaguar racing boss] Lofty England to tell him. The fact that I completed the race and got it back to the pits rather than retiring after the first lap helped me with Lofty because I hadn't shown up his brand new car as being unreliable - good PR!"

Tony also contested three non-championship races in the HWM during and after his GP season and scored a couple of good results. On 23 August 1952 he was fourth in the Scotland National Trophy at Turnberry and on 14 September he finished fifth in the Cadours Grand Prix in France, his HWM this time a works entry. The last race in the HWM was on 11 October at Charterhall in Scotland and disappointingly resulted in a DNF when its Alta engine's crankshaft broke, putting an end to the car's career in Tony's hands.

But greater things had preceded that. On 22 June 1952 at the famous Spa-Francorchamps circuit in Belgium, Tony Gaze made his significant bit of motor racing history by becoming the first Australian to start a World Championship Grand Prix race. It was the Belgian Grand Prix (also known as the European GP) and the third round of the championship including the largely irrelevant Indianapolis 500. Tony qualified 16th but the race was very fraught for him, starting with a fuel pump problem which caused methanol fuel to spray onto his face.

He remembers: "Everything went wrong. The main thing in the race was the fact that the fuel pump played up and the fuel pressure went off the clock which meant a pit stop to rebuild the pump." Tony recovered from that fairly well in the wet conditions but on the last lap another somewhat unexpected problem emerged: "Then right at the end I had a bird fly in my face and I was down to a crawl because I'd got double vision. I put my hand up and saw flesh and blood and thought 'my God, that's my eye!', but it was only the guts of the bird."

He crawled around the last 14 kilometres that constituted a lap at Spa in those days and was repassed by many of the cars he had overtaken on his comeback after the fuel pump incident. Despite all this he still finished 15th, six laps behind the winning Ferrari of champion-in-waiting Alberto Ascari.

At the British Grand Prix at Silverstone on 19 July Tony qualified 26th but had an had an oil pipe burst early on: "I hadn't realised the rules because I crept around to the pits, put another pipe on but they wouldn't let me out again until I'd been re-scrutineered. So that put me properly out, even though it was a long race but it was hardly worth going again." As a result, the records show a DNF Silverstone. Two of the three works HWMs (Peter Collins and Duncan Hamilton) also failed to finish the British GP while Lance Macklin brought his home in 15th place.

In the German Grand Prix at the old Nürburgring on 29 July Tony qualified an excellent 14th out of 30 starters and had gained several positions by the time six of the 18 laps had been completed: "I was going quite well and just when I was beginning to feel confident but then I flew off the road after the Karussel. I got back on thinking 'that was a silly thing to do' and went off again at the next corner. I looked over my shoulder and there were the rear wheels at funny angles." The HWM's De Dion axle had broken, putting him out of the race.

That turned out to be the last World Championship Grand Prix Tony started because at the Italian GP at Monza on 7 September his and the two works HWMs all failed to qualify. In the meantime there had almost been a bit of high drama in qualifying involving Tony, Alberto Ascari and his Ferrari 500, a car that Tony would later own.

Tony explains: "For some reason they accepted entries from far more cars than were allowed to start and none of the HWMs were fast enough to start because Ferrari and Maserati fielded four cars each, there were three Gordinis, there were teams of Connaughts, HWMs, Cooper-Bristols and so on.

"Qualifying was very difficult, especially for me on such a fast circuit because being so tall I stick a long way out of a single-seater. My car was always about five miles an hour slower than everyone else on the straights - I had a built-in headwind! But I was desperate to get starting money because it's a long way to Monza and we'd already travelled all that way. I was then quickest for a bit, even faster than Peter Collins, but then he appeared going past the pits with his head virtually disappeared into the cockpit to cut drag. I tried to do the same but couldn't, I was just too tall.

"I saw Ascari coming up behind me in his Ferrari going around the Curva Grande [at the end of the main straight] and I thought that if I could stay in front of him through the Lesmo curves until the start of the back straight, get a tow and stick with him until the main straight I'd certainly qualify.

"I knew I'd have to go flat out into the second Lesmo, and I did and got the whole thing sideways and nearly wrote Ascari off as he was coming past. He went by me looking slightly puzzled and when practice was over and I hadn't qualified I went over to him and apologised. I don't think anyone had ever done that before because he slapped me on the back and said 'okay, now we go and have a cup of tea', so we did and from then on whenever we bumped into each other [not literally!] at a motor race we'd go and have a cup of tea together.

"Luckily for us the Italians felt a bit sorry for us because the whole HWM team hadn't qualified. They said they'd misled us and paid the starting money anyway."

It seems that Tony was blissfully unaware of the history he was making as an Australian. Did he understand the significance of being the first Australian Formula One driver? "Not really. I just enjoyed being in it." Did anyone point out to him that he was the first? "No. The only thing we did was when we had a bunch of Australians coming to Spa as gophers. I think they said something to me because I hadn't put anything on the car.

"I still had Stirling Moss's Union Jack on the side and they said I ought to do something so we thought of the green and gold and got some gold paint and painted a stripe around the front of the windscreen. Scrutineering was very strict in those days when it came to markings, like having exactly the right size number and so on.

"You had to be in the colour of your country, you weren't allowed anything on the side of the car except the manufacturer's name and your own name. The gold stripe had them a bit bluffed so I came up with a story – we'd spilt methanol on it and as we couldn't paint the same [British racing] green we just covered up the stain with the gold band. They knew what I was doing of course but said 'oh well, in that case we'll let it through'".

As noted earlier, Tony ended the 1952 season with a broken crankshaft in his HWM's Alta engine, the damage sustained in the race at Charterhall in October. It was time for a rethink and a change of direction in 1953.

TWELVE
CHANGE OF DIRECTION

AT THE END OF 1952, Tony Gaze found himself with no car to drive as the crankshaft in his HWM's Alta engine was cracked and in Geoffrey Taylor's hands for repair. Based on previous experience, it was reasonable to assume the engine would be out of action for some time! Taylor had no spare engine Tony could use, so the car was mothballed for the moment. Tony had engaged the services of HWM's head mechanic Frank Nagle to help him with his 1952 campaign but with no further employment on offer from the Australian, he returned to HWM.

Tony searched for a competitive car to contest the 1953 Grand Prix season (which was once again for F2 cars) and even spoke to Enzo Ferrari who offered him an ex-works machine, an offer declined because there would be no support from the factory. It was obvious that if he wanted to stay in Grand Prix racing, Tony would have to part with a great deal of money.

He looked at continuing with an HWM-Alta but was concerned about reliability: "They tried to make it go faster but it was developed as far as it could go so it started getting unreliable through silly things like pistons hitting the head. So I decided the way to go for me was get into sports cars where you still had a chance to go to races where the factory cars didn't go."

The HWM part of the equation was not the problem, it was Alta: "One of the good things about HWMs was that they had a lot of proprietary parts on them from other manufacturers so getting parts was no great problem, unlike Alta where everything was made by Geoffrey Taylor and he never seemed to keep any spares."

So sports cars would provide the next phase of Tony Gaze's international motorsport career, but in the meantime there was an interesting diversion for Tony and fellow Australian racers Lex Davison and Stan Jones - the 1953 Monte Carlo Rally. The trio drove 'Australia's Own Car', a Holden 48/215, sometime known as the 'FX' and affectionately nicknamed the 'Humpy Holden'. The first of a long line Holdens which continues today, the 48/215 had been launched with considerable fanfare in April 1948.

Powered by a 2.2-litre (132.5 cubic inch) straight six, the car had been developed by General Motors' Australian subsidiary based on an existing

Chevrolet chassis. It dated back to 1940 but had never been put into production and suitably re-engineered for Australia with a new body design, became the first Holden.

Lex Davison and Stan Jones had already achieved some rallying successes in Australia in addition to their circuit racing activities. The Light Car Club of Australia (LCCA) Peninsula 100 Trial in February 1950 saw Jones the winner in a Ford Customline and Davison second in a Holden. More Holden rallying successes were recorded by a number of drivers including Jones and Davison, while even future triple Formula One World Champion Jack Brabham notched up a couple of rallies and trials in the marque.

Australian rally fans' excitement levels increased in December 1952 with the news that Davison, Jones and Gaze would take a Holden to Europe to contest the famous Monte Carlo Rally the following month, the entry having been arranged by fellow racer John Barraclough. This would be the first time a Holden competed in an overseas event.

After unsuccessfully seeking factory backing for the effort, a 1952 model 48/215 with 6,000 miles on the clock was purchased. It was fitted with a larger fuel tank, had two driving lights mounted on the bonnet and recessed fog lights added below the headlights, and a heater/demister and windscreen washer system was installed. The water supply for the washers was stored near the exhaust manifold to keep it warm during the European winter event. An emergency electric fuel pump was also fitted.

Tony notes that the engine had been prepared by leading Holden 'hotting up' firm Repco and therefore went a lot better than the standard 48/215. As a result, he was a little concerned about scrutineering but was told by Lex Davison not to worry about it: "We'll get through alright because they don't know what the hell a Holden is or what it should be!"

Car 177 with Gaze, Jones and Davison aboard left the start of the event in Glasgow on 20 January 1953, travelling via Wales, London, Lille, Brussels, Amsterdam, Paris and Clermont-Ferrand in the Alps where they took a wrong road but recovered in time to reach Valence with 18 minutes in hand.

In fact they reached Monte Carlo with no points lost, then with Jones driving finished eighth in a special braking-acceleration test - equal with Stirling Moss - to be in the top 100 for the final test, a maintained average speed section through six controls. They finished 64th, a little disappointing because previous form on the rally had shown them to be consistently much better than that. The result was nevertheless good enough for Holden to toast their achievement with a new car for each crew member plus a cheque to help with expenses.

"Unfortunately, we made a complete mess of the final elimination," remembers Tony. "We didn't have a practice car like just about everyone else and hadn't been able to recce the route. Our car was in the *parc ferme* and we couldn't get at it. So we ended up 64th on that one, but the Holden went very well – we were keeping up with the Jaguars."

When the Australians returned to England after the Monte Carlo they stayed with Tony and Kay Gaze at their estate Caradoc Court in Herefordshire. The engineless HWM was there and spotted by Lex Davison who asked Tony what he was planning to do with it. The answer was "probably sell it", prompting Davison to buy the car complete with a number of spare parts which were piled into the Holden, taken back to Australia and successfully passed through customs as spares for the saloon!

Davison had been looking for something to replace the pre-war Alfa Romeo Tipo B monoposto he'd been successfully campaigning in Australia since 1948. The idea was to install the Alfa's engine into the more modern HWM chassis but it wouldn't fit because the blowers were on the side of the engine, making it too wide. Instead, he installed a Jaguar engine from a wrecked XK120 he had, updated to the latest C-Type specifications. Lex Davison went on to achieve numerous good results in the car for two years from late 1953 including victory in the 1954 Australian Grand Prix at Southport in Queensland.

· · · · · · · · · · ·

Tony's decision to go sports car racing in 1953 led him, Stan Jones and Lex Davison to form 'Ecurie Australie', intended to comprise three HWM-Altas to contest the potentially lucrative European season where the starting money paid was relatively generous. It must be remembered that during the 1950s and into the early 1960s, sports car racing was arguably the world's number one motor racing category, attracting large crowds and quality fields and surpassing even Formula One in many areas.

Some of the world's most famous races were and are for sports cars – Le Mans 24 Hours, Sebring 12 Hours, Daytona 24 Hours, Targa Floria and so on – and manufacturer interest was high with marques such as Aston Martin, Jaguar, Ferrari, Alfa Romeo, Maserati, Mercedes-Benz, Porsche and later Ford all competing. The World Sports Car Championship was instigated in 1953 and the winning manufacturer gained enormous prestige.

Unfortunately, the Ecurie Australie idea came to nought when Alta entered into an exclusive engine supply deal with Connaught. The alternate plan of installing a different powerplant in the HWM chassis was also a non-starter because HWM didn't have the capacity to build three new cars in the required time.

Thoughts of an Australian sports car team racing in Europe were therefore put on hold but would re-emerge a couple of years later as the 'Kangaroo Stable' involving Tony, motoring journalist and champion driver David Mackay, Jack Brabham and others. The Ecurie Australie name was revived a few years later in Australia, the team led by Lex Davison.

For Tony, however, the immediate need in early 1953 was to get something organised for himself. At that time, Aston Martin's racing manager John Wyer got in touch with him to ask if he'd be interesting in going to Monza and help test the DB3 sports car for Le Mans. A full 24 hours simulation would be part of the tests and despite the fact it was still winter in Europe.

Tony remembers that it didn't quite go as planned: "It was all a joke really because on the first lap the crankshaft pulley that drives the fan failed and everything broke, so I didn't even get a clean lap. There was a chap who was a friend of Peter Collins who had an ordinary road-going Aston Martin there and the next thing he was missing the pulley from his car because it was pinched and put on the DB3.

"But by the time we'd had lunch and repaired my car it was snowing and we were doing tests around Monza in the snow! What we were proving I just don't know but we just went on and on and on until they did the 24 hours. Wyer said he was interested in me driving for them and if I'd like he'd sell me a DB3. Graham Whitehead was also looking for one so we bought one each.

"Wyer stitched us up. We were promised that Aston Martin wasn't going to come out with something new to make us obsolete the moment we got these things. So the first race meeting I go to Reg Parnell turns up in a works DB3S which was a lot lighter and more powerful!"

Tony's car was chassis number DB3/9 (registered as TPB 639) and Graham's DB3/10. After driving the car in the Silverstone International Trophy meeting and at Charterhall, Tony and Graham shared DB3/9 in the 12 Hour race at Hyeres in France's Southern Provence on 7 June. They failed to finish when a piece of casting came off in the timing case and broke the chain early in the race. The winner was Peter Whitehead in his Jaguar C-Type.

Two weeks later Tony took DB3/9 to the Grand Prix of Portugal at the Oporto circuit, a rough, fast and dangerous 7.5 kilometres of 'around the houses' public road complete with tramlines, cobblestones and a fish drying factory at the finish line! Opened in 1950, Oporto closed a decade later for safety reasons. Tony Gaze probably wishes the track had been shut down well before that, because on 21 June 1953 he came close to losing his life there on the second lap of the race.

In fact there were two serious accidents in rapid succession, both of them caused by errant Ferrari drivers. The first was when Duncan Hamilton's privately entered C-Type was punted off by an amateur driver who was apparently subsequently banned for life. Hamilton was injured. Then it was Tony Gaze's turn when a driver called Palmieri hit the DB3, catapulting it into a tree at high speed. The car broke in half and burst into flames, leaving Tony lying semi-conscious in the middle of the road.

He was dragged off the track to safety by spectators who risked being injured themselves as the cars raced by, while officials took him to a nearby cottage, stripped off his driving suit – and the normal clothes he was wearing underneath it – and treated his cuts with industrial strength alcohol.

Jaguar engineer Len Hayden was part of Duncan Hamilton's team at Oporto and recounted the events of the day: "On the same lap [as Hamilton's accident] we saw a pall of smoke from the other side of the circuit and when neither Duncan nor his friend Tony Gaze appeared, Angela Hamilton and Katie Gaze were obviously getting panicky.

"All I could do was get some brandy and wait, telling them their husbands were sure to be together by now, and a car would deposit them back at the pits slightly merry when it was all over. I was half right. At the end of the race a car drew up and out got this figure literally covered in sticking plaster and wearing only underpants.... it was Tony, drunk as a lord, so Katie was alright." It was subsequently rumoured that Palmieri never drove again, so upset was he by the accident.

The crash caused Tony considerable angst in terms of his planned racing programme as he'd had entries accepted for several prestigious and potentially lucrative events including the 1,000 kilometre races at the Nürburgring and Monza. He sent a telegram to Monza saying, "Can't drive, car written off" and got a reply offering double the starting money! They thought he was trying to wrangle a better deal.

Tony got onto to John Wyer and offered to purchase one of the works DB3s because he knew he could make a fair bit from starting money but Wyer wouldn't be in it. Then the insurance company tried to get a second-hand Aston because that was a cheaper option than paying out. Tony reckons that John Wyer and Aston Martin didn't want him to find out how much faster the works cars were than the customer cars. If so, it wouldn't be the first or last time that particular scenario had arisen in the history of motorsport!

The insurance money eventually arrived and Tony approached Lofty England at Jaguar to sell him a car but a deal couldn't be done. Instead, he went back to HWM which had just completed a new Jaguar-powered open sports car for company co-owner George Abecassis to drive. As HWM didn't use chassis numbers, the car was recognised by its registration number, HWM 1. Based on the F1/F2 chassis, the car was quickly recognised as being a potential winner, so Tony asked HWM to build him a replica.

HWM – conveniently located just down the road from Geoffrey Taylor's Alta premises at Walton-on-Thames on the south-western outskirts of London – produced something of a trendsetter with its new sports car, one which inspired a number of other Jaguar-powered specials. John Heath developed a triple Weber carburettors installation to feed its XK engine and Indianapolis-style quick change Halibrand spur gears for the rear axle, allowing an easy change of ratios to suit any circuit.

It was immediately successful. In George Abecassis' hands HWM 1 led the works Aston Martins for a while in the 1953 Goodwood Nine Hour, was sixth in the Reims 12 Hour and beat the works Aston Martins and Jaguars in the 1954 Silverstone International Trophy with only Grand Prix driver Jose Gonzalez's Ferrari ahead of it at the end.

Tony's 'VPA 9' took a while to be built, not emerging from the factory until June 1954. Tony says that although his car was a later chassis than George Abecassis', it was never quite as good. But before VPA 9 became available, he did some more sports car racing in other peoples' cars as well as heading south in early 1954 for some racing in New Zealand and Australia, as related in the next chapter.

In August 1953 Tony teamed up with American Tom Meyer to contest the 12 Hour at Pescara driving Meyer's Aston Martin DB3/7, the pair classified sixth. He also shared Graham Whitehead's DB3/10 on several occasions including a successful outing in the Ulster Tourist Trophy at Dundrod near Belfast. At Liverpool's Aintree circuit he took HWM 1 to a fine fourth place in heavy rain behind two Jaguar C-Types (with Duncan Hamilton driving the winning car) and Carroll Shelby's Aston Martin DB3S.

At Aintree, Tony started from pole. It was a Le Mans start but HWM 1's engine was slow to fire so Tony found himself in the middle of the 2-litre class on the opening lap. He got through them fairly quickly until he was held up by the number three Ecosse Jaguar of Scott Douglas and then to a lesser extent the team's number two car with Ninian Sanderson at the wheel. Sanderson later apologised.

"After that," remembers Tony, "I caught up with the leading bunch and was only feet away from Jimmy Stewart - in the number one Jaguar - and a car length to Carroll Shelby and the same to Duncan Hamilton. I must have gained about ten or fifteen seconds, got the fastest lap by two seconds and the lap record. A great opportunity lost."

Tony and George Abecassis drove HWM 1 in the 1954 Hyeres 12 Hour and after gaining pole position recovered from a poor start to get back to second place only to be disqualified on the last lap following a minor pit infringement by Abecassis. To add insult to injury, HWM 1 had to be pushed across the finishing line as a result of a brush with a Ferrari on that final lap.

. . . .

VPA 9 made its debut at the Reims 12 Hour on 2-3 July 1954, the event won by Peter Whitehead and Ken Wharton in a Jaguar D-Type in what was the first victory for the famous sports-racer that went on to win the Le Mans 24 Hour race three times. It was Whitehead's second Reims 12 Hour win in succession - the previous year he'd taken a C-Type shared with Stirling Moss to victory.

The HWM marque was well represented with George Abecassis and his co-driver in HWM 1 and Tony and Graham Whitehead in VPA 9, which eventually finished seventh. Tony's new car - which was racing as a works entry - was a little disappointing. It was supposed to have the most powerful 3.4-litre Jaguar engine that had been built, but it wasn't as quick as HWM 1. There was also a handling issue that took some time to sort out.

Tony tells the story of VPA 9's debut: "It didn't really matter [that Abecassis was faster] because they were having problems with HWM 1. George came in during practice and said 'the engine's tightening up'. John Heath said 'nonsense', gave the throttle a twist under the bonnet and got a rod in his face! So that was the end of HWM 1.

"Our car was so tricky that before his second stint Graham Whitehead was physically sick. I had a problem with it - I did the first stint, the race started at midnight. For the first time I really thought I was mad going motor racing because at the start it was pouring with rain, it's the middle of the night and all the cars were parked for the Le Mans start. I thought, 'I'm going to run across the road and jump into two inches of water, pouring rain and set off down the straight at 160 miles an hour' - we are crazy.

"On the first lap I nearly came into the pits to get the lights adjusted until I realised I had them on dip [low beam] and shortly afterwards I was going down the pit straight at 160 miles an hour and went straight off the end up the escape road and through a barricade. When I had to reverse with all the 100-watt headlights coming down the hill towards me I couldn't see for the dazzle. I'd just passed Tommy Wisdom in a Bristol and I caught him up again the next lap and I did it again!

"The gearbox was running castor oil and it was leaking. I'd got it on my goggles and was trying to clean them but the more I wiped the more I smeared it. So I took them off. On the first lap my eyes hurt like hell and then I was okay and finished my three hours and Graham Whitehead went out.

"My eyes were red but I could see alright so I started my second stint just as it was beginning to get light. I still had the oil on my goggles so I went back to driving without them. The car went well enough but there was something that just wasn't quite right. Anyway, Graham took over for the last spell and we finished seventh. We never found out what was wrong with the car until about a year later."

Tony was then entered in a race at London's Crystal Palace circuit, by then basically 'an oval with kinks', according to one description and quite short at only 2.2 kilometres per lap. It was regarded as being a 'small car' circuit and when Tony arrived in the HWM he was bailed up by British Grand Prix and sports car racer Roy Salvadori who asked, "Why the hell have you brought this bloody great thing? A Cooper-Bristol is as big as you'd want!"

To his great pleasure, Tony won the race with the nearest big car nearly a lap behind. "But I missed a gearchange during the race," he remembers, "and I think the tachometer tell-tale was at about 6900rpm. They should have changed the valves - I didn't realise that Jaguar engines were that twitchy."

The next race was the Ulster TT at Dundrod and it dropped a valve: "The valves would apparently hit if the revs went over about 6800. Everyone else knew it and my crew knew it because I'd left the tell-tale on 6900. I think they tested the compression and it was alright so it was left. It did practice alright but the valve dropped an hour or so into the race.

"I didn't realise what had happened – I just thought a plug lead had come off because the car went onto five cylinders and it was only when I looked behind me and saw a cloud of smoke that I realised what had happened. The whole cylinder was wrecked. The trouble at Dundrod was there was nowhere to stop – bloody great slab walls, nowhere to get off the track. I found the first cross-road and stopped but by then the engine was pretty well wrecked.

"I never had that engine again because they sent it off to the factory to be repaired but at Goodwood [on 25 September 1954] it was pointed out that the engine now in the car was not the original but 'Jaguar's worst old engine'. Anyway I did practice and qualified somewhere in the middle of the field – but faster than George – but then I was asked to drive the single-seater instead." Tony agreed and it was an almost fatal decision.

This was the HWM 54-Alta Formula One car that Lance Macklin had driven in the French Grand Prix shortly beforehand. It had failed to finish that race and had been re-engined with a Jaguar motor by the time Tony drove it at Goodwood. It also nearly proved to be the undoing of Tony Gaze thanks to its pedal layout – from left to right: clutch-accelerator-brake (a not uncommon arrangement in openwheeler racers of that and earlier eras) instead of the normal clutch-brake-accelerator in VPA 9 which he'd been driving immediately before taking to the track in the racing car.

Tony had obviously instinctively trod on the accelerator pedal in the middle when he thought it was the brake, but even now he's not convinced about that: "I did two laps in practice in it and nearly killed myself. I don't know to this day what happened but Stirling Moss reckoned I trod on the wrong pedal. I came into the bottom of Lavant Straight into Woodcote and the thing wouldn't stop. I'd got my foot on something and it wasn't the accelerator," he insists.

"Anyway, whatever the reason it wasn't going to stop so I spun it down the escape road and hit the eight feet high dirt wall and got tossed out over the top of it and ended up in the crowd. The car was a write-off. There was a bit of a joke about the car because they salvaged what they could out of it at – the engine and things – and put the rest of it up against the wall ready to try and straighten it and sell it to some unfortunate bloke. But the scrap metal man arrived and took it without asking!"

Tony was hospitalised as a result of the accident, suffering severe concussion and back injuries which kept him out of racing until late 1954

Before the accident, Tony had driven VPA 9 in several other events including at Oulton Park near Chester where he had gearbox troubles. John Heath had found a cheaper way of doing up Jaguar gearboxes and proving the adage 'you get what you pay for' is correct, George Abecassis had a problem in practice with HWM 1 and had changed the box, using the team's only spare.

As Tony changed down to third for Old Hall Corner at the end of the pit straight in VPA 9, everything locked up. He thought the engine had seized and let the clutch out which didn't make the slightest difference and then found himself spinning around and around, about five times. The corner marshall didn't know which flag to wave there was so much happening! The team later discovered the gearbox had slipped into two gears at once and solidly locked up. There was absolutely nothing that could be done and Tony didn't get to race because there was no spare gearbox.

There was a comedy of errors at the famous Zandvoort circuit in Holland. Esso called the team in shortly before the race started to put a different oil in the cars because it was going to be very hot. But they substantially overfilled the sump, causing Tony in VPA 9 to miss out on what he reckons should have been a win. He and George Abecassis had done identical lap times in practice.

It looked pretty good for Tony, at least at first: "We had Duncan Hamilton with us but he'd run engine bearings in practice and was only a 'starting money special'. George sheared a driveshaft at the start and I thought I had this race won because I was seconds faster than even the Ecurie Ecosse outfit [which was becoming an unofficial Jaguar works team] and its C-Types. I led the first lap but then got on the straight and everyone passed me. The thing just wouldn't go.

"I looked and the oil temperature was 130 and the oil pressure about 10, and I was too late to stop for the pits so I had to do a lap like that. I came in and George said 'throw it away you've done the bearings' and I said 'no, I reckon there's too much oil in the sump'. The mechanic crawled underneath and drained a gallon of oil out – at 130 degrees centigrade – and away we went, laps down.

"As the event was two heats – one a Le Mans start and the other an ordinary start, time added – you could almost forget it, but I drove the second heat, started from the back obviously and got caught behind a Dutchman in a C-Type who was driving me mad baulking me all the time. I eventually got by and was going quite well, enjoying myself, and gaining on everyone but I was damn near a lap behind.

"Going into the Hugenholtzbocht [an almost 180 degrees hairpin] immediately behind the pits I was going a bit too quick and thought rather than losing it I'll just go over the grass and come out the other side. But the grass was wet and I got bogged! I looked at the pits and saw Duncan Hamilton having hysterics!"

At this stage Tony and the HWM people still hadn't been able to work out why VPA 9 was so unreliable and the handling so unsure. An incident involving George Abecassis and the fact that he declined an opportunity to drive VPA 9 at one race meeting when his own HWM 1 was out of action illustrates how bad everyone knew Tony's car was.

"We went to dinner," remembers Tony, "leaving the mechanic to put a new driveshaft in HWM 1. We came back to see if he'd finished and there was a very bent HWM 1. What the hell had happened? The mechanic had taken it for a spin to impress a girlfriend, came hurtling over the top of a hill and into a roundabout he didn't know was there. He immediately ceased being a racing mechanic and became a sales manager, I think. So there's George left with no car. You can tell what he thought of mine because he didn't ask if he could borrow it!"

VPA 9 verged on the uncontrollable under some circumstances. It was later discovered the dampers on the front were failing quickly, leaving just the coil springs and no damping - the wheels were just doing what they felt like. The problem was cured by adding some friction dampers. In a race, the friction was tightened up at the first pit stop and everything was fine after that. Simple!

HWM continued to build and develop cars over the next two years but there was a tragic end to its story in 1956 when John Heath - who was regarded as a competent driver but not in the same class as George Abecassis - died when his HWM crashed and overturned on the Mille Miglia. Abecassis had recently married Aston Martin chief David Brown's daughter Angela and retired almost immediately. Only one more HWM was built, a Jaguar-engined Alta-based vehicle for hillclimber Phil Scragg.

THIRTEEN

DIVERSIONS DOWNUNDER

SIX MONTHS BEFORE Tony Gaze's European sports car adventures in VPA 9 had taken place, he had ventured to the southern hemisphere at the beginning of 1954 to contest two important races in New Zealand, the Grand Prix at Ardmore near Auckland on 9 January and the prestigious Lady Wigram Trophy at Christchurch on 6 February. In between there was a quick trip across the Tasman Sea to contest Australia's first 24 hour race at Mount Druitt on the outskirts of Sydney, sharing a Jaguar C-Type with his friend and 'team mate' Peter Whitehead.

Gaze and Whitehead were by now operating pretty much as a team despite driving different makes of car in New Zealand, sharing resources including their engineers Alan Ashton and Stan Ellsworth. Everyone got on and worked together well, so it was a logical arrangement.

Tony had a 2-litre supercharged HWM-Alta for the New Zealand races while Peter drove a Ferrari Type 125 (chassis no F1/114) fitted with a supercharged 2-litre V12 engine. Built in early 1950 for Formula One, the Type 125 was the first car to carry the 'Ferrari' brand. This one originally had a 1.5-litre supercharged V12 and was one of the factory cars for part of that year before being sold to the Englishman. As a 2-litre normally aspirated Formula Two car, he campaigned it with some success until late 1953 when he installed the supercharger and took the car to New Zealand.

The 1954 New Zealand Grand Prix was an interesting race, attracting a quality field and at the end of it, some controversy. Apart from the Gaze and Whitehead entries there was British driver and occasional Grand Prix competitor Ken Wharton and his screaming 1.5-litre V16 BRM. Most pundits predicted the winner would come from this trio with another Brit, Horace Gould in his 2-litre Cooper-Bristol, considered an outside chance. Local hero Ron Roycroft and his Alfa Romeo had the crowd behind him and the chance of a good placing if some of the others had problems.

Other Australian entrants included Lex Davison in the ex-Gaze HWM-Jaguar, Lou Molina in a Holden Special, Tom Hawkes in an Allard Special and Stan Jones in the ex-Charlie Dean Maybach Mk.1 Special, one of Australia's most famous racing cars of the era which had been built up around a Maybach engine from a captured World War II German half-track vehicle. Another interesting competitor was (to quote one report) ".... a quiet, fresh-faced 27-

year-old ex-speedway champion named Jack Brabham, just finding his feet and hands in a Cooper-Bristol called the Redex Special...."

Practice resulted in Wharton gaining pole position ahead of Whitehead, Gould and Jones. Davison was seventh and Brabham eighth, but Tony Gaze was further back due to some gearbox problems: "I had a Jaguar gearbox in the HWM. After three laps third gear went and Alan Ashton had a hell of a job finding bits to fix that. We had to put in standard [Jaguar] Mk.VII road car gear ratios which were pretty hopeless for racing so I ended up with in effect a two-gear car, third and top."

Seventy thousand eager New Zealanders turned up to watch the 100 lap race which was eventually won by Stan Jones ahead of Ken Wharton (whose BRM had no front brakes for the second half of the race), Tony Gaze and Horace Gould. Peter Whitehead's race ended when his clutch disintegrated and Jack Brabham was sixth.

It was after the race that the real fun started, Gould protesting the result and claiming he'd actually completed 101 laps and won, and that he'd deliberately stayed behind Jones on the last lap because he knew he was a lap clear. The protest was upheld by the stewards, who strangely decided he'd finished second - which even Gould didn't believe - but then a series of counter-protests, investigations and examination of lap charts followed with the upshot that the original placings were confirmed several weeks later.

As for Tony Gaze, third place on the face of it was a good result but it should have been better. His effort was thwarted by the fact that his fuel supplier - Shell - failed to supply him with any fuel for the race! But for some 'creative procuring' by his crew, Tony would have ended up with 'did not finish' against his name.

We'll let Tony tell the frustrating story: "We turned up on race day and went to the fuel depot to collect our fuel and there wasn't any! The only fuel we had was what was left in the tanks after practice. We were running on pretty specific mixtures. I was on the Mercedes thing of 85 per cent methanol, five per cent nitro-benzine and 10 per cent acetone and Peter was on I think 85 methanol, 10 petrol and five benzol.

"We went around the depot and thought it's got to be here somewhere because we'd wanted a couple of 44s [gallon drums] because the fuel consumption of those blown things was enormous. But there wasn't any. I suggested we put all the fuel we've got in one of the cars and see how far it'll go. Peter said no because as we'd been contracted to start and we'd been paid to be here, we'd better start. The mechanics disappeared trying to find fuel – I think trying to borrow it from someone else who had something similar – and I was left on my own.

"It came to start time and as there was no-one to help me. I thought I'd just get someone to give me a push and I'll run on the plugs it's got in it instead of the warming plugs because I didn't have a plug spanner or any plugs. So I did that and it seemed to be running alright but when I drove around for the start it went onto three cylinders.

"At the start of the race I set off on three cylinders and came into the pits – it had stub exhausts so you could feel which one wasn't firing – and Peter Manton was in the pits and he said 'change all four, you're going nowhere, you haven't got fuel for halfway'. In the meantime the BRM came by so I was a lap behind anyway.

"So I went back out and I was rumbling around, not particularly trying but going fast enough to enjoy myself when I saw Peter's car pulled up at the side of the road. He'd had his clutch disintegrate – he was very lucky that he had any genitals left because his legs straddled the transmission – and on the next lap there are my mechanics with drums and syphon tubes syphoning the fuel out of his Ferrari.

"I thought I'd better speed up because we might be in this race after all. So I did and came into the pits when I was signalled in – they'd worked out when I'd be running out of fuel – and put all the fuel they'd got in, sent me out and told me to go as far as I could. I did and passed the BRM which was running out of brakes to take second. I was gaining three seconds a lap on the Maybach and I started thinking that we might possibly win this.

"But a few laps before the end [lap 92 of 100] it ran out of fuel but I had enough speed to coast into the pits. For the benefit of the crowd I opened the fuel filler to show them the reason for stopping. The next thing I know there's a funnel put in it and a churn of fuel but they had to push me the whole length of the pits because the fuel lines were empty and the fuel pump on an Alta engine's on the camshaft. The crew was absolutely exhausted but it had pumped up enough fuel to start.

"After the race I asked Alan Ashton where the hell he'd got the fuel from. He said 'don't ask!', but then told me that the BRM had finished refuelling so one of their cans was borrowed when they weren't looking! So I finished on BRM fuel. I ended up third on the same lap as the Maybach and BRM.

"When we met the Shell bloke afterwards he told us they'd got a message to him and with the race half over he'd got some fuel in the back of his car but they wouldn't let him across the track. We're supposed to be professionals so I got onto Shell about the fuel thing. We'd come 12,000 miles to do this and there was no fuel on race day.

"We haggled and we haggled and they said 'yes, but if you'd had fuel you mightn't have finished!' I said 'but we did bloody well finish!' They went on – 'you might have gone off' and so on. They just went on and on and didn't seem able to grasp the fact that not only had we finished, we were third on the same lap as the two in front and might have had a chance to win!"

Annoyed and frustrated by the Shell peoples' attitude, Tony pointed out that it was probably just as well for him that Peter Whitehead's car expired for mechanical reasons in the race because if it had run out of fuel they'd probably have had a court case to deal with "because he's not short of money and I am!"

This suggestion of even the possibility of legal action obviously had some effect: "The Shell bloke offered me 200 quid or something to shut up about the 'misunderstanding' of the fuel situation. But it wasn't a misunderstanding, it was a complete balls-up! Then I thought that 200 quid's better than nothing. I might as well take it."

Four weeks later it was down to New Zealand's South Island and Christchurch for the Lady Wigram Trophy on 6 February. The 2.2 miles (3.5km) Wigram circuit was like many others of the time, built around an airfield's runway and perimeter tracks. What made it unusual was that it was (and remains) an operational Royal New Zealand Air Force base.

The 48 lap race provided Whitehead and Gaze with a great result – first and second, respectively – but only after some issues with tyres. The circuit was highly abrasive and practice revealed that tyre life was going to be a problem. Dunlop insisted that both drivers have a tyre change in the race, its primary motivation for this being to save the company the embarrassment of the world witnessing its products failing.

Tony and Peter came to an agreement which was supposed to see whichever of the pair was in front come in first for a tyre change. Whoever was second would get the benefit of the crew having already performed a change. Tony was leading the race at the time Dunlop insisted on a tyre change but the stop created a problem for him:

"We didn't need fuel but while they were changing the wheels someone thought they'd chuck in a can of fuel. Might as well, you know, what with one-and-a-half to the gallon or whatever it was we were doing. But an official made me get out of the car for safety reasons. I pointed out that the car had stub exhausts, it won't catch fire. If there was a red hot exhaust pipe it would be a different matter. By the time I finished arguing we'd had a 40 second pit stop rather than a 20 second one."

Tony thinks he probably wouldn't have won the race anyway because Peter Whitehead decided to gamble on his tyres lasting the distance, refusing to come in to change them and going on to win comfortably. He'd taken a big risk – his Ferrari's tyres were pretty well shredded by the end – but he got away with it and gained a big advantage by not stopping.

. . . .

In between the New Zealand races, Tony and Peter Whitehead teamed up in Peter's C-Type Jaguar to contest what was a first for Australia – a 24 hour race at the now defunct Mount Druitt circuit in Sydney's west on 31 January-1 February. This 2.2 miles (3.5km) circuit had been an emergency airfield during the war but was in poor condition and prone to breaking up. Tony and Peter recruited popular local veteran Alf Barrett to join them in what was the fastest car in the mixed field and the one the bookies had at the shortest price.

The race was described as a "brave venture" by one motoring writer with the condition of the circuit "far from perfect" even before heavy rain in the three days leading up to the race caused further damage to the track surface. The paddock area was a quagmire, there were no covered pit facilities, no seating for spectators and wholly inadequate paddock lighting.

Twenty-two cars started the race, a mixture of road and racing sports cars and saloons, the latter category including a Bristol, Humber Super Snipe, various Holdens, Renault 750, Peugeot 203 and even a Fiat 500.

The promoter – Belf Jones – had got in touch with Gaze and Whitehead and asked them to compete as he knew Peter's newly-acquired C-Type would be a crowd-puller. The pair flew to Australia from New Zealand in between races to have a look at the track and weren't overly impressed as Tony remembers: "I'd been there once before when it was basically just running up and down the runway and we said it's not on because there's only a skin of bitumen and the cars will break it up.

"They said they'd be replacing everything and it'll be perfect and they offered us quite good starting money. That was the clincher! So we came over thinking we should win this easily because we had the fastest car. We'd got caravans and things to sleep in and by the time we'd each done one stint of driving – about two hours at a time - we were 100 laps ahead or something. Maybe that's a slight exaggeration....!"

The C-Type was, as expected, dominant from the start and was comfortably in the lead after completing 282 laps. But at that point the breaking up track surface claimed the Jag: "My second stint came around and it was dark," recalls Tony. "We'd been working on a fuel consumption as if we were driving at Le Mans because we didn't want full tanks as we needed to keep the weight down as we knew the track was going to break up. I hopped in and was heading down the back straight for the first time and drove into a great hole which the others probably knew about but I didn't.

"It felt as if the wheel had come off so I stopped and got out to have a look. The wheel was still there but the big arm holding the rear suspension together was broken. I managed to get it back to the pits to get it welded up. We found that the car had the full 40 gallons of fuel in it because we'd been using far less than we thought and we were carrying all that weight.

"So there's the mechanic with 40 gallons of fuel over him welding the arm by torchlight! He welded it up and I went back out, finished my stint and went to bed. Two or three hours later I suddenly realised there was three of us in the caravan, so I knew it had happened again. We welded it again and sat at the side of the track for the last part of the race ready to drive across the line at the finish. We were the only sports car still 'running' so we won the sports car class! We took the money and got out of the way before we became too unpopular!"

Only seven cars finished the race which was won by an XK120 Jaguar driven by Mrs Doris Anderson, Charlie Whatmore and Bill Pitt. They completed 572 laps or 1,258 miles (2,024km) at an average speed of 52 miles per hour (83km/h) and just managed to stagger to the finish with the car's engine mountings shot to pieces and one carburettor about to fall off!

As Tony notes: "The race was a good idea but at the wrong place...." An interesting diversion nevertheless.

FOURTEEN

FORZA FERRARI!

THE INFORMAL TEAM Tony Gaze and Peter Whitehead had established in early 1954 when they contested the New Zealand Grand Prix and Lady Wigram Trophy races - plus their joint effort in the Mount Druitt 24 Hour race in Whitehead's Jaguar C-Type - led them to think about expanding the association in 1955 and running a pair of identical openwheeler racing cars to contest events in New Zealand and elsewhere as a proper team.

The New Zealand events were gaining prestige and starting to attract some big names. Tony and Peter had noted the quite substantial starting money a couple of competitors had been paid in 1954, notably Ken Wharton and his BRM. The decision was therefore made to purchase two cars which would not only be potential race winners but also interesting enough to race promoters and spectators to attract good starting money.

A plan was drawn up to contest a couple of races in New Zealand in early 1955 including the Grand Prix (there was no Lady Wigram Trophy that year) followed by a visit to Australia and then South Africa. The idea of Gaze and Whitehead more formally joining forces was a good one which had worked well in 1954 under the looser arrangement when Tony drove the HWM-Alta and Peter Whitehead his Ferrari 125.

Everyone worked together well, the two drivers were good friends and they were both fast. Moreover, experience had shown that given the same machinery or when sharing a car, their lap times were virtually identical.

First thoughts centred around acquiring a pair of 4.5-litre Alfa Romeo 159s of the type driven by Giuseppe Farina to victory in the last race of his 1950 World Championship-winning year and by Juan Manuel Fangio throughout the 1951 season for his first World Championship. But investigations revealed that only a single 159 was available and that spares were a scarcity because the engines from these cars had been finding their way into speed boats!

Plan 'B' involved going to Ferrari to buy two 4.5-litre Type 375 cars which they thought would bring good starting money and be quick and reliable. Naturally aspirated and producing up to 380 horsepower at 7,000rpm from the V12 engine, the 375 had been a worthy opponent to the Alfa Romeo in the 1951 World Championship season in Alberto Ascari's hands. With the rules changed to the 2-litre formula for 1952, it was made suddenly obsolete just as it reached its prime. Ascari drove one in the 1952 Indianapolis 500 but retired with a broken wheel.

Tony and Peter went to see Enzo Ferrari who had a bit of a soft spot for the Englishman because the Type 125 he had used to win the 1954 New Zealand Grand Prix was the first car Enzo had sold to an outside customer. Whitehead had also provided the marque with an early victory when he won the 1949 Czech Grand Prix in the 125.

Enzo Ferrari agreed to sell them two 4.5-litre cars and all the arrangements were put in place. But just before the contracts were signed he suggested they perhaps they should consider buying two Formula One cars instead, a pair of Type 500s. These had started life as 2-litre Formula Two cars and had won two World Championships for Ascari in 1952-53 when the title was contested by that category. They had subsequently been modified to accommodate 2.5-litre Type 625 engines to comply with the new Formula One rules introduced in 1954.

Enzo Ferrari told Tony and Peter that he would enlarge the engines to 3.0-litres from 2.5 "which we've been doing for Farina in South America" when they returned from South Africa and then they could do a season of Formula One. He also pointed out that as the Indianapolis engine had twelve cylinders and the 500/625 only four "instead of changing twenty-four spark plugs when you warm them up in the morning, you'll only have to change eight!"

Tony and Peter considered the new option and agreed. Although a 500/625 wouldn't be as quick as the 4.5-litre it would be cheaper to run, less complex and would allow them to follow their southern hemisphere events with a season of Formula One in Europe. That's what they decided to do, but as this was Ferrari they were dealing with, it didn't quite work out that way. But for the moment a grand plan was in place.

Enzo Ferrari's reference to running Farina's car with a 3-litre engine in South America rather than the required 2.5-litres is interesting. Tony wonders if they told the organisers about the bigger engine because you couldn't tell any difference just by looking at them. There's probably no need to answer that question!

So Tony Gaze and Peter Whitehead took delivery of a pair of identical Ferrari Type 500/625s, numbers five and four, respectively, out of six built. Most historians note that the cars' chassis numbers were simply '4' and '5', but some sources refer to them as 500-004 and 500-005. Regardless, when they were upgraded to Type 500/625 standards new chassis numbers (GP.0480 and GP.0482) were applied.

Tony's car (0480) had a particularly distinguished history as this was the example used by Alberto Ascari to win his World Championships in 1952 and 1953. He won 11 championship Grands Prix in this car, six in 1952 (Belgium, France, Britain, Germany, Holland, Italy) and five in 1953 (Argentina, Holland, Belgium, Britain and Switzerland).

Ascari also won several non-championship Grands Prix in '5'. His 1952 World Championship campaign had seen him victorious in all but the first round – Switzerland – because he was contesting the Indianapolis 500 in a 4.5-litre Ferrari 375 at the time. His victory in 1953's opening race in Argentina is interesting because it is known that the car was using an illegal 2.5-litre engine which was changed back to the proper 2-litre unit when the car returned to Europe! Standard practice at Ferrari, apparently. The more things change....

For the 2.5-litre formula in 1954 Ferrari introduced a new car, the Type 555 Squalo. This proved to be not as competitive as hoped so a couple of the Type 500s were pressed into service upgraded as Type 625s. Tony's car was one of them, results in its new guise including third for Frenchman Richard Trintignant in Germany and a win by Mike Hawthorn in the non-championship Rouen Grand Prix. In its Type 625 form, the 2,498cc four-cylinder double overhead cam engine developed 240 horsepower at 7,000rpm.

The 3-litre engine was of similar configuration and although it produced only five more horsepower than the 2.5 it was at a relatively lazy (and potentially more reliable) 6,500rpm but with a useful increase in torque. As before, the engine was fed by twin double choke Weber carburettors.

· · · · · · · · · · ·

And so to New Zealand for the 1955 Grand Prix at Ardmore on 8 January. The serious competition was small in number but strong in quality, headed by Bira in a Maserati 250F, the Gaze and Whitehead Ferraris and Australian Reg Hunt in his newly-acquired ex-factory Maserati A6GCM.

The Ferraris were slightly disadvantaged, however. "We made a mistake," remembers Tony. "To try and make certain we didn't have the fuel problems we'd experienced the previous year we ran the cars on 100/130 aviation fuel and the first thing we found up against Bira's Maserati was that we could stay

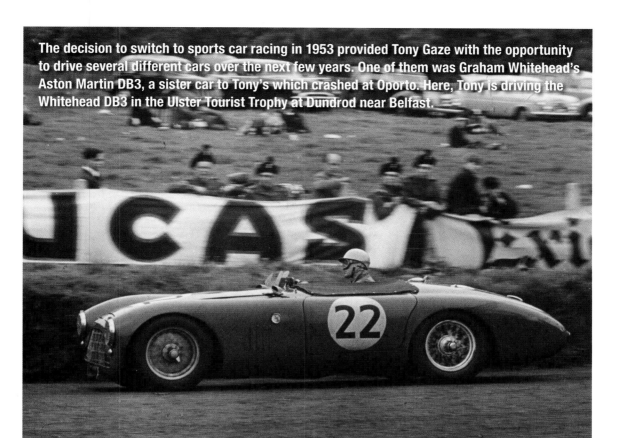

The decision to switch to sports car racing in 1953 provided Tony Gaze with the opportunity to drive several different cars over the next few years. One of them was Graham Whitehead's Aston Martin DB3, a sister car to Tony's which crashed at Oporto. Here, Tony is driving the Whitehead DB3 in the Ulster Tourist Trophy at Dundrod near Belfast.

Tony's association with the HWM-Jaguar sports car began in 1953 through driving HWM 1, the works car campaigned by company co-owner George Abecassis. Tony's own car - VPA 9 - wasn't ready until 1954. Here, Tony is driving HWM 1 at a very wet Aintree (Liverpool) in the Daily Telegraph International meeting in May 1954, heading for fourth place behind two C-Type Jaguars and Carroll Shelby's Aston Martin DB3S. Note how much of him is sticking up out of the car!

Tony prepares to go out in George Abecassis' HWM-Jaguar at the May 1954 Aintree Daily Telegraph International meeting. He started from pole but HWM 1's engine was reluctant to fire at the Le Mans start, costing him considerable time.

Tony took delivery of his own HWM-Jaguar (VPA 9) in June 1954 and campaigned it in Britain, Europe, New Zealand and Australia before selling it to Lex Davison in 1956. This shot was taken at Silverstone in July 1954 in the sports car race supporting the British Grand Prix.

A 2-litre supercharged HWM-Alta openwheeler was acquired to contest the major New Zealand races in 1954, the Grand Prix and Lady Wigram Trophy. The fuel supplier failing to supply any fuel (!) caused problems at the GP but Tony managed to finish third and was second behind 'team mate' Peter Whitehead's Ferrari in the Trophy. Kay and Tony look on while the mechanics momentarily stop work on the HWM to have their picture taken.

Ferrari driver - Tony in action in South Africa in 1955 driving his ex-Alberto Ascari Ferrari 500/625, the car that took the Italian to two World Championships in 1952 and 1953.

Friends and team mates. Peter Whitehead and Tony Gaze with their first and second place trophies from the 1956 Lady Wigram Trophy race in New Zealand. The pair had previously run as an informal team but in 1955-56 formalised the arrangement, each driving a Ferrari 500/625.

Tony Gaze had considerable success in the Ferrari 500/625, never finishing worse than third in it apart from once in South Africa when he spun on some else's oil in a minor race. Subsequent owner Lex Davison added more important chapters to this significant car's history.

The Gaze and Whitehead Ferraris running 1-2 early in the 1956 Lady Wigram Trophy in New Zealand. The positions were reversed by the end of the race.

The establishment of the three-car, all-Australian Kangaroo Stable team with Aston Martin DB3Ss in 1955 was a bold move. The team's second and most successful outing was the Hyeres 12 Hour in May 1955 in which the Tony Gaze/David McKay car (illustrated) finished second and the other two cars third and fourth.

The Gaze/McKay Kangaroo Stable DB3S in the pits on its way to second place in the 1955 Hyeres 12 Hour. Tony Gaze has just got into the car and David McKay (in pudding basin helmet and checked shirt) is standing just to the right.

Kangaroo Stable team manger Jim Roberts provided this pic with the caption: "Kangaroo car at garage in Hyeres with self and French garage employees." Number 28 (OXE 474) was Les Cosh's DB3S and number 24 (OXE 472) was jointly owned by Tony Gaze and David McKay. Part of the third car (Tom Sulman's OXE 473) can just be seen on the far right of the picture.

Tony Gaze's last major race was the Le Mans 24 Hour on 28-29 June 1956, sharing this 2-litre Frazer Nash Sebring-Bristol with fellow former Spitfire pilot Dickie Stoop.

Sadly, Tony's last race at Le Mans ended like this when Dickie Stoop crashed the Frazer Nash after ten hours of racing and while the pair was leading the 2-litre class. "Dickie going off was unheard of," Tony notes, "he wasn't the sort of bloke to crash." Except for this once.

Tony Gaze in the late 1950s - nudging 40 and looking for something to do. Gliding provided that something.

Tony contested the 1960 World Gliding Championships in Germany, representing Australia and flying a borrowed Slingsby Skylark 3. He was given the number '1' because the competing nations were ranked alphabetically and Australia was first on the list.

Tony owned several gliders over the years including this Slingsby Dart, a high performance sailplane which he brought with him to Australia in 1977. In this shot Tony is in the aircraft and waiting to be launched.

Huntin', shootin' and fishin' kept Tony partially occupied at the family stately home, Caradoc Court at Ross-on-Wye in Herefordshire.. He became expert at salmon fishing, this 1966 shot showing him with the biggest one he caught, a 40-pounder.

One of Tony's British gliding records - set in April 1960 for a two-seat 200km triangular flight - recognised in this British Gliding Association certificate.

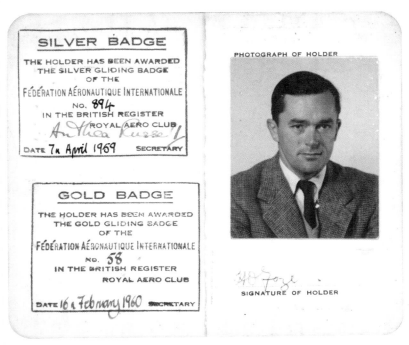

Once he started gliding in 1958, Tony Gaze quickly progressed, eventually gaining qualifications at the highest level. He also set a couple of British records on the way. This page from his *Fédération Aéronautique Internationale* Gliding Certificate booklet shows two of his earlier badge awards.

Three Jags - some of Tony's cars at Caradoc Court circa 1963: E-Type Series 1; customised Mk.VII estate with a standing platform at the rear and used for towing horse floats and gliders; and Mk.II 3.8.

Kay Gaze took up race horse training with some success. Here she is in 1971 with one of her winners outside Caradoc Court.

Lord (Charles) March and Tony Gaze at the re-opening of the Goodwood circuit in 1998. Tony was naturally an honoured guest due to the original establishment of the circuit being very much down to him. The annual Goodwood Revival meeting is regarded as one of the great motor sport events of the year. Charles March pays a personal tribute to Tony in the foreword he wrote for this book.

Tony and his HWM-Jaguar VPA 9 reunited at Goodwood.

Tony and Diana Gaze - friends since the late 1940s and married in July 1977.

The sign may be a bit wonky but the tribute certainly isn't. Tony and Diana at Goodwood in 2005 outside the circuit's media centre - the Tony Gaze Building.

Tony at the Temora Aviation Museum in rural New South Wales in October 2001. He is with the museum's then newly-acquired Gloster Meteor F.8 painted in the colours of a Meteor III he flew with 616 Squadron RAF in the closing stages of WWII. This is the only airworthy single-seat Meteor in the world and was purchased from Britain where it was well-known as *Winston*.

Six decades later, Tony is reunited with a Spitfire at Westhampnett. This was his first operational base and part of the Goodwood Estate. This shot was taken in the same spot as a 1941 snap that appears earlier in this book.

All togged up and ready to go. Tony and Diana have been regularly invited to events around the world. One of them was in 1991 to celebrate the 75th anniversary of one of Tony's wartime RAF squadrons, No 41. Part of his visit was to fly one of the squadron's Sepecat Jaguar strike jets, under supervision of course! Flying kit had changed considerably since 1940....

Tony and Diana "ready to party" in their Melbourne flat in 2002.

with it everywhere except on the straights – towards the end of the straights it would begin to pull away. Someone asked me if there was anything I wish I'd brought with me and I said 'some methanol pistons!'"

Bira's Maserati was running on a methanol blend and the speed difference between it and the Ferraris on the straight was noticeable. Gaze and Whitehead had to consider reliability as they had several other events to contest during their southern sojourn and wanted no major engine overhauls, so their motors were detuned to run on normal fuel to reduce wear and tear at the cost of some performance.

Bira's tactic in the 100 lap New Zealand Grand Prix was to get in front from the start and stay there as long as possible by going as hard as possible. This increased the risk of mechanical problems but he got away with it, the Maserati holding out and providing its driver with a win and lots of lap money. Despite this, either of the Ferraris could have won the race if they'd had a little luck.

Practice for the race quickly showed that the battle would be between Bira, the two Ferraris and Hunt's Maserati. Gaze and Whitehead were, of course, still learning about their cars – as was Hunt – but settled down to a pace only fractionally slower than Bira's.

There were two qualifying heats before the main event, Peter Whitehead winning the first from Hunt, and Bira the second ahead of Tony Gaze. Grid positions were decided by the lap times achieved in these heats, leaving Tony Gaze fourth behind Whitehead, Bira and Hunt with less than a second separating the four of them.

The Gaze and Whitehead Ferraris just beat Bira off the line, but the Maserati quickly took the lead after the first lap from Whitehead, Hunt and Gaze. From there, it appeared to the casual observer that Bira pretty much controlled the race. He made no pit stops and was never headed, but towards the end he was struggling with no brakes.

Both Ferraris had to make brief pit stops which may well have cost them the race. Whitehead lost 23 seconds having a minor adjustment made and Tony Gaze dropped a lap while a jammed throttle linkage was cleared.

Tony recalls what happened: "I had no trouble catching Bira after he had lapped me while I was in the pits clearing the stuck throttle. I stayed behind to try to push him into a mistake as there was no hope of making up a lap. I had some more trouble when I was pushed off into a 44 gallon drum by

McLaren and Jensen who gave way to Bira but didn't see me right behind. I unlapped myself near the end but the gravel [from the off] broke the lenses of my goggles and I had gravel rash on my face."

The result was Bira winning by 23 seconds from Whitehead, with Gaze 63 seconds further back in third and all of them on the leading lap. Fourth place went to Jack Brabham in his obsolescent Cooper-Bristol, two laps in arrears. These margins show that Bira's apparent dominance was nowhere near as great as it seemed. Had it not been for those unscheduled pit stops, the result might have been different.

The next stop for the two Ferraris was Australia at the end of January for the South Pacific Championship race at the Gnoo Blas circuit at Orange in the central western district of New South Wales. Some higher compression pistons had been shipped out for Gaze and Whitehead but for Tony they made little difference because he had clutch problems, the result of allowing Peter Whitehead to do a couple of practice starts with a tall axle ratio and breaking a finger on the clutch. Despite this, Tony finished the race third with Peter taking the win.

Then it was onto South Africa for a couple of races before the cars were to be shipped back to Ferrari to have 2.5-litre engines installed so a season of Formula One could be contested – or so Tony Gaze and Peter Whitehead thought!

Both cars reverted to standard pistons for the South African races in March. At Capetown Tony finished mid-field in a handicap race after spinning on someone else's oil but in two scratch races he finished first and second. At Johannesburg's Palmietfontein circuit he won the Queenstown Settlers Trophy with Whitehead third after suffering some timing gear problems.

The whole idea of returning the two Ferraris to Formula One specifications fell apart after Johannesburg. As arranged, the cars were shipped back to the factory but once there, Enzo Ferrari flatly refused to allow the necessary work to be done. It was pointed out to him that this was part of the contract signed when the two cars were purchased but he would not budge. No explanation was offered, just a flat refusal.

Tony and Peter examined alternatives. They went back to Motorworks – which looked after the cars in England – and were told they could get crankshafts and conrods made to bring the 3-litre engines back to 2.5-litres. At first, Tony thought the idea had some merit: "We didn't want to alter the heads and things – we just wanted to alter the stroke. It mightn't be as good as the factory but it would be a 2.5. We knew we'd have to rev it a bit harder but the valve gear was the same as F1 so that shouldn't be a problem. The only snag was maybe there was something we hadn't thought of.

"Anyway, we went into it until we spoke to a couple of Ferrari people who said 'he [Enzo] will never let them out on the track and on top of that you'll never get any spares'. So the cars just sat at the factory for the rest of 1955 and we didn't do a season's racing in Formula One."

The grand plan had come to nought, unfortunately. The lesson learnt – when it came to Enzo Ferrari – was that even a proper contract 'ain't worth the paper it's written on'! Tony Gaze and Peter Whitehead were not the first and certainly not the last to be shafted by *'Il Commendatore'*. Both Ferraris would be resurrected for 1956, but the balance of 1955 saw Tony doing some more sports car racing, as described in the next chapter.

. . . .

Tony Gaze and Peter Whitehead planned a substantial programme of racing in New Zealand in early 1956, using the Ferraris again. Tony also took his HWM-Jaguar sports car 'VPA 9' with him while Peter Whitehead had the Cooper-Jaguar he had raced at Le Mans. These races were significant for Tony as they formed the last major campaign of his career as a racing driver.

He had already decided that he would retire from full time racing and especially from openwheelers. This was due largely to the wishes of Kay, who was becoming increasingly concerned about his safety. Perhaps she just figured that the odds were shortening as time went on. Drivers were regularly dying in those days and no-one was immune, regardless of how good they were. Tony had got away with a couple of close calls already, but perhaps it would be better to quit before his luck ran out.

Tony promised her he'd stop racing because she'd always felt responsible for her first husband, Johnny Wakefield, being killed because she'd been able to help get him transferred from the Fleet Air Arm into testing Seafires at Supermarine. He died in an aircraft collision when he was taking off crosswind and hit someone who was landing into wind.

Casualties in 1955 included double World Champion Alberto Ascari who was killed while testing a Ferrari sports car at Monza in May. There was also the tragic accident at Le Mans the following month when one driver and 82 spectators were killed. This accident had a profound effect on many people and on the sport itself.

But first, there was a campaign of racing to conduct and the need to get the Ferraris away from the factory in Italy and prepared for action. Both cars had been overhauled and re-engined with the 3-litre Monza Type 750S four-cylinder sports car engine which ran on a methanol blend and produced 260 horsepower at 6,400rpm.

It had been suggested by one of the Ferrari people that the five-speed gearbox from the Type 555 Squalo Formula One car should be installed instead of the existing four-speed unit. It seemed like a good idea in theory but Tony checked with Mike Hawthorn - who had driven for the factory in 1955 - and was told not to bother.

Hawthorn told Tony that he didn't like new gearbox as much as the old one because it was much less predictable to drive. He also said that having five-speeds was a myth because first was only a starting gear which had a lockout catch in it so it couldn't be selected again. "Put a bit of grit under your back wheels at the start and you'll find it works just as well," he said.

Tony discovered an ongoing problem that plagued his car while he owned it: "My car handled better than Peter's but the engine was hopeless. I'd got a terrible flat spot. It was so bad I had to get police permission to use the main road outside Auckland to try to get rid of it - they couldn't believe us until we did a couple of gear changes in front of them and it just went flat and then picked up."

Tony had to live with that flat spot for all of his New Zealand campaign and despite enormous effort it just wouldn't go away. Peter Whitehead's engine was fine and everything on Tony's was checked: "We played around, we checked all the timing, our engine was the same as Peter's except the camshafts may have been slightly different. We played around with accelerator pumps and things and got rid of that part of the flat spot but it was still costing a minimum of a second a lap and probably a lot more. Changing up you just had to just wait while it decided to clear itself.

"I thought I could over-rev it and probably get rid of the flat spot but then when we'd done that accidentally at Orange the previous year we'd had a piston break. When we pulled them down at Cape Town before the race there we found a lump of piston in the sump of Peter's car. We thought, 'well it's a great big 3-litre piston and if you over-rev it'....

"And also in New Zealand we had four races to do. Part of our contract was that we did the four races so if we blew the bloody thing up in the first event – the Grand Prix – we wouldn't get the money. I didn't dare over-rev it so I had to put up with it." By comparison, Stirling Moss was also contracted to appear in New Zealand but only for one race, the Grand Prix in his Maserati 250F. He could therefore afford to go for it, knowing he didn't have to worry about ongoing reliability.

Tony and Peter had come to an agreement regarding who would win what in New Zealand. The Grand Prix would be a case of 'may the best man win', but if they were in a position to do so, the other race victories would be shared between them. A possible fly in the ointment of this neat little plan was Peter Whitehead's strong desire to repeat his victory of two years earlier in the Lady Wigram Trophy.

The 1956 New Zealand Grand Prix was held at Ardmore on 7 January, the lineup headed by the Moss Maserati, the Gaze and Whitehead Ferraris and Jack Brabham's Cooper-Bristol. Another entrant was Reg Parnell and his Aston Martin DB3R sports-racer but its engine threw a conrod through the side of the crankcase on the main practice day and there wasn't enough time to repair it.

In order to make sure that Parnell was able to make it to the grid – and therefore collect his all-important starting money – Peter Whitehead lent him his Cooper-Jaguar sports-racer. Parnell 'paid' for the loan by being seconded help cure the flat spot in Tony's Ferrari, but like everyone else he failed to do so. "It's the flattest flat spot I've ever come across," he remarked.

Many competitors also had logistical problems to worry about because "shipping arrangements went haywire," according to one report with several cars taken to Wellington instead of Auckland including Moss' Maserati and the two Ferraris. Cases of spares were still missing the day before the race, although most them were delivered to Ardmore in time for the Grand Prix itself.

The 1956 New Zealand Grand Prix turned into something of a Stirling Moss benefit, although as had been the case with Bira the year before, his almost flag-to-flag win was not quite as comfortable as it seemed. Moss was on pole ahead of Whitehead, Gaze and Brabham, but as the latter made a pre-race warmup run through the paddock before going out to the grid, his car's gearbox destroyed itself and he was out.

Tony Gaze led the field away from the flag followed by Moss, Whitehead and Alec Mildren's Cooper-Bristol. Moss took the lead along Hangar Straight on the first lap and stayed there for the next 200 miles, building up an ever-increasing lead. He was nearly a lap ahead of Gaze and Whitehead near the end of the 100 lap race when he felt what he thought was rain on his face and goggles. It wasn't water but petrol spraying from a broken fuel pipe.

Partially blinded and chocking on the fumes, Moss slowed and made a pit stop eight laps from home to have the pipe patched up and a bit of fuel thrown in to make up for what had been lost overboard. He continued at reduced pace and went on to win but Tony Gaze - who had been second throughout the race - gradually began to catch him. Moss then showed his class by responding with a new lap record on the 98th tour to make sure his lead was not seriously threatened.

Tony came home second, 43 seconds in arrears while Peter Whitehead was third a lap down after surviving a spin in the closing stages. Tony also drove VPA 9 at the Grand Prix meeting for a third place the sports car event.

Next was the Lady Wigram Trophy at Christchurch on 21 January and Peter Whitehead got his wish for a second victory in this race, beating Tony into second place after starting from pole. Tony got his own victory at that meeting when he took VPA 9 to the flag in the sports car event. Whitehead obviously had a liking for the Lady Wigram Trophy - he also won it in 1957 driving a Ferrari 555 Super Squalo.

Then it was to the Dunedin Wharf circuit for the Eighth New Zealand Road Race Championship event on 28 January. Under the terms of his agreement with Whitehead it was Tony's turn to win and he duly did, taking the Ferrari to victory from second on the grid ahead of Reg Parnell's repaired Aston Martin. Peter Whitehead was fourth after starting from a relatively lowly ninth.

The fourth and final event for the Gaze and Whitehead Ferraris' 1956 'Tour of New Zealand' was the inaugural Southland Road Race over 240 kilometres on 11 February. This time Peter Whitehead was in line to collect the major honours, starting from pole and leading Tony Gaze to the finishing line 41 laps later. The two Ferraris were the only cars on the leading lap - Reg Parnell finished third, two laps behind.

It had been a successful and profitable campaign for both drivers, Tony ending it with a win and three second places and Peter two wins, a third and a fourth.

Although it wasn't generally known at the time that he was retiring, these results also provided a fitting conclusion to Tony's career as a full-time racing driver.

. . . .

Tony had been contracted to drive his Ferrari at the Moomba meeting at Melbourne's Albert Park circuit on 10-11 March 1956 but by the time the car had been shipped to Australia from New Zealand it had already been agreed that Lex Davison would buy it, along with VPA 9. One of Davison's conditions of purchasing was that he would be able to race it in the Australian Grand Prix later in the year.

This created some problems, firstly with the Australian Government over its import duty regulations. Tony had to go to Canberra to get permission for Lex to buy the Ferrari because under the letter of the law it should have gone back to Italy and then re-imported. This somewhat ludicrous situation existed for many years and caused a large number of racing car sellers and buyers what at the end of the day was unnecessary grief and money.

Tony' second problem was due to some backing he'd received from the *Argus* newspaper to drive the Ferrari at Albert Park. After some negotiation, the contract was altered so that the newspaper backed Tony driving VPA 9 at the meeting while Lex Davison was able to take possession of the Ferrari - along with a bag of grit courtesy one F A O Gaze! Tony's time driving the car had been very successful. Apart from that minor handicap race in South Africa in 1955 when he spun on someone else's oil and finished in the pack, he never came worse than third in it.

That Albert Park meeting in March 1956 was also the last time Tony raced in Australia and he scored a pair of good results to go out on driving VPA 9 - third in the Argus Cup and first in the Moomba TT the following day, beating Bib Stillwell's Jaguar D-Type and Stan Jones' Cooper-Jaguar, a car that previously belonged to Peter Whitehead. After that, Tony's HWM joined the Lex Davison racing stable.

"In the meantime," remembers Tony, "We were still trying to get rid of that damn flat spot in the Ferrari's engine, trying different chokes and God knows what. Then Lex complicated matters because he wanted to repaint it, but we wanted to get rid of the flat spot and we took it up some back roads near Altona [Victoria] somewhere to try it out. I drove it - it was better but it wasn't anything like it should have been.

"At Albert Park for Lex's first drive in it I warmed it up for him because he knew he'd rev it – with the Ferrari you had to warm up by idling. I handed it over to him and said 'use 6,300 or 6,400 revs – 6,500 if you're desperate. He came back after the first few laps with the tacho's tell-tale showing 7,100! He'd never had a tell-tale before and said 'I didn't do it' and I said 'so what is that?!'

"I think the reason Lex didn't have any problems with the flat spot – although Alan Ashton may have got rid of it – was the fact that he was over-revving it. When he was in New Zealand where he did so well against more modern machinery he rang up and said 'I've found out how you can go as fast as the new stuff – take it to 7,500! The only trouble is that after about 20 miles a rod comes through the side of the block!'"

Lex Davison went on to achieve substantial success in the Ferrari including wins in the 1957 and 1958 Australian Grands Prix (the former after considerable controversy over lap scoring), the 1956 Bathurst 100, 1957 Victorian Trophy, 1957 Queensland Road Racing Championship and 1957 New South Wales Road racing Championship.

When Lex Davison moved into a rear-engined Cooper Climax in 1960 the Ferrari was sold and subsequently passed through several other owners. This enormously significant car – both in Australian and international racing terms – came perilously close to be being cut up and made into a sports coupe by one of its owners but was rescued just in the nick of time by Jim Harwood, who rebuilt it to its former glory.

For some years the Ferrari has resided in England's Donington Collection alongside many other very famous racing cars. Still powered by the 3-litre 750S engine used by Tony Gaze and Lex Davison, it is not just a static exhibit at Donington. Fully operational, it gets the occasional outing at historic race meetings in Britain.

FIFTEEN
KANGAROOS AND LE MANS

WITH TONY GAZE'S plan to contest some Grands Prix in 1955 thwarted by Enzo Ferrari's refusal to honour their agreement to convert the Australian's Type 500/625 to Formula One specifications after completing its early season southern hemisphere races, he had to find some other racing to do.

The opportunity came with the concept of establishing an all-Australian sports car team to compete in British and European races using three cars under the name Kangaroo Stable. The idea was not new, remembering that Tony's decision to go sports car racing in 1953 had led him and fellow Australian drivers Stan Jones and Lex Davison to form Ecurie Australie.

The plan then was to run three HWM-Altas in the potentially lucrative European season with its generous starting money, but the idea foundered when Alta entered into an exclusive engine supply deal with Connaught. The option of installing an alternative powerplant into HWM chassis was closed because HWM didn't have the capacity to build three new cars in the required time.

The idea of the Kangaroo Stable came from Tony Gaze and experienced driver Les Cosh in late 1954, who approached veteran racer Tom Sulman with their proposal. This tied in nicely with the aspirations of leading Australian motor sport journalist, racing driver (winner of the inaugural Australian Touring Car Championship in 1960) and later team owner David McKay, who also became involved in the project. Like Tony Gaze, McKay was an 'internationalist' in his motor racing outlook. Tony helped get the team together by at first attempting to acquire some Jaguar D-Types but none were available.

He then went to Aston Martin's John Wyer and was able to secure three production DB3Ss. Powered by a 2,922cc six-cylinder engine developing 210 horsepower at 6,000rpm, the DB3S was built in both open roadster and coupe versions and went on to be highly successful, especially the works cars. Kangaroo Stable's cars were all roadsters.

Customer DB3Ss had slightly less power than Aston Martin's own racers, this no great surprise as factory cars are always a little faster than those supplied to privateers because they have the latest and best 'go faster' bits.

What did surprise Tony and the others was just how *much* faster the factory cars were when they were supposedly pretty much the same: "It was interesting in the Goodwood Nine Hour race [in August 1955] the difference between the factory cars and ours - there was just no comparison. Going by St Mary's corner, for example, with one of the factory cars, by the time you got to the end of Lavant Straight it would be around the corner [Woodcote] at the far end! They were just so much faster."

The three Kangaroo Stable DB3Ss were chassis numbers DB3S/102 (registered OXE 472) co-owned by Tony Gaze and David McKay, 103 (OXE 473) for Tom Sulman and 104 (OXE 474) for Les Cosh. The team made some modifications to the cars including moving their batteries to under the passenger seat and radiator header tanks from near the exhaust manifolds to the scuttle. Of interest is that DB3S/105 was acquired by Graham Whitehead, who co-drove it with his half-brother and Tony Gaze's friend Peter a couple of times.

The Kangaroo Stable was managed by Australian Jim Roberts who had previously been Tony's mechanic on the HWM-Jaguar 'VPA 9'. Being Aston Martin, the cars were predictably delivered considerably later than John Wyer had promised and even then there were some unserviceabilities and setup issues to deal with including faulty shock absorbers. Tom Sulman made the Kangaroo Stable's debut appearance in 103 on 7 May 1955 when he took the far-from-sorted DB3S to a cautious 18th place at Silverstone. Reg Parnell and Roy Salvadori finished first and second driving their works DB3Ss in the 40 lap event.

The team's next race was the first in which all three cars competed and the one which provided its best result. The Hyeres 12 Hour in the picturesque Mediterranean port town near Nice on 29 May paired Tony Gaze with David McKay in DB3S/102, Tom Sulman and Jack Brabham in 103 and Les Cosh and Dick Cobden in 104. They represented the first time a multi-car team driven exclusively by Australians had competed in a major international motor sport event - or perhaps any overseas race.

Their performance was impressive: second (Gaze/McKay), third (Cosh/Cobden) and fourth (Sulman/Brabham) behind winners Andre Canonica and Gino Munoran in a Ferrari 750 Monza after 1,604 kilometres of racing. Tony believes that he and David McKay actually won the race but were victims of a timekeeping error which incorrectly put them a lap behind the winning Ferrari.

There was some consolation for the Australians as they won the Teams Prize but there was apparently no trophy for presentation to them until an official was sent home to find what was described as "a very ugly sculpture of an eagle.... with no plaques it was handed over very quickly at the prize-giving ceremony.... McKay handed it to Jim and told him to do with it what he liked...."

Two weeks after Hyeres the sport suffered a major tragedy at Le Mans when more than 80 spectators were killed during the 24 Hour race. Many European races were cancelled as a reaction to what was by any measure a catastrophe and some circuits, like the original Albi in the south of France, were closed on safety grounds.

Motor racing was banned completely in Switzerland, a ban that remains in place today. Switzerland's reaction may well have been at least in part fuelled by the fact that its main circuit - Bremgarten near Bern - had a reputation for being dangerous. Trees overhanging the track made it particularly treacherous in the wet and since its opening in 1931 had suffered more than its share of serious accidents and fatalities.

The overall effect for the Kangaroo Stable and others in 1955 was fewer opportunities to race, especially for the 3-litre sports cars as a number of races were limited to 2-litre cars. As an aside, Tony was listed as reserve driver for the Whitehead brothers' Cooper T38 Jaguar in the ill-fated Le Mans race but was not required. The car failed to finish.

Despite these issues, the team was still able to compete in a number of other events during 1955, either individually or collectively. In the Grand Prix of Portugal at Oporto on 26 June - the scene of Tony's major accident in the DB3 in 1953 - he finished eighth, five laps behind winner Jean Behra in his Maserati 300S. Les Cosh was ninth, another two laps in arrears.

All three Kangaroo Stable DB3Ss contested the Grand Prix of Lisbon on 24 July which was won by American Masten Gregory in his Ferrari 750 Monza. Les Cosh was the best of the Australians, finishing 11th while Tom Sulman was 12th. Tony had brake problems and failed to finish.

Tony had been offered an alternative to the Lisbon race by Bira, who asked him to drive his Maserati 250F at Albi just before it closed, but he had to turn it down: "It clashed with Portugal but it was David McKay's turn to drive the Aston Martin so I suggested that he drive it at Lisbon and I'd take Bira's Maserati to Albi. But the Portugese said that if I didn't drive the Aston they'd call it off! Also we [the team] needed the starting money, so I drove the Aston.

"I drove the Maserati at Silverstone which was interesting because both it and Bira were very small. I said 'I can't drive it' and he said 'get in it'. I was driving it around Silverstone to see what it felt like getting hell from everyone saying 'you're a Ferrari driver, what the hell are you doing in a Maserati!'"

Tony and David McKay ran in the Goodwood Nine Hour on 20 August and recorded a 'did not finish', although perhaps they should have gained some sort of result but for a slight misdiagnosis of a problem with the car's distributor. They were up against a strong field which included three works and several private DB3Ss, an Ecurie Ecosse Jaguar D-Type and a works Ferrari 750 along with a number of other strong privateers.

Given the already observed superiority of the factory Aston Martins over the private 'customer' cars, but also the fact that the works DB3Ss used up tyres as a greater rate, Tony and David McKay decided to limit their speed and try and go through the race with fewer pit stops. If there was some attrition they reasoned there was a chance of getting a decent result.

One way or the other it was an eventful race for the Australians, as Tony describes: "The first thing was that the car wouldn't start – it was a Le Mans start – and I was sitting there trying to get it to go so I was right at the tail of the field when it did. There was a bloke in a DB3 who I'd had trouble with in practice driving in the middle of the road making it impossible to pass. I came up behind him and he pulled over on me and I just touched him, enough to make a little dent. But it spun me and there I was stopped in the middle of St Mary's with everyone going by me.

"Just as I was about to get going there was a hell of a bang in the back and a Lotus, I think, had run into me. My car was still perfectly mobile but the other car wasn't. So I went into the pits to have a look at the damage which was minor so I went back out.

"The car was alright. We were going at our agreed lap time so we weren't wearing the tyres too much but then it just suddenly stopped. So I got out and did all the checks I could. I took the cap off the camshafts and pressed the starter to make sure they were going around and then had a look at the distributor and the arm was going around.

"So I thought 'the bloody drive's gone to the distributor'. I put the bonnet down and started to walk away and there was a hell of a bang and Mike Keen had killed himself in the Cooper-Bristol almost next to me. We took his helmet off and his head was not looking too good. I said to the doctor who was there 'it doesn't say much for these helmets, does it?' He said 'well you wouldn't want to look at his head if he hadn't had it on'. Anyway he was taken to hospital and died.

"I went back to the pits and the Lucas bloke apologised for the failure [of the distributor drive] and that was that. An hour or two after we'd packed everything up he came back and said 'it's a different sort of apology now, isn't it?' I said 'why is that?' He said 'pity you didn't pull the rotor arm off because the only thing that happened was that the little key in the rotor arm had broken'. Woops! We did fifty-one laps."

The race was won by Peter Walker and Dennis Poore in their works DB3S with 309 laps completed ahead of a D–Type and the more fancied works DB3S of Peter Collins and Tony Brooks. The number one Aston Martin (Roy Salvadori and Reg Parnell) lasted only three laps before a wheel hub broke.

The Kangaroo Stable's final outing was at Oulton Park on 27 August. Tony didn't drive there but Les Cosh managed 13th in the 355km event while Tom Sulman was entered but did not start. The race provided another win for a works Aston Martin, this time driven by Reg Parnell.

The team was disbanded and DB3S/102 was taken to Australia via New Zealand by David McKay in early 1956. There it achieved some fame in April 1957 when McKay set an outright Australian land speed record of 143.19mph (230.43km/h) over a flying kilometre at Carrathool in the Riverina district of New South Wales, the event staged as part of an article for *Modern Motor* magazine. By then, the car was fitted an updated twin spark plug engine which gave the full 210 horsepower of the factory cars.

Tony believes the Kangaroo Stable idea was worth the effort and was "a lot of fun." He also believes his HWM-Jaguar sports car would have been a better choice of equipment than the Aston Martins and would have gained better results.

After that, the latter part of 1955 was spent getting his and Peter Whitehead's Ferrari 500/625 openwheelers ready for the New Zealand races they would contest in the early part of 1956. As described in the previous chapter, this would be Tony's last major racing campaign as he deferred to his wife's desire for him to hang up his helmet.

. . . .

But Tony Gaze's career was not quite over yet. There would be one more race and it would be at the biggest sports car event of all - Le Mans on 28-29 June 1956. Kay was happy that he had stuck to his undertaking to give up openwheeler racing so there was no problem with doing the odd sports car event because of the perception that it was safer: "She was so happy that she let me drive the Frazer Nash at Le Mans in 1956 as that was a different sort of race," he remembers.

The car was a works-entered 2-litre Frazer Nash Sebring-Bristol he would share with British driver Richard 'Dickie' Stoop who had flown Spitfires with Tony in 610 Squadron Royal Air Force during the war. Tony remembers him as "a bit of a weird bloke - he stayed on in the RAF even though he was completely colour blind and ended up as an instructor at the test pilots' school. Then someone was rude to him so he just resigned! He wasn't interested in rank, he just liked flying. He was shot down in the war and was with us at Westhampnett."

When Stoop left the RAF after the war he joined the motor industry and eventually became chief engineer of the Rootes Group which manufactured Hillman, Sunbeam, Singer, and Humber cars. He remained an enthusiastic sports car racer, entering the Le Mans 24 Hour race ten times. He died of a heart attack in 1968 while racing a Porsche 911 in England. He was just 47.

Tony says that Stoop was a "very careful driver and skilled engineer" who was not prone to crashing. Unfortunately, he choose the 1956 Le Mans 24 Hour to have a crash, while he and Tony were leading the 2-litre class. Tony didn't even realise they were in front until just before Stoop's accident. He tells the story of their race:

"I think the mistake we made was that after practice, the fuel consumption was so good we decided to do three or four hours each. He did the first stint and I did the next one and I ran into terrible trouble because during practice he'd taken the new rule about full length, full size windscreens literally. We had this bloody great ordinary touring windscreen - everyone else had a bit of perspex cut.

"We had got it covered from the passenger seat to try and stop the suction from that and we ran into terrible trouble with flies on this great big windscreen! So we had a look at other people's bug deflectors and we made a perspex one. In the middle of the night with all the flies at Le Mans we wouldn't be able to see through the big screen and it was too high to look over the top.

"So all this was put on. Dickie went off and he had no trouble - presumably because his head was well down - but my head was almost at the top of the windscreen. I got halfway down the Mulsanne Straight and my goggles were sucked off and went behind my head! I pulled to the side of the road and tightened them right up, which gave our timekeepers a fright because they thought I'd crashed. But the goggles flew off again - the airflow from the bug deflectors was curling over and pulling them off.

"So I thought I'd bloody well drive without goggles - with the big windscreen it was okay. I'd been smelling petrol - the thing smelled of petrol anyway - and the engine stopped after coming around Arnage. I got out and thought what could I do? I'd got a torch and thought I'd better have a look around and there's all these yellow lights flashing.

"I found that the fuel pipe had broken off at the pump. I thought it's too far to push the thing to the pits so I'll hold the pipe and wriggle the pump until I've filled the carburettors. What I'd forgotten was that on those racing carburettors it's all float, there was damn all petrol in there. When I got in and started it, it only ran for a very short time so I had to stop and start my way around. I passed a Porsche that was on fire [the works Max Nathan/Helm Glöckler 356 Carrera 1600], forgetting that when I was running fuel was spurting out of the fuel pump everywhere!

"I got almost to our pit and thought 'to hell with this - I'm going to be a hero and push it in'. I pushed it about five yards and there's officials with me saying 'we are not allowed to help you' so I thought I'll start it again and did and went in.

"We had the necessary spare bits to fix it, so I hopped back in and Kay said 'you're not going out in that thing again are you?' But I did, finished my four hours and went off to have a cup of tea and a bit of a sleep and Wolfgang von Trips [driving the class-winning 1.5-litre Porsche 550] was there.

"He asked me how I was going and if I was enjoying. I said 'oh, just creeping round, getting in everybody's way - I'm not used to the smaller cars'. And he said 'but you are leading the two-litre class - what do you expect to do - win the bloody race?!'

"The only reason we were leading really was because all the Porsches had expired or caught fire or something. Anyway I had a bit of a sleep and waited for Dickie to come back in. When he was due I put on my gear. Dickie was given the signal to come in the next time around but he walked in! He'd crashed in the esses. I said I'd go out to see if I could fix it but he said not to bother so that was the end of that. [they completed 100 laps and ten hours].

"Dickie going off was unheard of – he'd done a lot of races in Frazer Nashes and things and wasn't the sort of bloke to crash. All we had to do was cruise – there was no [2-litre] opposition left, virtually."

The race was won by Ron Flockart and Ninian Sanderson in their D-Type after logging 300 laps with the Stirling Moss/Peter Collins works DB3S second, a lap behind.

. . . .

Le Mans 1956 was Tony's last 'proper' race – there were still a couple of hillclimbs in his future – but he did do some laps around the famous circuit a year later when he was named as reserve driver for the Duncan Hamilton/ Masten Gregory D-Type which finished sixth outright. Unfortunately for Tony he didn't get to drive in the race, although he had to qualify without pushing too hard. The car was an ex-factory D-Type [long nose chassis number XKD 601, carburetted 3.8-litre].

Tony found the car interesting, and fast: "I saw the 4.5-litre Costin Maserati coming up behind me going through the esses, but I wasn't going to have a go there because I was determined not to hurt the car. So I decided to follow it down Mulsanne Straight to see how it went.

"I thought it would leave me for dead – 4.5-litres, streamlining – and I was exactly the same distance behind him when we got to the kink. When I got back to the pits I asked how fast 5,750rpm in top gear just before the kink was. I was told that allowing for tyre growth, about 187 miles an hour [300km/h] which was quite quick really! We had about 310 horsepower because the car was on carburettors rather than fuel injection which was good for about another ten.

"For Le Mans the D-Type was ideal because the Aston Martin people had to absolutely break their necks on the twisty bits only to be left for dead when they got onto the Mulsanne Straight."

All went well for the first part of the race but Masten Gregory came in after his second stint saying there was fire in the car. The exhaust had fractured and the heat had melted a hole in the floor. As nothing could be done to repair the exhaust a sheet of steel was found and bolted to the floor over the hole.

It also seemed that the auto advance and retard of the distributor had failed. The retard had burned the hole, so the ignition was advanced. The car ran well at high revs but not so well down low. Tony had been trying to get Lofty England to change the distributor but couldn't.

The car went on to the finish sixth, but after Duncan Hamilton took over for the last spell Masten approached Tony to say that as Duncan had had couple of brandies – he was known to enjoy a drink before, during and after a race – could he take over for the last part of the race? "The car's not going well but it's fun," Masten told him, "so get into your gear and I'll call him in." Tony stood alongside him and tried to wave Duncan in but he "did a Nelson and refused to look," so Tony missed out on driving in the race.

D-Types won Le Mans in 1955, 1956 and 1957 and one of the winning drivers was Brit Ivor Bueb who had been involved in the first and last of those victories. For the 1958 24-Hour Bueb was paired with Duncan Hamilton in his D-Type while Tony was back at Le Mans assisting the team in a managerial role. He was also listed as reserve driver but didn't get to drive.

The car was well on the pace and in fact led much of the time it was running but it ended in disaster when Hamilton crashed in the wet with only four hours to go. At the time, he was duelling for the lead with the Ferrari 250TR driven by Phil Hill and Olivier Gendebien that went on to win. Tony's mates Peter and Graham Whitehead were second in their DB3S.

"I had to talk to Duncan and Bueb," remembers Tony, "and said 'look, if we're running second halfway through this event and it's obvious we haven't got the quickest car, are you going to settle for second or are you still going to try to win?' They said they'll still try to win and I said 'well okay, as long as I know so I know what sort of signals to give you'. We were the fastest car in the dry but it when it rained Duncan was being caught by Phil Hill's Ferrari.

"We were leading at midnight when Ivor Bueb's driving caused a couple of other drivers to come to me saying he'd gone absolutely mad – crazy driving in the fog and rain while leading and that he was going to get into trouble. Duncan – who really fancied himself in the wet – took over and there's Phil Hill in the Ferrari catching him. I thought the next lap would be really interesting because Hill will be right behind Duncan. Hill went past but Duncan didn't – he'd crashed.

"We went out to try and get to him because we heard he'd been injured. We found the car and him – he'd just got in the ambulance – and followed the ambulance. We had his wife Angela with us but they wouldn't let us follow the ambulance the short way to the hospital, an official saying we had to go right around the town which during the race is miles. We said 'but the driver's wife is with us, she must be taken to the hospital' and the official replied 'but she was not driving!' Work that one out!

"Duncan was not badly hurt but when Angela arrived she saw him being attended to by nuns and thought the worst, that the last rites were being delivered or something! Despite claims in his subsequent book that the accident had been caused by a slower car, the real reason was that he simply hit a puddle at high speed and lost it. Lofty [England] went down to where he'd crashed to inspect the damage and all the spectators he spoke to who'd seen it said the same thing – there was no slower car, he just lost it."

. . . .

Le Mans 1958 was effectively the end of Tony Gaze's involvement in motor racing at the high level he'd generally enjoyed during his career. His achievements were very substantial and he was – to coin a phrase – 'almost famous'! He'd raced with and against the best drivers, teams and cars of the era, earned enormous respect in the process and knew just about everyone worth knowing in the sport.

He'd driven or owned an interesting array of openwheeler and sports cars including a couple that were quite famous, notably the ex-Ascari World Championship-winning Ferrari 500/625 and the ex-Stirling Moss HWM-Alta he'd used to make history by becoming Australia's first World Championship Grand Prix driver in 1952.

All of Tony Gaze's racing was in the era of 'gentleman racers' and a smaller number of professionals at a time before the massive commercialism we know today took over the sport. It was the era of front-engined racing and sports cars. The rear-engined revolution instigated by father and son Charles and John Cooper was about to hit when Tony retired. Jack Brabham won the 1959 World Championship in a Cooper-Climax and Grand Prix racing changed forever.

Whom did Tony Gaze most respect as a driver? "Stirling Moss," he says, "because he could drive anything. Ascari was a funny bloke but a bloody good driver. Fangio was remarkable but he couldn't translate his skill in openwheelers to sports cars. Even in the streamlined GP Mercedes he hit drums and bales. He liked to be able to see the wheels. Mike Hawthorn was an 'on and off' driver. On his day he was brilliant, extraordinarily fast and damn near unbeatable, but you couldn't rely on him. Peter Collins was also very good.

"But Stirling Moss was the best in my eyes. He never won a world championship because he insisted on driving British cars which were usually inferior, and he switched cars so often. But he proved when he drove the Mercedes that he was the equal of anyone. He was a great thinker and tactician."

SIXTEEN

COUNTRY GENTLEMAN

YOU'RE 38 YEARS OLD and you've spent your entire adult life flying fighters, fighting Germans and driving racing cars. Exciting stuff, but what happens next? What could possibly top that?

This is what Tony Gaze had to face in 1958 after he'd given away motor racing. Certainly there were substantial compensations in his life including living in 1,000 acres of English country estate - Caradoc Court at Ross-on-Wye in Herefordshire near the Welsh border - complete with stately home, salmon fishing, shooting, horses and all the other trappings of the 'country gentleman'.

There was no shortage of money, either, allowing him to indulge in nice cars and most other things that took his fancy. It was all very pleasant, but....

One very unpleasant thing Tony had to deal with in 1958 was the death of his great friend and motor racing 'partner-in-crime', Peter Whitehead. He'd had a successful motor sport career, his racing funded largely by his family's successful wool business. But he was much more than just a rich bloke playing with racing cars, he also had considerable talent as a driver.

Whitehead had participated in 12 World Championship Grands Prix between 1950 and 1954 and stood on the podium once. He also drove in numerous non-Championship Formula One races and many other major openwheeler events including as a team with Tony Gaze in New Zealand, Australia and South Africa. He won the 1938 Australian Grand Prix at Bathurst (meeting Tony for the first time during this trip) and raced sports cars extensively. These provided him with his best result - victory in the 1951 Le Mans 24 Hour sharing a Jaguar C-Type with Peter Walker. Other wins included the Reims 12 Hour twice.

His last major success was also at Le Mans in the 1958 24 Hour when he and half-brother Graham finished second in their Aston Martin DB3S. Three months later - on 21 September 1958 - he was dead at the age of 43, killed while contesting the Tour de France race in a Jaguar saloon with Graham. Graham was driving and Peter navigating when the car crashed off a bridge into a ravine at Lasalle. Graham suffered only minor injuries but Peter died instantly.

Tony found dealing with his friend's death difficult, especially since it appears that the only reason the Whitehead brothers were in the Tour de France was that for the first time, Peter had made a profit from his motor racing in 1958, largely due to the Le Mans success. His accountant had told him that he needed to purchase another car quickly or he would be liable for heavy taxes. The Jaguar was duly acquired and off they went to France.

Peter was a much better driver than Graham, a point that rankled with Tony in the context of the accident. As noted earlier in this account, Peter and Tony were capable of turning out almost identical lap times in the same or equal cars, while Graham was substantially slower than either. Tony notes that when he and Graham shared the Aston Martin DB3 at Hyeres and the HWM-Jaguar 'VPA 9' at Reims, he – Tony – was "seconds faster."

Graham Whitehead turned up at the Gazes' home a couple of days after the accident, smiling and happy, which seemed odd. "He was probably in denial," says Tony, "but he was always a bit peculiar." Graham continued sports car racing until 1961 but then seemed to go into a long decline, dying an alcoholic in 1981 at the age of 58.

Unfortunately, Peter Whitehead left a financial mess behind him when he died which nearly brought his very large family business down. He'd failed to get his estate in order, made no provision for tax minimisation and when death duties of over a million pounds had to be paid it was almost fatal to the company which had to take out massive loans to cover this and other debts.

· · · · · · · · · ·

It didn't take Tony long to start getting a little restless after his retirement. After all, enjoyable and scientific as it was, salmon fishing didn't have quite the same buzz to it as flying Spitfires and driving Grand Prix racing cars. Tony was quite successful with his salmon fishing because he was taught by a highly skilled expert – a reformed poacher who was now the estate's gamekeeper! He knew all the tricks like reading the water to identify where the fish were and passed his knowledge onto Tony. It certainly wasn't just a matter of throwing a line in and hoping for the best.

It was Kay (or 'Kate' as she was by now usually called) who suggested he might go back to motor sport on a lower level – hillclimbs and sprints – to satisfy his competitive urges. "When I gave up racing it was because I'd promised my wife," Tony reminds us.

He acquired one last HWM single-seater in 1958, powered by a blown Alta engine, but it didn't work out: "It was a big mistake. I should have bought myself a pair of shotguns or something because it got to the stage where hillclimbing was getting professional and there was four-wheel-drive specials and things and I just had an HWM with a very powerful engine. The only thing I won with it was a class sprint thing at Brands Hatch.

"George Abecassis at HWM got shirty about something I'd done and wouldn't supply me with the ZF diff I needed to handle the power. Without that all it would do is spin the inside rear wheel, so I got rid of it. I had a bit of fun with it, I suppose - but not really."

Of course Tony was a man who enjoyed nice and preferably fast cars, something that always stayed with him. Some of the road cars he has owned over the years while living in England are worth recalling and make for a very nice collection worthy of any enthusiast. Jaguars dominate, naturally, and include at various times Mk.I 2.4 and 3.4, Mk.II 3.8, S-Type 3.8, XK 120, E-Type S1 and V12, Mk.IX and a Mk.VII especially converted to an estate car with a standing platform at the rear and used for towing horse floats and gliders. Others were the Alvis Speed 25 he'd bought during the war, Daimler Double Six, Ferrari 250GT Lusso and 330GT, Lotus Cortina, MG TF and Jensen FF.

Tony had the Double Six 'hotted up' by the factory with an E-Type manual gearbox, bigger valve springs, hotter cams, faster steering ratio and stiffer suspension. It was a very fast car which he took to Australia with him and derived a great deal of pleasure from blowing young hotshots in their Torana SLR/5000s, XU-1s, Falcon GTs and the like into the weeds with it. He'd let them overtake him, suck them right in and then.... blat! A couple of truisms come to mind here, notably those about 'boys and their toys' and 'once a petrol head, always a petrol head'!

Since then, Jaguars have dominated Tony's garage, residents including XJ6, XJ12 and XJ-S. Even today a couple of modern Jags adorn the Gaze garage and driveway,

. . . .

It was Tony's friend and fellow racing driver Prince Bira who provided him with the idea for something to do after retirement, something that would not only get him back into the air but also provide a new challenge - gliding. Bira was an accomplished pilot and one of the pioneers of gliding in England. He'd been a gliding instructor with the Air Training Corps during the war and afterwards helped re-establish the sport.

Bira owned several aircraft over the years and there is one delightful story about him which relates to this and the fact that he was Siamese royalty. He'd ordered an Auster J/1 Autocrat light aeroplane in 1946 at a time when there was considerable demand for them and the factory at Rearsby in Leicestershire was having trouble meeting that demand.

Like many other customers, Bira was getting impatient about the delay and rang the factory to see how things were going with his aeroplane. In an attempt to satisfy some of the customers, airframes were being switched from one to another. Some telephone calls to Auster were inadvertently received by the production works rather than the main office. One of them went like this:

Caller: "When am I going to get delivery of my Autocrat?"
Works Manager: "What's your name?"
Caller: "I am Prince Bira of Siam."
Works Manager: "And I'm Oliver bloody Cromwell!"

Bira and Tony were talking one day and Tony was asked what he was going to do after finishing with motor racing. Tony muttered something about "doing salmon fishing, I suppose" but Bira suggested that he ought to take up gliding. "I hadn't really thought about it," says Tony. "The only gliding I'd seen was sitting on a ridge and watching. He said I should think about it, so I did.

"The nearest gliding club to me was at Bristol, so I went along and ran into Peter Scott [well-known ornithologist, artist and son of Sir Robert Scott of Antarctic fame], got to know him and asked if I could have a flight. I got in and the instructor asked me if I'd flown before and I said 'yes, a bit' so he gave me control of the glider, a Slingsby Tutor. No instruction at all and I was flying it! He then told me to do a circuit and land, so I did and he said 'okay, we'll send you up in the single-seater.' So off I went.

"Then I thought that if I'm going to do this I'd like to get into competition so I bought myself a two-seater Slingsby T42 Eagle because Peter Scott had one, put an experienced bloke in the back and learnt quickly. After about a year I got myself into the Nationals and gained a Gold C certificate. I also set a couple of British distance and time records and became vice-president of the Bristol Gliding Club."

Peter Scott and Tony always got on well together and had much in common. They regarded each other almost as 'kin'. Both their fathers had been involved in different ways with Captain Robert Scott's Antarctic expedition. This expedition had left behind huts and a large stock of food that along with seal and penguin meat, eggs and equipment.

This had enabled Irvine Gaze and the rest of the Shackleton expedition's Ross Sea party to survive and also to carry our the laying of food depots. These were left abandoned for two years after their still unloaded ship was carried away by the sea ice. Both Peter and Tony left the Bristol Gliding Club as Vice Presidents.

After taking delivery of the Eagle in September 1958, Tony threw himself into his gliding and quickly progressed. He gained his Silver C height, distance and duration badge in April 1959 after completing the necessary flights, the duration sortie lasting 5 hours 15 minutes. Other long cross-country and closed circuit flights regularly followed including one 315 kilometres effort lasting eight hours in July 1959, followed by a 6 hours 35 minutes, 288 kilometres flight a few days later.

Many more such flights followed throughout the remainder of 1959, culminating in the awarding of his Gold C badges in February 1960 after completing the required flights which involved a minimum distance of 300 kilometres, a height gain of at least 3,000 metres and a duration of not less than five hours.

In April 1960 Tony established a new British and United Kingdom speed record for a two-seater glider flying a 200 kilometres triangle in the Eagle. Miss Rosemary Storey was his passenger on the flight from Nympsfield in Gloucestershire and back via Didcot and Stratford-on-Avon.

"I was very lucky," notes Tony, "because having learnt to fly in England I didn't have any navigation problems which a lot of glider pilots did. The moment they broke the umbilical and got out of range of their local airfield, they just couldn't map read and got into trouble. The cross-countries I did were dead easy because I knew most of the places from flying over them during the war."

By now, Tony was an experienced and well-qualified glider pilot with nearly 150 flights and some 200 hours in his log book. The 1960 World Gliding Championships were being held at Cologne in West Germany in June and it was suggested to Tony that he might write to the Gliding Federation of

Australia and ask if they'd be interested in him flying for them. He did that, saying he was available if they wanted him. They answered in the affirmative noting that they wanted two people competing but could only afford to send one to Germany. If Tony could pay for himself they'd very much like to have him on the team.

Tony borrowed a high performance single-seater Slingsby Skylark 3 from the Handley Page Club and took it to Germany for championships, competing in the Open Class. As competition numbers were allocated alphabetically by country and Australia was first on the list, Tony found himself carrying number '1' on the Skylark. Twenty-four nations were represented at the event.

The competition was flown from the old Cologne airport at Butzweilerhof on the north-western outskirts of the city. Acting as his crew were Kay along with Alwyn Sutcliffe, Ted Chubb and Peter Philpot from Bristol Aircraft's structures department and Bristol Gliding Club members. The Gazes' modified Jaguar Mk.VII estate tow car was there and the tug aircraft for the competitors was a Dornier Do 27 provided by the German Army.

The championships were spread over two weeks and involved a number of tests involving speed and/or distance and navigation. A couple of the flights were very long including one of 450 kilometres from Cologne to the village of Gross Koenigsfoerde near the Kiel canal which took nearly seven hours to complete. This involved a very long retrieval and recovery drive by the crew in the Jaguar.

Alwyn Sutcliffe described the normal procedure for the crew: "Having satisfied ourselves with the aid of a pair of binoculars that our glider had got away, we would hitch the trailer to Tony's Jaguar Mk.VII tow car and set off in the general direction of the course, telephoning the control office at Butzweilerhof each hour until we received details of where our pilot had landed. When the task was a closed circuit, however, we would generally wait at base."

Unfortunately the crews' first recovery on the opening day of competition on 1 June was not a happy one. The task was a 172 kilometres out-and-return race and Tony had landed just short. By five o'clock in the afternoon most of the competitors had completed the course but there was still no sign of Tony. The public address system told the story, first in German, then French and English: "Achtung! Nummer ein ist ausgelandet" - "Attention please. Number one has landed outside the airfield."

It had came unstuck for Tony because he'd misread the guide chart he'd borrowed from the English team captain. Because speeds were being measured in nautical miles per hour Tony assumed that the distances noted on the chart were also in nautical miles. But they weren't – they were in statute miles and as one statute mile equals 0.869 nautical miles, there's the potential for a 15 per cent error.

Tony describes how it happened: "Near the end of the first competitive flight I figured I had about 20 miles to go, consulted the chart, calculated I needed so much height to get there, added a bit for safety and set off for the finish. I arrived within sight of the finish but it became clear that I was not going to reach the airfield. I might have just scraped it in - maybe - if there hadn't been radio masts in the way, so I had to put it down somewhere.

"I thought God, I'm over the middle of bloody Cologne. The only thing I could see to land in was the railway marshalling yards so I thought I'd have to go there if I couldn't get to the airfield. Then I saw this tiny little park and went into there, half a kilometre from the finish. I narrowly missed a courting couple in the long grass with the wing tip, but they were so engrossed they didn't even notice!

"I then rang the airfield and an unhappy team arrived wanting to know why I'd landed half a kilometre from the finish. I said I didn't know, I showed them the chart, I thought I'd done the right thing. I wanted to do well and I just couldn't understand what had happened.

"That's when they told me about the chart being in statute rather than nautical and that's why I'd come down short. But of course it doesn't matter because even if you're only half a kilometre from the finish you still haven't finished, so that cruelled me for the whole event. I ended up coming 14th in the Open Class - which I suppose isn't all that bad - but I would have been well inside the top ten but for that which cost me a lot of points."

It in fact cost Tony 400 points out of a possible 1000 but he did well in most of the other tests. Finishing 14th out of 27 starters in the Open Class was quite an achievement, especially considering that the vast majority of his opposition were pilots with very substantial competition experience.

Tony continued gliding for many years after that and owned several more sailplanes including a German Schleicher Ka 6CR he purchased in Cologne from a championship competitor who wanted to sell it before he returned home to South Africa. Of the 35 entries in the 1960 championship's Standard

(15 metres wing span) Class, 16 were Ka 6s, one of which was flown by the winner, Heinz Huth.

Other gliders he owned included a Standard Austria with its distinctive V-tail. This had been designed for the Austrian Aero Club and some were built by the club in its workshop but series production was undertaken in Germany by Schemm-Hirth which developed the design. Tony's was a high performance German example with a laminar flow wing which sacrificed some lift for additional speed.

Tony also owned another high performance single-seater, a Slingsby T51 Dart which he brought to Australia when he permanently moved from England in 1977 and flew it out of Tocumwal in southern New South Wales near the Victorian border for a time. Meanwhile, he set another British record in May 1961 in his Eagle, this one a 'goal and return' mark for two-seaters of 170 miles out of Nympsfield. As with his previous record, Rosemary Storey was his passenger.

Other achievements followed including the awarding of his Diamond Gain of Height badge following a visit to Australia and New Zealand in early 1962. In Australia he flew from Berwick (Casey) airfield and Benalla in Victoria plus Waikerie in South Australia before crossing the Tasman for three flights in a Skylark 2 from Dunsandel in the South Island. The third of them was a marathon 7 hours 15 minutes effort which took him to 24,700 feet. The requirement for Diamond Gain of Height badge is a net gain of not less than 5,000 metres (16,404 feet).

There was a most unusual flight in 1963 in the Standard Austria - searching for the Loch Ness Monster! Organised through Peter Scott, Tony was part of that year's major effort to find 'Nessie', the theory being that if a silent glider was used to observe from the air, the Monster would be less prone to being frightened away than it would be by noisy powered aeroplanes.

Tony flew his Standard Austria at 7,000 feet in clear air while Scott flew his Olympia Type 419. Both gliders were towed by Tony's Auster, flown by the club's chief flying instructor, Peter Collier. Tony was very nearly caught out by a sea fog that suddenly rolled in. He received a radio call to immediately return from the Loch, saw the fog approaching Dalcross airfield on the northern tip of the lake and just squeaked it in as the fog completely enveloped the field.

Did he spot anything interesting? He reckons he saw what looked like two rocks in close formation moving towards deep water and reasons that as they were moving, they couldn't have been rocks! A local clergyman swore he'd seen the Monster, his word perhaps or perhaps not able to be taken as gospel, so to speak....

In June 1965 Tony entered the Standard Austria in 295 kilometres race across England from Nympsfield to Great Yarmouth on the east coast in Norfolk. Twenty-one started and 12 completed the event with Tony winning at a speed of 111km/h, just shy of the record for the distance. Tony reckons that his real time was "actually faster as it was my landing time that was noted because the finish line was not manned until later."

The 1965 World Gliding Championships were held at South Cerney in the Cotswold district of Gloucestershire, England and Tony offered to help by providing his Standard Austria to the Australian team. He suggested they arrive in England early to give them a chance to familiarise themselves with the country over which they'd be flying so they wouldn't get lost. He had an Auster tug aircraft so he said he'd tow them and teach them.

Tony notes that despite that help they didn't go too well: "They did all that but they just got lost and made the most dreadful errors. They flew all right but couldn't navigate. Also, the Austria with laminar flow wing was a 'hot ship' - they needed something with a little less speed and a little more lift. I'd thought about flying in the competition myself. Perhaps I should have!"

Tony ended up flying gliders for two decades, including after he returned to Australia in 1977. One of his later achievements was in January 1979 when he flew the Dart from Tocumwal to West Wyalong in the central west of New South Wales and return. The 507.8 kilometres flight was sufficient to earn him Diamond Distance and Goal Flight badges, giving him the full set of gliding's top certificates.

Recognition of his previous Diamond Height badge by the Gliding Federation of Australia proved to be difficult. The GFA pointed out that it "cannot endorse certificates issued by other countries.... the task must be endorsed on the GFA for, by the FAI certificates officer.... and then sent, with the certificate and appropriate fee, to the country of origin.... I am holding your claim etc until I hear further from you."

Tony wrote a cheque for the three dollars fee but never sent it as the whole thing was becoming too difficult: "Too idle to forward this," he noted. He still has the cheque!

Tony thoroughly enjoyed his gliding "but I got embarrassed because not having a family, I had to get crews from the club to help me. Some of them gave up their holidays to do that so I began to feel I was imposing. But I won a couple of competitions and got a couple of records."

· · · · · · · · · · ·

Taking up gliding also got Tony back into powered flying. Since his last flight in an RAAF Mustang in July 1950 he'd only flown a Chipmunk twice in 1955 but in 1961 he purchased a Beagle-Auster 6A Tugmaster (G-ARRX, c/n 2281, ex-VF512). The 6A Tugmaster was a civil conversion of former British Army Auster AOP.6s for glider towing while the more refined 6B was intended for touring. Tony's 6A was the second conversion, first flown in its new form on 5 July 1961.

He regained his civil licence credentials in June 1961 after performing four familiarisation and check flights in Auster V G-ANHW and picked up his own aircraft from Rearsby on 29 July. It was immediately pressed into service as a glider tug and also used for general flying.

Tony logged nearly 400 hours in the Auster between then and February 1968 when he sold it and purchased Socata MS.893A Rallye Commodore 180 G-AVVJ (c/n 10752). Equipped with towing gear, this was also used as a glider tug and for transporting himself, Kate and perhaps a jockey around the country when she took up a career as a race horse trainer. The Rallye was used extensively and regularly until October 1976 when it was sold shortly before Tony returned to Australia. He added another 580 hours to his log book in the Rallye, bringing his overall total to 3,055 hours plus his gliding time.

Tony flew a couple of other light aircraft types during this period including a Robin DR.400 in August 1974 and a Victa Airtourer out of Staverton in September 1968, doing some aerobatics while he was at it.

"The Auster was from the factory," says Tony, "but they couldn't guarantee anything and give you a full life because they had bought a whole swag of them from the Army and they weren't quite certain that each aircraft had its original wings and other bits. I used that until my wife got a bit sick of sitting in the back when we went to horse races. It was a really nice aeroplane – I thought it was the nearest thing to a proper light aircraft.

"I thought of trading the Rallye in on something bigger and flying that out to Australia, calling in at gliding clubs across the world on the way, earning myself a little money and moving on. But I thought better of it. The amount of paperwork necessary to do that was incredible and others had told me of problems in certain countries. It would have been easy to end up in jail in some places!"

· · · · · · · · · ·

After retiring from motor racing, Tony had spent two decades in England before returning permanently to Australia following the premature death of Kay in 1976. In the meantime there had been the various ups and downs in his private life which effect everyone during the course of a lifetime. There had been a couple of attempts to return to Australia with Kay but the first one was thwarted by Tony's widowed mother-in-law. Tony reckons he was conned into staying in England by her:

"We were getting ready to go back to Australia. I'd been down salmon fishing and I came up for lunch. She was sitting in my chair, pointed to the chair at the head of the table and said 'that's where you are from now on'. I said 'what's going on?' and she said she was fed up with the arthritis she suffered – she was on two sticks and had two nurses – 'I'm going to bed, there's no-one around this property, your father can run his property [in Australia] without you. I want you stay and run the place because we can't run it without you.'"

That surprised Tony and Kay because everyone thought she was going to stick it out until she died. "She was sort of typical Victorian," remembers Tony. "I think she thought she *was* Queen Victoria occasionally! She'd been on two sticks as long as I'd known her and she just suddenly decided she'd had enough."

Tony thought about it and decided he was enjoying it in England, a thousand acres in the Herefordshire countryside, salmon fishing, a good shoot. He liked the country and decided to give it a go, with the proviso that he could go back to Australia every couple of years to see his father and keep his Australian citizenship going: "I did that until she died. I did my gliding and an awful lot of salmon fishing and of course I went to all the motor races and kept an interest in that."

Shortly before he returned to Australia, Tony became involved in helping a young Australian racing driver called Alan Jones who was trying to establish himself in the tough world of European racing. The son of Tony's old friend and champion driver Stan Jones, Alan certainly did manage to establish himself. He made his Formula One debut with Hesketh at the 1975 Spanish

Grand Prix, recorded his first win in Austria in 1977 with the Shadow team and gave Williams its first world championship in 1980.

Kay liked horses and decided she wanted to train them, going to a lot of effort to gain her trainer's licence. But in the meantime the thought of moving to Australia had re-emerged because like her mother, Kay suffered from arthritis and the theory was that moving to Australia's warmer climes would help her.

Tony and Kay went to Australia to look at properties in Victoria and found one they liked. Tony paid the deposit but when they got back to England they discovered that Kay's trainer's licence had been approved. The Australia idea ended then because Kay knew that if she had to go through the entire process again and in a different country, it would take many years to get the licence she wanted so badly.

Tony wasn't overly enamoured with the horse training idea but nevertheless fully supported Kay in her venture, although he was concerned about the amount of money it was eating up: "They only really gave the licence to her in England because she lost her temper with them because she wanted a permit to race her own horses and they wouldn't do it. So she qualified a few really good horses and won some important events.

"I think to shut her up they gave her a full trainer's licence. She did very well and was the only woman trainer to train two winners at the Cheltenham Festival, for example. But the way she was going through money I don't think it could have gone on for long. She was pretty crazy about horses but she was rapidly going broke, I think. She had so many horses. When she had some good ones she thought if she bought more she'd have more winners. It doesn't work like that."

Other issues put considerable strain on the Gaze marriage as time went on. There was a number of infidelities on Kay's part - sometimes with little or no attempt at discretion - and an attempt at suicide. She was obviously a very unhappy lady with some psychological problems that played heavily on her. For Tony, it was an extremely difficult time.

"She just couldn't handle getting old and she really wanted out. When she tried to commit suicide I got her pumped out and she didn't forgive me for that. I think that when she did die she wouldn't have been too unhappy about it. I was seriously wondering what was going to happen when she tried to knock herself off...."

Kay passed away in 1976 two days after undergoing a hip replacement operation which in those days was a much more complex, difficult and dangerous procedure than it is now. "I went to see her one day and the next day she'd been moved and everyone was looking a bit serious about it. By the time I got home she was dead," says Tony. "These days you'd sue but then you accepted it as an embolism or something. But you don't expect to get killed by having a hip replacement done." Kay was 62 at the time of her death and Tony 56.

Kay's death created another problem for Tony, the matter of inheritance. Kay's mother had apparently left them a large interest in her estate but with the proviso that if Kay predeceased Tony, it would go to their children, cutting Tony out. They had no children as Kay wasn't able to conceive and the washup was that everything went to the next in the Heywood family line, a nephew.

Left out in the cold, Tony took care of the death duties and other necessary paperwork tasks that had to be dealt with and returned to Australia to settle at his property 'Gilgai' near Nagambie in central Victoria. In Australia, he would establish a new life and a new relationship with an old friend.

SEVENTEEN
DIANA

"YOU MARRIED the wrong man, you know," Tony Gaze said to Diana Davison while they were dancing at a Light Car Club of Australia trophy presentation evening in December 1948. Tony was of course not very subtly suggesting that he was perhaps the *right* man! Having just given birth to her's and Lex's twins - Jonathon and Peter - and having snuck out of the Mercy Hospital to attend the event, Diana was "very affronted" by the remark, especially since Tony had visited her in hospital the day before.

Tony was wrong, of course. Diana *had* married the right man. After all, she and her husband, champion racing driver Lex Davison, and Tony and Kay Gaze were and would remain very good friends over many years, both socially and professionally. The Davisons were regular visitors to the Gazes' home in England, Tony and Lex raced with and against each other and Tony would sell several cars to his friend.

Diana reflected on Tony's arrogance in making that comment - the perception that pilots and racing drivers sometimes think they're 'God's gift' comes to mind - and told her close friend Bun what a frightful remark she thought it was. Bun also just happened to be one of Tony's ex-girlfriends. Diana notes that "I was only a 22-year-old and wasn't experienced in the ways of racing drivers - except one - let alone fighter pilots."

Tony was, of course, single at the time. He and Kay Wakefield were still six months away from marrying, although they had been very much a permanent 'item' for a couple of years. Diana and Lex didn't know Kay well then, "although they had stayed with us in our very small cottage at Lilydale," Diana remembers.

"Little did I know then in what grand manner she lived in England. I have a memory of her sitting on the back step cleaning her brown shoes. Probably a first! Our first introduction was at the 1948 Australian Grand Prix at Point Cook in the unbelievable heat of that meeting when she - poor girl - was sitting in the back of Tony's tender truck looking like a very melted human."

Tony's words on the dance floor that night were unfortunate and ill-considered when they were uttered but also a little prophetic. He married Diana more than a quarter of a century later, but it took two tragedies to make it possible.

The first was the death of Lex Davison in 1965 and the second the passing of Tony's wife Kay in 1976. Diana was a great comfort to both Tony and Kay during Kay's decline and to Tony afterwards. They then discovered feelings for each other that went beyond friendship and were married at Christ Church of England in Hawthorn, Melbourne on 14 July 1977. It turned out to be an excellent match which has provided them both with great happiness.

Alexander Nicholas ('Lex') Davison, racing driver, farmer and businessman was often described as being 'larger than life'. He was a legend in Australian motor sport and remains the only driver to have won the Australian Grand Prix four times as well as three Australian Hillclimb Championships. He was also the inaugural winner of the CAMS Gold Star as Australian Champion Driver.

His main business interests included the Holden dealership Monte Carlo Motors, Killara Park Aberdeen Angus stud and later a share-farming dairy at Lilydale, Victoria and Paragon Shoes and its associated retail outlets. The profits from the businesses allowed him to indulge in motor racing at a high level.

Most of those profits came from the Paragon Shoe Company which was a very substantial business in its heyday. The company had been started by Lex's father and Diana tried very hard to hold it together after Lex's untimely death in 1965 but due to numerous extenuating circumstances it had to close down. This was heartbreak for Diana.

Monte Carlo Motors was established by Lex and Stan Jones after they and Tony had achieved some success in the 1953 Monte Carlo Rally driving a Holden 48/215. Unfortunately, Lex's idea of how to run a business was rather different to Stan's, so there was conflict. Diana remembers that "Lex's mother always said 'don't go into business with friends', but Lex did so twice – again with another friend in a business called Malvern Motors and that didn't help the friendship either.

"But Paragon Shoes was the goose that laid the golden egg. I gathered up all the historic ledgers, wages sheets, sample shoes and my own collection that had grown over the years. I gave the books to the State Library of Victoria and the shoe collection to the National Gallery of Victoria. In 2007 it was decided that the Museum should have the collection and an amount of money was allocated to put it together."

Lex died while at the wheel of his Repco-Brabham racing car at Melbourne's Sandown Park circuit in February 1965 after suffering a heart attack during practice for the Tasman Cup race being held there. The heart attack caused him to crash and he died from the resulting head injuries.

His loss at only 42 years of age rocked everyone involved in Australian motor sport and the public who followed it as well as hundreds of people from the business and art worlds. The British Racing Drivers' Club air freighted a wreath in the shape of its insignia from the UK and Diana received at least 2,000 letters, many of them from people who had never met the most beloved of Australia's 'gentleman racers'. His death was a major news event all over Australia.

A permanent tribute to him was immediately organised with the creation of the Lex Davison Trophy for the winner of the Australian Grand Prix. Designed and built in Britain by Mr Rex Hays, the trophy incorporates a silver model of the Austin Seven driven to victory by Arthur Waite in the first Australian Grand Prix in 1928.

Lex left Diana and seven children behind, five boys and two girls aged between seven and seventeen. Three of them – Jonathon (born 1948), Chris (1951) and Richard (1954) went on to race. Jon Davison was a leading Formula 5000 driver and later the head of Sandown Park raceway; Chris and Richard both raced Formula Fords and in Richard's case he went on to win the 1980 Australian Formula 2 Championship and then raced Formula Pacifics and Mondials in the 1980s.

The Davison racing dynasty continues today in its third generation with Jon's son James a professional racing driver in the USA, contesting the US Formula BMW series and then the Atlantic series, supported by Jon.

Richard's sons Alex and Will are both well-known to Australian motor racing fans, Alex mainly for his successful exploits in the Porsche Cup and Will as a driver for the Dick Johnson V8 Supercar team. Will won the 2001 Australian Formula Ford Championship before heading to Europe for some F3 racing, but like so many others, a lack of finance thwarted his ambitions to progress further, including into F1.

Alex also drove Porsches in Europe for some years where he had a number of podium finishes as well as success in the USA at Indianapolis, as did James. Diana is rather proud of the fact that only two Australians have won races at the 'brickyard', both of them her grandsons!

In early 2008 Alex travelled to the USA as a guest of Porsche Germany to test for a drive in the Le Mans series, while Will recorded a great result in the 2007

Bathurst 1000 when he and Steven Johnson brought their Ford Falcon home to a podium finish. He scored his maiden victory in the Australian Touring Car/V8 Supercar Championship at the Eastern Creek (Sydney) round in early 2008.

The connection between Tony Gaze and the Davison family has always been very strong and continues to be. In August 2005 the Lex Davison Society was launched, this comprising a group of individuals who have pledged part of their estates to assist young Australian motor sport competitors competing internationally. The Society provides a vehicle whereby pledges from the estates of members can be utilised to assist the careers of young Australian motor sport competitors embarking on international campaigns.

The Society has two eminently appropriate patrons, Tony and Diana Gaze. As its literature notes: "Tony holds the honour of not only being a great friend of the late Lex Davison, but he was also Australia's first ever driver to compete in Formula One. He has an amazing history in motor sport and brings a lifetime of passion and knowledge of the sport to his position as joint patron. Diana Gaze is the widow of the late Lex Davison and is the matriarch of Australian motor sport royalty; the Davison family. Diana is loved and respected by both the Australian and international motor sport communities."

· · · · · · · · · · ·

Being married to a famous racing driver meant that Diana's own achievements behind the wheel and her connection with cars are often forgotten. She was a pretty good steerer in her own right and in between having her tribe of children managed to get a fair bit of competition under her belt.

Rob Roy hillclimb in Victoria was a favourite venue for her at a time when success in hillclimbing carried with it a great deal of prestige: "Anthony was a baby [1947] and Lex said he was off to Rob Roy. I said we'd rather just stay at home because taking a new born baby was a bit of a handful. Lex said 'why don't you drive too?', which I thought was good lateral thinking, and he got me into the MG TC he'd given me for my twenty-first birthday. So I used to drive that at Rob Roy.

"I think after about the second time I was the fastest TC – I held the Ladies' record for some years. But sadly, Lex rearranged the TC. It was a beautiful looking black car. We adapted the area behind the seats and made it a tiny little bassinet and put mattresses and things in there – that was for Anthony so he could go everywhere with me. It was my shopping car.

"Then Lex thought he might drive it one day and that was the end of it. He drove it at Lobethal in South Australia where they were instructed to only pass on one certain side and the accident resulted largely from confusion over that. The event's organisers decided to use the international overtaking rule for clockwise circuits. This was the reverse of the long-standing Australian system that everyone was used to."

Lex was behind well-known racer and car collector Gavan Sandford-Morgan, who was driving his racing MG TC C-Type SS 750. Lex started darting from side to side trying to get past and eventually decided which way he was going to go. Unfortunately, Sandford-Morgan went in the same direction and they collided, sending Diana's MG into a metal power pole. The car was as good as written off and Lex suffered a quite serious back injury.

"Years later," Diana remembers, "when on a rally we arrived at Lobethal where we met Gavan who took me on a drive around the circuit, pointing out the H-section metal power pole that had caused all the damage to car and driver."

Diana also had some fun in their massive 7.6-litre Mercedes Benz SSK 38/250 which Lex took to third place in the 1947 Australian Grand Prix at Bathurst. He also ran the SSK in other races and hillclimbs before replacing it with a 2.9-litre Alfa Romeo Monoposto.

"I started to drive the SSK Mercedes and that was a big challenge getting it up Rob Roy," remembers Diana. "Lex would stand at the side giving me instructions at the start line but it was such a long change from first to second that sometimes I had to move both hands from the steering wheel to put it into second gear. It had a supercharger that you could bring in at will and make this wonderful howling noise. I was never sure how it was going to stop at the top of Rob Roy, it was a handful." Handful or not, Diana set a new Ladies' record at Rob Roy in the SSK in 1948.

She also managed a bit of mischief in the Mercedes: "Driving it back to the farm was probably the greatest fun because we had an elderly gentleman, Mr Drakeford, who used to live in the cottage. He and I were driving along sitting on the chassis of this mad-looking thing with no body and a car full of hoons came past making fun of me driving this great big car.

"And Mr Drakeford says 'go on Mrs D, you show 'em!' So I planted my foot, engaged the blower and left a car full of gaping mouths behind – and a very satisfied look on mine and Mr Drakeford's faces! This was just out of Yarra Glen in Victoria."

Diana also did some rallies, or trials as they were usually called in those days: "The first trial I drove was in the Monte Carlo Holden that Lex, Tony and Stan [Jones] had driven. My navigator was Evelyn Ward, the wife of Peter Ward who was Lex's navigator. Evelyn and I got lost in a timber mill somewhere in East Gippsland late at night and had to walk out, which was pretty frightening.

"By the end of the 1950s I wasn't driving anymore, I was too busy at home with seven kids to look after and I thought it was time that one of us kept our feet on the ground. But for a while I was known as the 'fastest little bitch on the track', which I took as a great compliment!"

"A Davison family relic" is how Diana describes another car with which she has long been associated, the Alfa Romeo 6C 1.5-litre (chassis no 0111522) purchased by Lex's father in chassis form in 1928. Known as the 'Little Alfa', Lex took over the car in 1946 when his father died, by which time it had 130,000 miles on the clock and had been rebodied twice. Lex had the Alfa completely stripped and rebuilt again and another bodied fitted.

In this form he competed in the first post-war race meeting at Bathurst's Mount Panorama circuit, which was also the newly wed Davisons' honeymoon. Another major rebuild was subsequently performed, work done including shortening the chassis, lightening the brakes and axles, fitting a Rootes supercharger and moving the engine back six inches. Yet another body was fitted at this stage.

The Alfa was hillclimbed until the early 1950s including by Diana who ran it at Winton, Mount Tarrengower and the Geelong Sprints, or Speed Trials as they were sometimes called. She occasionally won her class in the car, at least "when it didn't play up," she notes.

After that it fell into disuse, remaining on the Davison family farm 'Killara Park' until the property was sold in 1980. It was subsequently rebuilt yet again after many years of inactivity and campaigned at Winton, Mount Tarrengower and Phillip Island while Tony and Chris drove it and Sandown Park and Amaroo Park in historic events "with many infuriating episodes of unreliability," notes Diana.

"When I met Lex in the early 1940s it had a two-door saloon body on it," she says. "I think it had red mudguards and a black body - it was pretty smart. Lex's mother had learnt to drive in it and so had Lex. I think the first time I ever drove a car was when Lex had been partying too much so I drove it up Toorak Road and was very proud of myself - I passed a tram!"

Diana restored another Alfa Romeo, a 1934 supercharged 1750 SS Castagna-bodied car purchased from a Dr Burgess of Bathurst NSW. "It was in need of some TLC," she notes, "but I rather overdid it and changed its very English body of black and white to Alfa red. Rather a mistake. I drove it at Winton and Phillip Island and with my daughter Catherine in the inaugural Targa Tasmania in 1992."

The Alfa was a star of the Targa and was the first car away – well, away eventually! In the full glare of the media and a large crowd of onlookers, its cantankerous nature revealed itself. Targa organiser and startline commentator, well-known motoring journalist and former racer Max Stahl made the grand announcement: "Ladies in car 101, start your engine."

The Alfa then proceeded to put on a "non-starting exhibition", as Diana describes it, much to Max's and the girls' consternation! Happily, the car did start and went on to complete the 5,000 kilometres event.

Diana had meanwhile purchased an Alfa basket case – literally – "a basket full of bits with a very tragic, rusted chassis with chassis and engine number that was the 1929 1750 SS Zagato-bodied Alfa. I call it the biggest jigsaw puzzle in the world and looked all over the world for original parts for it. I found a good source in northern Italy."

Restoring this car was a huge undertaking that took over a decade to complete and involved a vast amount of international parts sourcing by Diana, Tony, David Rapley ("the magician who completed the puzzle") and other friends. The rebuild – which included constructing a new chassis – was completed in 1999. Diana threw a party for all those involved to celebrate – at a restaurant appropriately called 'Nuvalari'. Diana drove this car in the Adelaide Classic event with Catherine's husband Glenn.

· · · · · · · · · ·

Tony and Diana lived together at 'Gilgai' for some years after they were married before moving to a smaller property in the same general part of Victoria, near the town of Seymour. With the permission of the Duke of Richmond the 30 hectares property was named 'Goodwood Farm'. On it they built the most magnificent rammed earth house which has in it the memorabilia of Tony's achievements – his medals, documents, trophies, paintings of his exploits both in the air and on the racetrack and thousands of photographs chronicling a remarkable life.

They have travelled extensively, often as the guests of organisations or even governments. There has been several visits to the Goodwood Revival meetings where both Tony and Diana have naturally been honoured guests. Tony has been reunited with some of his cars at Goodwood and even had the chance to drive a couple of them. In July 2007 Tony and Diana were invited to Portugal to mark the 45th anniversary celebrations of the *Club Internationale des Pilotes de Grand Prix F1.*

Tony was invited to the Battle of Britain 65th anniversary commemorations in London in September 2005. He felt a little strange about being there because he wasn't directly involved in that pivotal event. When the Battle was raging Tony was still undergoing flying training and was posted to his first operational squadron just after it officially ended.

On the day now commemorated as Battle of Britain Day – 15 September – Tony was at No 5 Flying Training School at Sealand near Chester performing two flights in the Miles Master advanced trainer. He'd soloed on the Master the previous day.

Another invitation had an exciting element to it: 1991 marked the 75th anniversary of 41 Squadron Royal Air Force, the unit with which Tony flew in Germany in the closing stages of the European war. He scored his last three 'kills' with 41 Squadron, flying Spitfire XIVs.

It turned into something a bit special for Tony: "We were invited to 41 Squadron's 75th anniversary at Coltishall and it was going to be a really big show with full security because they were worried about the IRA. There was a black tie dinner which was a big secret because they didn't want the IRA to know all these senior RAF officers were going to be in the one place.

"I was sitting alongside one Air Commodore who said, 'before I talk to you about flying do you mind if I look at your chest to see if you know anything?' He looked and saw the DFC and two bars and decided I worth talking to!

"The next day we were introduced around and there was a huge air display – the Red Arrows, lots of different fighters – and halfway through it a chap alongside me in civilian clothes asked what I thought of it. I said, 'fantastic, the Arrows, aerobatics and all that'. He asked what I'd flown during the war so I said 'Spitfires and Meteors at the end'.

"He then asked if I'd like to fly a Jaguar and I said 'don't be silly, of course I'd like to'. He said I had a choice – I could either fly a Jaguar or a Hawk – I chose the Jaguar. It turned out he was the Senior Air Staff Officer in Germany and he said he'd be in touch. I went away thinking I'd hear no more about that.

"I got a message a day or two later saying that if I reported to RAF Coltishall – at my convenience – I could have a flight in a Jaguar! I hoped to do some aerobatics and enjoy myself that way, but when we went to the briefing we were told that we were going to do a simulated Gulf mission – some of the squadron was just back from there – 450 knots at 200 feet up a valley and back over the bombing range."

Tony says that "Di had snuck into the back of the briefing and said 'my God, here we go, they'll kill themselves!'" Diana emphasises that she was *invited* to the briefing and "was appalled at the detailed discussion on ejection procedures and other terrifying likely happenings. I was certain I was about to become a widow again!"

Tony continues: "So out we went and it was very interesting. I thought they might just let me fly a bit but they let me do the most of the show except for the landing, and I'd liked to have done that! I followed the pilot through on the controls on the takeoff. Anyway we did what we were supposed to, went to the bombing range and dropped two bombs – except they didn't fall off – but the range officer said he could tell where they 'went' because the electronics worked. If they had dropped we would have been reasonably accurate.

"We'd been up for an hour and the fuel was running low. The pilot said to fly it back to Coltishall which I did but he did the landing. The Jaguar had very high fuel consumption at that low level. The pilot said that in the Gulf they'd stopped doing the really low level missions and gone up a bit to about 8,000 feet where the fuel consumption was noticeably lower. It was most enjoyable."

Tony was awarded an Order of Australia Medal in the 2006 New Year's Honours list for his "services to the sport of motor racing", a fitting tribute given his importance in the context of being an Australian competing on the world stage at a time this was extremely rare. He was a pioneer of bringing 'internationalism' to Australian motor sport.

That, his extraordinary record as a fighter pilot and the number of 'firsts' he notched up over the years add up to what is nothing less than a very significant list of achievements by a remarkable, modest and always understated man.

"Almost unknown" indeed!

APPENDICES

SQUADRON LEADER F A O GAZE DFC** RAF RECORD OF SERVICE

DATES	UNIT/BASE	MAIN AIRCRAFT	NOTES
9/1/40-25/7/40	Various	--	Iinduction and basic training, Aircraftman 2nd Class (2AC)
26/7/40-7/9/40	7 EFTS Desford	Tiger Moth	Leading Aircraftman (LAC), initial flying training
8/9/40-10/1/41	5 FTS Sealand/Turnhill	Master	Advanced flying training, awarding of 'wings'
15/1/41-9/3/41	57 OTU Hawarden	Spitfire I	Operational training
10/3/41-29/8/41	610 Sqn Westhampnett	Spitfire IIA/B	Pilot Officer; first operation 19/3/41; first 'kill' (Bf 109E) 26/6/41; first DFC awarded
29/8/41-19/11/41	610 Sqn Leconfield	Spitfire I/II	Convoy patrols
20/11/41-3/6/42	57 OTU Hawarden	Spitfire I/II, Master	Flight Lieutenant, instructing
3/6/42-8/7/42	616 Sqn Kingscliffe	Spitfire VI	'A' Flight Commander
8/7/42-29/7/42	616 Sqn Kenley	Spitfire VI	
29/7/42-8/8/42	616 Sqn Great Sampford	Spitfire VI	
8/8/42-11/8/42	RAE Farnborough	Spitfire VI	UP Flight (air-to-ground unguided rocket testing)
11/8/42-31/8/42	616 Sqn Great Sampford	Spitfire VI	Became 'ace' 19/8/42
31/8/42-8/9/42	64 Sqn Hornchurch	Spitfire IX	Squadron Leader
8/9/42-7/11/42	64 Sqn Fairlop	Spitfire IX	Eagle Squadron incident 26/9/42, demotion
8/11/42-2/1/43	616 Sqn Westhampnett	Spitfire VI	Flight Lieutenant; second DFC awarded
8/1/43-22/4/43	Air Ministry	--	PR3 unit - pep talks at factories etc
24/5/43-20/6/43	453 Sqn Hornchurch	Spitfire V/IX	RAAF squadron
20/6/43-19/7/43	268 Sqn Odiham	Mustang I, Typhoon	Army-Co-operation, instructing
20/7/43-14/8/43	Sector HQ Hornchurch	Spitfire IX	Supernumerary to Station Flight
14/8/43-25/8/43	129 Sqn Hornchurch	Spitfire IX	
25/8/43-4/9/43	66 Sqn Kenley	Spitfire V	Shot down over France 4/9/43, returned to England 28/10/43
10/2/44-21/7/44	FAU Swinderby	Spitfire II, Martinet	Fighter Affiliation Unit
22/7/44-11/9/44	610 Sqn Friston	Spitfire XIV	Anti-Diver patrols
12/9/44-3/12/44	610 Sqn Lympne	Spitfire XIV	
4/12/44-31/12/44	610 Sqn Evere (Belgium)	Spitfire XIV	
1/1/45-27/1/45	610 Sqn Ophaven (Belgium)	Spitfire XIV	
28/1/45-4/3/45	610 Sqn Eindhoven (Neth)	Spitfire XIV	Shot down Me 262 14/2/45
6/3/45-6/4/45	41 Sqn Eindhoven (Neth)	Spitfire XIV	Third DFC awarded
7/4/45-16/4/45	41 Sqn Twente (Neth)	Spitfire XIV	10th 'kill' (Ju 52) 11/4/45
17/4/45-1/5/45	41 Sqn Celle (Germany)	Spitfire XIV	Last 'kill' (Fw 190) 30/4/45

2/5/45-7/5/45	616 Sqn Luneberg (Germany) Meteor III		Squadron Leader; first jet flight (Meteor) 2/5/45
8/5/45-30/8/45	616 Sqn Lübeck (Germany)	Meteor III	Flew captured Fw 190, Si 204 etc
31/8/45-1/9/45	263 Sqn Lübeck (Germany	Meteor III	616 Sqn renumbered
1/9/45-21/9/45	263 Sqn Manston	Meteor III	
22/9/45-1/12/45	263 Sqn Acklington	Meteor III	
3/5/46-9/5/46	56 Sqn Bentwaters	Meteor III	
10/5/46-26/8/46	691 Sqn Exeter	Meteor III, Spitfire XVI	Navy liaison/target-towing etc
27/8/46-24/7/47	61 OTU Keevil	Spitfire XIV/XVI/XIX/21	CO of Test Flight; last RAF flight (Spitfire XVI) 15/7/47

RAAF SERVICE

23/1/49-2/7/50	21 Sqn Laverton Vic	CAC Mustang	'City of Melbourne' Squadron, Citizen Air Force

Abbreviations: EFTS - Elementary Flying Training School; FAU - Fighter Affiliation Unit; FTS - Flying Training School; OTU - Operational Training Unit; Sqn - Squadron.

• • • • • • • • • • •

SQUADRON LEADER F A O GAZE DFC** COMBAT CLAIMS

DATE	TYPE	LOCALITY	RESULT	AIRCRAFT	UNIT
26/6/41	Bf 109E	nr Gravelines	Destroyed	Spitfire II	610 Sqn RAF
26/6/41	Bf 109E	nr Gravelines	Probable	Spitfire II	610 Sqn RAF
6/7/41	Bf 109E	nr Lille	Shared dest.	Spitfire II	610 Sqn RAF
10/7/41	Bf 109E	nr Hardelot	Destroyed	Spitfire II	610 Sqn RAF
10/7/41	Bf 109E	nr Hardelot	Destroyed	Spitfire II	610 Sqn RAF
17/7/41	Bf 109E	Le Touquet	Probable	Spitfire II	610 Sqn RAF
13/7/42*	Fw 190A	nr Abbeville	Probable	Spitfire VI	616 Sqn RAF
18/7/42	Fw 190	nr Le Touquet	Destroyed	Spitfire VI	616 Sqn RAF
19/8/42	Do 217	Dieppe area	Destroyed	Sptifire VI	616 Sqn RAF
17/8/43	Fw 190	nr Antwerp	Destroyed	Spitfire IX	129 Sqn RAF
19/8/43	Bf 109G	nr Amiens	Probable	Spitfire IX	129 Sqn RAF
4/9/43	Fw 190	nr Beauchamps	Destroyed	Spitfire V	66 Sqn RAF
5/8/44	Fi 103 'V-1'	nr Beachy Head	Destroyed	Spitfire XIV	610 Sqn RAF
1/1/45	Fw 190D	Ophoven	Destroyed	Spitfire XIV	610 Sqn RAF
14/2/45	Me 262	Munster area	Destroyed	Spitfire XIV	610 Sqn RAF
11/4/45	Ju 52/3m	Bremen area	Destroyed	Spitfire XIV	41 Sqn RAF
12/4/45	Ar 234	Bremen area	Shared dest.	Spitfire XIV	41 Sqn RAF
28/4/45	Fw 190D	Schwerin airfield	Shared dest.	Spitfire XIV	41 Sqn RAF
30/4/45	Fw 190D	Elbe Bridgehead	Destroyed	Spitfire XIV	41 Sqn RAF

TOTAL: 12.5 confirmed destroyed (11 and 3 shared) and 4 probably destroyed plus 1 Bf 109E and 4 Fw 190s recorded as 'damaged'. Also (as noted in table) 1 Fieseler Fi 103 V-1 'flying bomb' destroyed.

*NOTE: The wreckage of this Fw 190 'probable' was found in 1994 during excavation work.

TONY GAZE'S RACING CARS

TYPE	CHASSIS NO	CATEGORY	NOTES
Alta Monoposto 2-litre	56S	Racing	1947-1951; ex-Johnny Wakefield; UK hillclimbs/sprints; Australia hillclimbs/races incl 1948 AGP; sold to Wally Feltham.
Alta Sports 2-litre	54S	Sports/Racing	1947-50; ex-George Abecassis; UK and Australia; TG's last Australian race 12/6/50 (Balcombe Vic) before going to Europe; sold to Mr Williams.
Alta F2 2-litre	F2/1	F2	1951-52; British and European F2 races.
Aston Martin DB3	DB3/9	Sports/Racing	'TPB 639'; 1953, crashed Oporto 21/6/53 and destroyed.
Aston Martin DB3S	DB3S/102	Sports/Racing	'OXE 472'; Kangaroo Stable 1955; to David McKay.
Ferrari 500/625	5/GP.0480	F1	1955-56; ex-works used by Ascari for his 1952/53 World Championships; used by TG for NZGP etc races; sold to Lex Davison 1956.
HRG Streamliner 1.5-litre	n/a	Sports/Racing	1947-49; purchased new in UK, to Australia late 1947; hillclimb/ racing; 'Woodside' bodywork fitted 1949; sold to Norman Steele.
Holden 48/215	n/a	Rally	1953 Monte Carlo Rally with Lex Davison and Stan Jones; finished 64th.
HWM 51/52 Alta	n/a	F2/F1	ex-Stirling Moss; 1952 Grands Prix, various F2; sold to Lex Davison 1953.
HWM-Alta 2-litre	n/a	Racing	NZGP/Lady Wigram Trophy 1954.
HWM-Jaguar	'VPA 9'	Sports/Racing	1954-56; UK and European sports car races plus New Zealand/Australia; sold to Lex Davison.
HWM-Alta	n/a	Racing	1958; for sprints and hillclimbs.
Maserati 8CM	3011	Formula Libre	ex-Whitney Straight/B Bira; various UK races 1951-52.

TONY GAZE - SUMMARY OF MOTOR RACING

YEAR/S   NOTES

1938   First race at Brooklands in Hudson.
1945-47 Sprints at RAF Keevil airfield, Prescott hillclimb (Alta Monoposto and Sport).
1947-50 In Australia - hillclimbs, road racing, 1948 Australian Grand Prix (Alta Monoposto, Alta Sports, HRG Streamliner).
1951   UK/Europe Formula 2 (Alta F2); Formula Libre (Maserati 8CM).
1952   World Championship Grands Prix and other events (HWM Alta); Formula Libre (Maserati 8CM).
1953   Monte Carlo Rally (Holden); various UK/Europe sports car (HWM-Jaguar, Aston Martin DB3), Pescara 12 Hour (DB3).
1954   NZGP etc (HWM-Alta); Mt Druitt 12-Hour (Jaguar C-Type); UK/Europe sports cars (HWM-Jaguar).
1955   NZGP, South Africa, Australia (Ferrari 500/625); Kangaroo Stable Europe/UK sports cars (Aston Martin DB3S); other sports cars (HWM-Jaguar).
1956   NZGP etc (Ferrari 500/625); Australian sports cars (HWM-Jaguar); Le Mans 24-Hour (Frazer Nash Sebring).
1957   Le Mans 24-Hour reserve driver for Duncan Hamilton/Masten Gregory (Jaguar D-Type).

INDEX